Existing Before God

Existing Before God

Søren Kierkegaard and the Human Venture

Paul R. Sponheim

Fortress Press
Minneapolis

EXISTING BEFORE GOD

Søren Kierkegaard and the Human Venture

Copyright © 2017 Fortress Press. All rights reserved. Except for brief quotations in critical articles or reviews, no part of this book may be reproduced in any manner without prior written permission from the publisher. Email copyright@fortresspress.com or write to Permissions, Fortress Press, PO Box 1209, Minneapolis, MN 55440-1209.

Cover image: Søren Kierkegaard, Oil on canvas. By Luplau Janssen; 1902. Frederiksborg Museum.

Cover design: Alisha Lofgren

Print ISBN: 978-1-5064-0563-6

eBook ISBN: 978-1-5064-0564-3

This book was produced using Pressbooks.com, and PDF rendering was done by PrinceXML.

Contents

Mapping the Tradition Series Paul Rorem, series advisor	vii
Abbreviations	ix
Preface	xi
Introduction: A Biographical Sketch	xv
A Volatile "Golden" Age	xv
The Melancholy Father	xx
Regine	xxi
Pseudonymity and Indirect Communication	xxiv
The Kirkekamp: Who Is a Witness to the Truth?	xxix
Part 1: *THE SICKNESS UNTO DEATH: A CHRISTIAN PSYCHO- LOGICAL EXPOSITION FOR UPBUILDING AND AWAKENING* by Anti-Climacus: **Analysis and Commentary**	1
Preface	5
Introduction	10
Chapter 1: The Sickness unto Death Is Despair	13
Despair Is the Sickness unto Death	13
Com.: The Algebra of the Spirit	13
The Universality of This Sickness (Despair)	19
Com.: Despair Common and Rare	19
The Forms of This Sickness (Despair)	21
Com.: The Morphology of Despair	21

DESPAIR CONSIDERED WITHOUT REGARD TO ITS BEING
         CONSCIOUS OR NOT, CONSEQUENTLY ONLY WITH REGARD
         TO THE CONSTITUENTS OF THE SYNTHESIS....
	21

DESPAIR AS DEFINED BY CONSCIOUSNESS	25
Com.: The Error's Mutiny	31
Chapter 2: Despair Is Sin	33
Despair Is Sin	33
Com.: The Logic of Intensification I: Before God	33
Com.: Making the End Fast: Against Apologetics and Socrates?	41
Com.: The Pathetic and the Dialectical	47

The Continuance of Sin	53
Com.: The Logic of Intensification II: Before Christ	63
Com.: The Logic of Intensification III: Sin against the Holy Spirit	69

Part II: The Theological Reception and Legacy — 75

Chapter 3: The Theological Reception of Kierkegaard — 77

The Nineteenth Century: Danish is a Minor Language	79
Norwegian Pietism and Henrik Ibsen	80
Denmark: Rasmus Nielsen and Hans Brøchner	83
Denmark and Beyond: Georg Brandes and Harald Høffding	86
The Twentieth Century: The Theological High-Water Mark?	93
The Bombshell: Barth, Brunner, and Bultmann	93
Kierkegaard as the Father of Existentialism?	101
American Appropriations: Paul Tillich, Reinhold Niebuhr, Colleges, and Commentaries	104
The Priority of the Future: Wolfhart Pannenberg and Jürgen Moltmann	112
The Feminist Interpretation of Kierkegaard	115
Taking Another Look: Emmanuel Levinas and Jacques Derrida	117
The Twenty-First Century: Plural Postmodern Perspectives	120
Mark Dooley and John Caputo	120
The Prophetic and the Pastoral	125

Chapter 4: The Theological Legacy of Kierkegaard for Our Time — 133

Getting the Direction Right: Confessing Faith . . . Sin	134
Meeting the World: Faith Facing the Other	137
Living in Hope, Honestly before God	141
Bibliography	147
Index of Names	163

Mapping the Tradition Series

Paul Rorem, series advisor

Mapping the Tradition is a series of brief, compact guides to pivotal thinkers in Christian history. Each volume in this series focuses upon a particular figure and provides a concise but lucid introduction to the central features of each thinker's work and sketches the lasting significance of that thinker for the history of Christian theology.

The series utilizes primary source works from each figure as an entry point for exposition and exploration. Guided by leading scholars in history and theology, primary source texts are reproduced with explanatory commentary and are accompanied by essays that orient readers to the context, contours, and historical and conceptual legacy of the corpus.

The series is designed for beginning and intermediate students, as well as interested general readers, who will benefit from clear, helpful surveys of thinkers, texts, and theologies from throughout Christian history and from introductions to major issues and key historical and intellectual points of development.

Volumes in the series:

Gillian T. W. Ahlgren, *Enkindling Love: The Legacy of Teresa of Avila and John of the Cross*

Paul Rorem, *The Dionysian Mystical Tradition*

Paul R. Sponheim, *Existing Before God: Søren Kierkegaard and the Human Venture*

Forthcoming:

Khaled Anatolios, *Irenaeus of Lyons: The Making of the Great Tradition*

Romanus Cessario, OP, and Cajetan Cuddy, OP, *Thomas and the Thomists: The Achievements of Thomas Aquinas and His Interpreters*

Robert Kolb, *Luther and Christian Freedom*

Andrew Louth, *John of Damascus: The Radiance of Orthodoxy*

Terrence N. Tice, *Schleiermacher: The Psychology of Christian Faith and Life*

Thomas G. Weinandy and Daniel A. Keating, *Athanasius: Trinitarian-Incarnational Soteriology and Its Reception*

Abbreviations

BA	*The Book on Adler*, trans. Howard V. Hong and Edna H. Hong.
CA	*The Concept of Anxiety*, trans. Reidar Thomte.
CD	*Christian Discourses / The Crisis and a Crisis in the Life of an Actress*, trans. Howard V. Hong and Edna H. Hong.
CUP	*Concluding Unscientific Postscript to "Philosophical Fragments,"* trans. Howard V. Hong and Edna H. Hong.
E/O	*Either/Or*, trans. Howard V. Hong and Edna H. Hong.
EUD	*Eighteen Upbuilding Discourses*, trans. Howard V. Hong and Edna H. Hong.
FSE/JFY	*For Self-Examination / Judge for Yourself!*, trans. Howard V. Hong and Edna H. Hong.
FT	*Fear and Trembling / Repetition*, trans. Howard V. Hong and Edna H. Hong.
IKC	*International Kierkegaard Commentary*, ed. Robert L. Perkins.
JP	*Søren Kierkegaard's Journals and Papers*, trans. Howard V. Hong and Edna H. Hong.
KRSRR	*Kierkegaard Research: Sources, Reception and Resources*, ed. Jon Stewart.
NRSV	New Revised Standard Version.
PC	*Practice in Christianity*, trans. Howard V. Hong and Edna H. Hong.
PF	*Philosophical Fragments / Johannes Climacus*, trans. Howard V. Hong and Edna H. Hong.
PV	*The Point of View*, trans. Howard V. Hong and Edna H. Hong.
RSV	Revised Standard Version.
SK	Søren Kierkegaard.

EXISTING BEFORE GOD

SUD *The Sickness unto Death*, trans. Howard V. Hong and Edna H. Hong.
TM   *"The Moment" and Late Writings*, trans. Howard V. Hong and Edna H. Hong.
WA   *Without Authority*, ed. and trans. Howard V. Hong and Edna H. Hong.
WL   *Works of Love*, trans. Howard V. Hong and Edna H. Hong.

Preface

Here is yet another book devoted to the study of the Danish writer Søren Kierkegaard (1813–1855). There's plenty of material to study. In less than two decades, he published over thirty works and left us voluminous personal journals as well. His voice seemed silenced with his death, for his writings were hardly noticed beyond the borders of Scandinavia for the rest of his century. But today his works are studied around the world. This book claims him as a Christian and investigates specifically his understanding of Christian teaching about the human self in all its complexity, as existing "before" God. I do not offer these pages as an original contribution to the Kierkegaard scholars surrounded by books aplenty. What's the point, then, of probing into this enigmatic author who was claimed as a resource by such opposing figures as Jean-Paul Sartre and Karl Barth?

One may begin a response by noting two distinctive features of the series in which this book appears. In Mapping the Tradition, after a brief biographical sketch, one begins with analysis of and commentary on central primary source material, here *The Sickness unto Death*. Then an effort is made to sketch the lasting significance of that thinker, here tracing Kierkegaard's reception from the nineteenth century's "misreception" through the theological high-water mark of influence in the twentieth century and into the present century's impassioned and innovative attention to his work, represented by deconstruction, postmodernism, and other streams carrying his contribution to new readers.

For whom may there be value in that distinctive combination in the case of Kierkegaard? In his own assessment in *The Point of View for My Work as an Author*, Kierkegaard claimed the category of "the individual" as his category. In the work we take here as our focus, his pseudonym, Anti-Climacus, resists speculation's grand sweep beyond the individual, writing, "perhaps instead the single individual human being and to be a single human being are the highest."[1] If that's his category, perhaps in this preface I may be permitted to address the individual reader, you.

If you are a curious person puzzled by how someone writing in a minor language can be claimed by figures who don't seem to fit together at all, you may find here an analysis that conveys so rich a depiction of human existence that discerning fragments seem free for the taking. If you are a student caught up in your academic pursuits in a senior division religion course, you may find here a way into this globally significant writer's precise and passionate understanding of Christianity. If you are a graduate student trying to grasp what Niebuhr or Tillich or Barth means by his praise and criticism of Kierkegaard, you may find here, particularly in the notes, a way to fuller discussion of these relationships. If as a pastor or therapist you are involved in trying to heal the human spirit, you may find here an unparalleled diagnosis of the architectonics of human despair along with a prescription that encompasses human psychological wisdom and yet appeals to divine revelation. If you are a member of a community of faith in this time of great religious confusion, you may find here the basis for what became a scathing critique of the cultural accommodations of established Christianity and a pointing toward a recovery of biblical faith. Most importantly, if you are simply a human being trying to find a way to navigate the turbulent currents of life's becoming, you may find here guidance for your venture, albeit put in the poetry of paradox.

I first found help from this mystifying Dane as a student of Reidar

---

1. Søren Kierkegaard, *The Sickness unto Death*, ed. and trans. Howard V. Hong and Edna H. Hong (Princeton: Princeton University Press, 1980), 119 (hereafter cited as SUD).

PREFACE

Thomte in the 1940s and later benefited from the guidance of Niels Thulstrup and Jaroslav Pelikan. I am deeply in their debt, as I am for the gadfly disturbance Paul Holmer provided in stressing the language *of* faith above and beneath the language *about* faith. These mentors are gone, but I have been fortunate in this writing to have the textual help of two college teacher friends, once my students, who read Kierkegaard thoughtfully, Kirsten Mebust and Curtis Thompson. Another friend, Ron Marshall, is a parish pastor who brings Kierkegaard to fruitful life in his parish in West Seattle and sends reports and recommendations to his old teacher in the Midwest. There are figures at institutions to thank as well. I have learned so much from students in teaching Kierkegaard at Luther Seminary for over forty years and am indebted to the faculty and administration who have supported this vocation. For this book, I am particularly grateful to Dr. Paul Rorem of Princeton Theological Seminary for his initiative and guidance throughout the months of researching and writing. At Luther, electronics services librarian Jennifer Bartholomew and circulation manager Karen Alexander have been most helpful. Finally, I am grateful to Gordon Marino at the Howard and Edna Hong Kierkegaard Library at St. Olaf College for his hospitality and guidance. Students of Kierkegaard beyond counting are deeply in debt to Howard V. Hong and Edna H. Hong for their path-breaking work of translation and to Princeton University Press for the handsome volumes in which the Hongs still bring readers to Kierkegaard most accessibly. I hope this book will help many readers come to a fuller understanding of this enigmatic Danish genius as they work their way through the Hongs' translation of *The Sickness unto Death*. At Fortress Press, Michael Gibson, Layne Johnson, and Allyce Amidon have been most helpful.

So it is that I place this small book in your hands and invite you to make what you can of it. May these efforts, mine and yours, contribute to fruitful human venturing before God.

Introduction: A Biographical Sketch

Søren Kierkegaard is today read around the world and claimed as a resource from a dizzying variety of perspectives. It is a daunting task to sketch the man who elicits this veritable flood of responses. I write as one caught up in those currents, often protesting, often convinced. Even a sketch may serve to help us get a sense of the "what" and "how" of this volcanic yet enigmatic Danish genius.

A Volatile "Golden" Age

The first half of the nineteenth century in Denmark has been called the Golden Age. All across Europe it was a time of radical change, with the development of a global market economy and the shift from semi-feudal monarchies to representative governments. Bruce Kirmmse describes this period in terms of a sharp contrast, even an "increasingly evident contradiction, between rapidly changing social and economic realities on the one hand, and the brilliant but blithely 'conservative'—apolitical, really—cultural productions of the period" on the other.[1] On June 5, 1849, Denmark became a constitutional monarchy featuring universal male suffrage. The first half of the century tells the story of the emergence of the peasant class, which was rooted in the agricultural reforms at the end of the previous century.

---

1. Bruce H. Kirmmse, *Kierkegaard in Golden Age Denmark* (Bloomington: Indiana University Press, 1990), 2. For a summary update of Kirmmse's 558-page analysis, see his "Kierkegaard and the End of the Danish Golden Age," in *The Oxford Handbook of Kierkegaard*, ed. John Lippitt and George Pattison (Oxford: Oxford University Press, 2013), 28–43.

The telling of the story of these changes drowns out the dying chords of an ambiguously golden "period of literary and artistic splendor, of a cultural blossoming" in which intellectual, artistic, and ecclesiastical life strikingly reflected conservative, aristocratic "stasis."[2] As Kirmmse summarizes: "It's almost difficult to believe that the great conservative aristocrat of the theatre, Johan Ludvig Heiberg, should have been so contemporaneous with Ibsen as to have prevented his works from being performed." We'll see that Søren Kierkegaard, "half peasant, half urbane aristocrat," may be said to have embodied the conflicts and tensions of the period.[3]

Looking beyond Denmark, three principal intellectual streams flowing through Europe at this time were represented by Immanuel Kant (1724–1804), Friedrich Schleiermacher (1768–1834), and Georg Wilhelm Friedrich Hegel (1770–1831). Does one go with Kant and identify religion as the "recognition of our duties as divine commands"? Or with Schleiermacher and find the key to our consciousness of God to lie in the feeling (*Gefühl*) or intuition (*Anschauung*) of our absolute dependence? Or shall Hegel lead us to see that "what is rational is actual and what is actual is rational," though religion may grasp the "positivity of negativity" only in "a way of imagining [*Vorstellen*] an other?"[4] In broad strokes, Kierkegaard's thought carries a response to each of these streams. There is clearly a strong emphasis on the ethical, but he wrote in 1843 of how faith entails a "teleological suspension of the ethical"[5] and in 1844 of how the concept of sin "belongs to ethics only insofar as upon this concept it is shipwrecked with the aid of repentance."[6] While Kierkegaard can praise "Schleiermacher's immortal service" to dogmatics in

---

2. Ibid.
3. Ibid., 26.
4. Georg Wilhelm Friedrich Hegel, *The Philosophy of Right*, trans. T. M. Knox (Chicago: Encyclopedia Britannica, 1951), 6. The second quotation is from Georg Wilhelm Friedrich Hegel, *The Phenomenology of Mind*, trans. J. B. Baillie (New York: Harper Torchbooks, 1967), 797. See also Immanuel Kant, *Religion within the Limits of Reason Alone*; Friedrich Schleiermacher, *On Religion: Speeches to Its Cultured Despisers*; and Friedrich Schleiermacher, *The Christian Faith*.
5. Søren Kierkegaard, *Fear and Trembling / Repetition*, ed. and trans. Howard V. Hong and Edna H. Hong (Princeton: Princeton University Press, 1983), 54–67 (hereafter cited as FT).
6. Søren Kierkegaard, *The Concept of Anxiety*, ed. and trans. Reidar Thomte (Princeton: Princeton University Press, 1980), 17 (hereafter cited as CA).

INTRODUCTION: A BIOGRAPHICAL SKETCH

recognizing that sin cannot be explained, his own pondering of this presupposition in *The Sickness unto Death* (1849) transcends the German's naturalistic framing. With Hegel, there is critique and dependence, but overall Kierkegaard insists that "despite all his outstanding ability and stupendous learning," "he was in the German sense a professor of philosophy on a large scale, because he *à tout prix* [at any price] must explain all things."[7] Very specifically, Kierkegaard will insist that the principle of contradiction applies in thought and life: the creature is not the Creator. We'll find him talking about an "infinite qualitative difference" between the two. It's a contradiction to blur the difference. Hegel could talk theology too, but his passion for unity led him to claim that "what is a contradiction in the realm of the dead is not one in the realm of life."[8]

These German currents made it north to little Denmark in varying adaptations. Kirmmse provides a helpful charting of the alternative intellectual-cultural positions available in Golden Age Denmark. It looks like this, with placement of figures yet to be warranted.[9]

		History	
		Romantic	Agnostic
Culture	Mandarin	J. P. Mynster J. L. Heiberg H. L. Martensen	H. N. Clausen Orla Lehmann liberalism
	Populist	N. F. S. Grundtvig	Søren Kierkegaard

The chart is constituted by how the figures involved respond to two

---

7. CA, 20. There is considerable disagreement among scholars regarding the mix of dependence and critique. Niels Thulstrup (*Kierkegaard's Relation to Hegel*, trans. George L. Stengren [Princeton: Princeton University Press, 1980]) was a definitive proponent of the primarily oppositional view. More recently, Jon Stewart, in *Kierkegaard's Relations to Hegel Reconsidered* (Cambridge: Cambridge University Press, 2003), sees Kierkegaard's attack against Hegelianism to be directed principally at his Danish contemporaries. But Merold Westphal ("Jon Stewart, Kierkegaard's Relations to Hegel Reconsidered," *Søren Kierkegaard Newsletter* 48 [September 2004]: 10–15), 10 stresses Kierkegaard's significant opposition to Hegel's own thought and contends that while Stewart's book "illumines Kierkegaard's relation to his fellow Danes, it obscures his relation to Hegel."
8. Georg Wilhelm Friedrich Hegel, "The Spirit of Christianity and Its Fate," 182–301 in *Early Theological Writings*, trans. T. M. Knox, with an introduction and fragments trans. Richard Kroner (Chicago: University of Chicago Press, 1948), 260–61.
9. Kirmmse, *Kierkegaard in Golden Age Denmark*, 245–47. I've added the names of Clausen and Lehmann.

questions. The first is "What is the importance of 'History' as the key to understanding the meaning and significance of one's present-day life?" Those who do find decisive significance in historical development, he labels "Romantic." Those who do not are termed simply "Agnostic" on this matter of historical development. The Romantic responses subdivide in their response to a second question: "What is the significant kernel of human experience that we call 'Culture' and who are its bearers or guardians?" One response, which he labels "Mandarin," would emphasize "a high literary tradition that is studied, guarded, and passed on by a relatively narrow elite." On the other hand, a position he calls "Populist" "would claim that that which is most valuable and significant in human life is the property of the entire people and that the greatest treasures are—potentially, at least—within the grasp of the lowliest citizen, regardless of his or her literary or formal education."[10]

Filling in the squares will serve us as we seek to understand Kierkegaard's work in his Danish context. Regarding the figures that concern us in this brief sketch, in the Mandarin-Romantic category, Kirmmse places conservative Golden Age voices thusly: J. P. Mynster (1775–1854) in the first generation and Johan Ludvig Heiberg (1791–1860) and Hans Lassen Martensen (1808–1884) in the second. For now, it must suffice to say that Mynster, who became bishop of Zealand in 1834, worked against the lay preacher revivalist movement, and in 1842, "he got the king to pass an ordinance for the forcible baptism of the children of Baptists."[11] Kierkegaard could praise Mynster in certain administrative respects, but he could not square the mild romanticism of Mynster's preaching with New Testament teaching. As a professor of theology at the University of Copenhagen, Martensen was

---

10. Ibid.
11. Julia Watkin, *Historical Dictionary of Kierkegaard's Philosophy* (Lanham, MD: Scarecrow, 2001), 172. Watkin's book is very useful in providing a chronology, maps for the period, the titles of Kierkegaard texts in Danish and in translation, and a comprehensive dictionary of categories and people who functioned in Kierkegaard's formulation and reception. Kirmmse, *Kierkegaard in Golden Age Denmark*, 74, points out that "up to 1849 belief and neutrality in matters of religion had no legal existence whatever, excepting as a crime," "though a limited legal recognition had been granted to the relative handful of Jews, Calvinists, and foreign Roman Catholics who found themselves in Denmark."

INTRODUCTION: A BIOGRAPHICAL SKETCH

Kierkegaard's teacher in his theological studies and earlier had been hired by Kierkegaard to tutor him on the main points of Schleiermacher's dogmatics. But it was Martensen's efforts to adopt and adapt Hegel's passion for unity that was their central point of contention.[12] Martensen was critical of the pantheistic turn in Hegel's thought and refused to identify finitude and sin. But his affirmation of the reality of human life came to be fitted within a Hegelian notion of divine development.[13] Martensen became Mynster's successor as bishop. As we turn to Kierkegaard's life, we'll take note of how Martensen's eulogizing sermon at Mynster's funeral became the match that lit the fuse for the final explosion of Kierkegaard's vehemence.

We'll pause to locate one more figure prominent in Kierkegaard's context. The Populist Romantic square in Kirmmse's diagram finds N. F. S. Grundtvig (1783–1872), the great hymn writer,[14] appropriator of Nordic mythology, and proponent of lay preachers and the folk school movement in Denmark. While Grundtvig's long life includes at least three very different periods, it was his "matchless discovery" (in the second phase of the second period, 1824–28) of the "living word" carried by the congregation's confessing of the Apostles' Creed through eighteen centuries that earned the devastating critique of Kierkegaard's pseudonym Johannes Climacus in *Philosophical Fragments* (1844) and *Concluding Unscientific Postscript to Philosophical Fragments* (1846). There were other voices in the cacophonous air over Copenhagen in this turbulent period, figures such as the liberals H. N. Clausen and Orla Lehmann, who represented a Christian cultural synthesis supportive of the rule of the urban upper classes. But it's time to turn to Kierkegaard himself, whom Kirmmse finds occupying

---

12. Curtis L. Thompson and David Kangas have helped us locate Martensen well in Hans L. Martensen, *Between Hegel and Kierkegaard: Hans L. Martensen's Philosophy of Religion*, trans. Curtis L. Thompson and David Kangas (Oxford: Oxford University Press, 1997). Martensen's early pieces stressing the reality of freedom had an important impact on Kierkegaard. See also Curtis L. Thompson, *Following the Cultured Public's Chosen One: Why Martensen Mattered to Kierkegaard* (Copenhagen: Museum Tusculanum Press, 2008).
13. For a brief summary of how Martensen's writing in dogmatics and ethics does seem to fall "between Hegel and Kierkegaard," see Paul R. Sponheim, *Kierkegaard on Christ and Christian Coherence* (New York: Harper, 1968), 58–65.
14. E.g., "O day full of grace that now we see," "Built on a rock, the church shall stand," and a half dozen other hymns in *Evangelical Lutheran Worship* (Minneapolis: Augsburg Fortress, 2006).

the Populist Agnostic square (on the decisiveness of historical development for faith).

Søren Aabye Kierkegaard was born on May 5, 1813, to Michael Pedersen Kierkegaard and Ane Sørensdatter Lund in Copenhagen. He was baptized June 3 in the Church of the Holy Ghost, Copenhagen. Ane had been a servant girl in the home of Michael and his first wife. There was some scandal; their first child was born less than five months after the wedding. One might characterize the relationship Søren had with his parents by referring to the brooding father and the absent mother. There's not a single reference to his mother in Kierkegaard's voluminous writings, even in his extensive private journals and papers. Yet the mother of Hans Lassen Martensen reported that receiving word of Ane's death left Søren "crushed by her loss."[15] Søren was the couple's seventh and last child. By the time of his mother's death in 1834, Søren had already lost two brothers and two sisters. A third sister died later that year. The family seemed cursed.

The Melancholy Father

That brings us to the brooding father. When he married Ane, Michael Pedersen Kierkegaard was a wealthy businessman in Copenhagen, having inherited his uncle's hosiery business and having proven himself a shrewd investor. But he had known poverty as well. He was born on a farm in the middle of Jutland, in western Denmark, and had worked as a shepherd boy until age eleven when he fled to Copenhagen. In 1846, Søren writes in his journal of how his father, "suffering painfully, hungry and exhausted, once stood on a hill and cursed God—and the man was unable to forget it when he was eighty-two years old."[16] That long memory of a boy's words of angry

---

15. Gary J. Dorrien, *Kantian Reason and Hegelian Spirit* (Chichester, UK: John Wiley & Sons, 2012), 262. There will be more to say later about Kierkegaard's thoughts on women and about feminist interpretation of Kierkegaard.
16. Søren Kierkegaard, *Søren Kierkegaard's Journals and Papers*, ed. and trans. Howard V. Hong and Edna H. Hong (Bloomington: Indiana University Press, 1967–78), 3:5874 (hereafter cited as JP). See also Joakim Garff, *Søren Kierkegaard: A Biography*, trans. Bruce H. Kirmmse (Princeton: Princeton University Press, 2005), 136. At this point in his lively and controversial eight-hundred-page work, Garff notes that when Søren's older brother Peter finished reading this journal entry, he said to Barfod (who was assigned the task of arranging Kierkegaard's papers for publication), "This is

INTRODUCTION: A BIOGRAPHICAL SKETCH

frustration might unreasonably plant a seed of guilt in the man and the religious streams of the time watered that seed for Michael. A stream of Pietism popular in Germany and Denmark was that of Count N. L. Zinzendorf (1702–1760), whose followers were known as the "Herrnhuters."[17] They emphasized the suffering Redeemer covered with wounds and blood. Søren was indoctrinated in this piety by his father, and the family regularly attended Herrnhuter Sunday-evening services. Sunday mornings, the family was to be found at the services of the Lutheran State Church where J. P. Mynster brought a message that shared the Pietists' concern for a deeply personal and emotional form of devotion, though in a mainstream way deeply infused with the influences of Romanticism.[18] In his brooding, Michael also bequeathed to his son a dark sense of melancholy, at least as Søren came to see things: "Merciful God, what a dreadful wrong my father did me in his melancholy—an old man who unloads all his depression on a poor child, to say nothing of what was even more dreadful, and yet for all that the best of fathers."[19] Indeed, he could make distinctions and write tenderly of his father: "I learned from him what fatherly love is, and through this I gained a conception of the divine fatherly love, the one unshakable thing in life, the true Archimedean point."[20]

Regine

That brings us to the second of four decisive crises John Updike highlights in his review of Joakim Garff's book: to 1837, when twenty-four-year-old Søren, now a University student and man-about-town, met fourteen-year-old Regina (known by the informal name of Regine)

---

my father's story—and *ours*, too." For a critical response to Garff's earlier work, see Sylvia Walsh, "Reading Kierkegaard with Kierkegaard Against Garff," *Søren Kierkegaard Newsletter* 38 (July 1999): 4–8, and Garff's response, *Søren Kierkegaard Newsletter* 38 (July 1999): 9–14.
17. Kirmmse, *Kierkegaard in Golden Age Denmark*, 30, clarifies that these true believers were so called "because they had organized in the 'shelter of the Lord' and built a house of worship on Zinzendorf's estate."
18. In his excellent *Kierkegaard: A Biography* (Cambridge: Cambridge University Press, 2001), 37–38, Alastair Hannay helpfully suggests the convergence of the two streams of Christian faith for Michael Pedersen Kierkegaard.
19. JP, 5:6019.
20. JP, 5:5468.

xxi

Olsen.[21] He was smitten with her and proposed marriage to her on September 8, 1840. Two days later Regine accepted. Kierkegaard almost immediately had dark second thoughts. He did not believe he was suited for married life, and thirteen turbulent months later, he broke off the engagement. He did manage to get her to be the one who publicly broke things off, protecting her good name. We edge here into the profound topic (to be discussed later) of Kierkegaard's understanding of communication. Regine had been troubled by his growing coolness and apparent efforts to break off the engagement, and Søren finally adopted a deceptive persona in responding to her question, "Will you never marry?" He said, "Well, yes, in ten years, when I have begun to simmer down and I need a lusty young miss to rejuvenate me."[22]

It is hard to know what all was involved in Kierkegaard's breaking off the engagement. Surely his legacy of melancholy was a factor.[23] But there were many components at play in this complex man. Julia Watkin summarizes for us: "Although in his journals and works Kierkegaard sometimes gives the impression that he hoped that their marriage might still be possible, there was also the thought that one must not marry and have secrets from one's partner."[24] There was also "a sense of his having a vocation that calls for the renunciation of marriage."[25] There is no question that the tempestuous time with Regine is at work in the authorship,[26] most explicitly in the pseudonymous works of

---

21. John Updike, "Incommensurability: A New Biography of Kierkegaard," *The New Yorker*, March 28, 2005, 71–76. I cite this reference in part to at least allude to one of the many theologically important literary figures (to name only two more: Walker Percy and Flannery O'Connor) whom Kierkegaard influenced.
22. Garff, *Søren Kierkegaard*, 188. Hannay, *Kierkegaard*, 158, offers a slightly different translation, but the same deceiving misrepresentation of Kierkegaard's feelings is conveyed.
23. See JP, 5:5664: "But if I were to have explained myself, I would have had to initiate her into terrible things, my relationship to my father, his melancholy, the eternal night brooding within me, my going astray, my lusts and debauchery, which, however, in the eyes of God are perhaps not so glaring." As to Kierkegaard's sense of guilt, see JP, 5:5515, and the reference to "the suffering I regard as God's punishment."
24. See JP, 5:5664 for the lament that "there are so many marriages that conceal little stories."
25. Watkin, *Historical Dictionary*, 2.
26. There are many questions that arise concerning Kierkegaard's multifaceted authorship. In a couple of pages in this sketch, we examine his use of pseudonymity and "indirect communication." In *On My Work as an Author* (1851), Kierkegaard claimed that "the issue . . . of the whole authorship [was] becoming a Christian." Søren Kierkegaard, *The Point of View*, ed. and trans. Howard V. Hong and Edna H. Hong (Princeton: Princeton University Press, 1998), 8

INTRODUCTION: A BIOGRAPHICAL SKETCH

1843. *Fear and Trembling*'s profound pondering of the Abraham/Isaac story is a clear instance and *Repetition*, published on the same day in 1843, had to be changed when Kierkegaard learned of Regine's marriage to one of her former tutors, Fritz Schlegel. There is a penitent tone to the sadness with which Kierkegaard writes in his journals: "My sin is that I did not have faith, faith that for God all things are possible."[27] One need not agree with the global tone of this dark self-estimation, but it is striking that in *Two Discourses at the Communion on Fridays* (1851), the dedication is "To One Unnamed . . . the entire authorship as it was from the beginning."[28]

Perhaps prominent in that not-suited-for-marriage vocation was the call to write. And write he did. But to what purpose? Well, way back in 1835, on a vacation (taken at his father's suggestion) in North Zealand, at Gilleleie, he had written in his journal that he needed "to get clear about *what I must do,* not what I must know, except insofar as knowledge must precede every action." And, "What matters is to find a purpose, to see what it really is that God wants *me* to do; the crucial thing is to find a truth that is truth *for me,* to find *the idea for which I am willing to live and die.*"[29] It took him a while to find and claim that calling. His father died in 1838, and perhaps that loss stirred him to the action of which he had spoken four years earlier. In 1840 he passed his university exam in theology, and in 1841 he publicly defended his doctoral-level dissertation on *The Concept of Irony with Continual Reference to Socrates.* Then in February 1843, he published the work that he considered the beginning of his authorship, *Either/Or,* followed in October by *Fear and Trembling* and *Repetition.* There then followed an incredible outpouring of pseudonymous works, including the works most cited from this period in his reception, *Philosophical Fragments* and

---

(hereafter cited as PV). Regarding the parallel double tracks of pseudonymous writings and signed writings, he distinguished between "what is offered with the left hand and what is offered with the right" (PV, 193). Was he so ambidextrous that the wildly diverse group of writings could serve to promote any single concern as "the issue"?

27. JP, 5:5521.
28. WA, 162. Robert Perkins points out in his introduction, ibid., 1, that "Kierkegaard did not write a book entitled *Without Authority*" but this expression is used to title a "collection of late writings" in which he refers to "his lack of authority and the issue of authority generally."
29. JP, 5:5100.

xxiii

The Concept of Anxiety (1844), *Stages on Life's Way* (1845), and *Concluding Unscientific Postscript* (1846). At that point, we are about at the end of what scholars call "the first authorship." He felt he had said what needed to be said to the Danish people; the *Postscript* was indeed to be "concluding." Kierkegaard writes in his journal of plans to take a country parish.[30]

It was not to be. Early in 1846, he became involved in a quarrel with the *Corsair*, a powerful and widely circulated paper that specialized in anonymous political satire. (This provides the third scandal Updike draws from Garff.) Julia Watkin points out that, despite the *Corsair*'s original aim to "serve the cause of political liberalism," "it degenerated into a publication that exploited fact, rumors and gossip."[31] In Kierkegaard's case, the ridicule took as its target not only his ideas but his physical appearance, and the caricatures showing the uneven length of his trousers became the talk of Copenhagen. It's fair to say that Kierkegaard's overreaction meant he could no longer present himself as a carefree walker of the streets of the city, but it also intensified his sense of disappointment over the minimal response to his call to the Danish church to clarify that being a Dane does not make one automatically a Christian. A second authorship would be needed, speaking more directly.[32]

Pseudonymity and Indirect Communication

That matter of the "how" of Kierkegaard's writing brings us to a range of issues that could arguably have been discussed earlier in this sketch. Perhaps engaging those issues will serve us well here, between the two authorships. While the pseudonymous works are probably the most studied in Kierkegaard's reception, it is essential to take note of the fact that in the same four years he was producing the aforementioned pseudonymous works, he also published religious works under his own

---

30. See JP, 5:5873: "It is now my intention to qualify as a pastor. For several months I have been praying to God to keep on helping me, for it has been clear to me for some time now that I ought not to be a writer any longer, something I can be only totally or not at all."
31. Watkin, *Historical Dictionary*, 98.
32. In 1851, Kierkegaard writes in his journal: "It ends with direct communication" (JP, 6:6786).

name, indeed eighteen pieces carrying the name *Upbuilding Discourses*. While these discourses do not employ specifically Christian categories, they give voice to themes that will be taken up in the second authorship. Thus, the first discourse in the final group of four bears the title "Man's Need of God Constitutes His Highest Perfection" (1844). As Johannes Climacus gave his "thought project" (*Philosophical Fragments*) a "historical dress" in a 550-page *Postscript*, the veronymous literature narrows the focus as well in *Upbuilding Discourses in Various Spirits* (1845). This two-track literature calls on us to consider what Kierkegaard meant by his use of pseudonymity and, more broadly, his understanding of what he called "indirect communication."[33]

We can begin with pseudonymity, noting at the outset that there is a dizzying plurality of voices here that stubbornly resist being reduced to a unity. Some interpreters have said that what Kierkegaard was up to was simply evoking the sheer literary opulence of plurality in positions. Of Kierkegaard, Roger Poole suggests that "the mystery is impenetrable to the end, and that this is because Kierkegaard's writing has made all solutions impossible."[34] *Either/Or* becomes then the first work in an authorship that might well be called Either/Or/Or/Or....

But we get suggestions that can be read as pointing to a structure. *Stages on Life's Way*, edited by Hilarius Bookbinder (1845), invites us into the stages or spheres of the aesthetic, the ethical, and the religious. There's more when we get to 1846 and find Johannes Climacus distinguishing between "Religiousness A and Religiousness B." Scholars have argued that a "Religiousness C" emerges in the signed *Works of Love* (1847) and *Christian Discourses* (1848) and the books written by Anti-Climacus (but "edited by [*udgivet af*] S. Kierkegaard"): *The Sickness unto Death* (1849) and particularly *Practice in Christianity* (1850). I am presenting Søren Kierkegaard as a Christian writer and hope that

---

33. See Howard V. Hong and Edna H. Hong, eds., *The Essential Kierkegaard* (Princeton: Princeton University Press, 2000), ix: "There is in the varied complex of thirty-eight works, in two parallel series of pseudonymous works and signed works, a dialectical structure, a 'coherence,' a 'comprehensive plan' [*total Anlaeg*]," citing JP, 5:5891.
34. Roger Poole, *Kierkegaard: The Indirect Communication* (Charlottesville: University Press of Virginia, 1993), 1.

the upcoming presentation of *The Sickness unto Death* will support that orientation. I believe the pseudonymity serves that purpose.[35]

But Kierkegaard doesn't make it easy for us. We can position ourselves somewhere between Kierkegaard's own remarks in a "first and last declaration" added to the *Postscript* (1846) and his *Point of View for My Work as an Author*, written in 1848 and published posthumously in 1859. In the former, he wrote that in the pseudonymous books "there is not a single word by me. I have no opinion about them except as a third party."[36] That would seem to settle the matter of the relationship of the pseudonyms to Kierkegaard's own views. But of course it turns out not to be a "last" declaration, for in *Point of View*, Kierkegaard asserts that his writing has been guided throughout by a religious pursuit as reflected in a threefold division of the authorship with the culmination in the religious. *The Point of View* is a strange work formally, as Garff notes: "The work hovers between autobiography and literary testament, but viewed properly it is neither one nor the other—its genre is rather that of a chameleon."[37] The eminent Kierkegaard scholar Emanuel Hirsch describes the book as "a religious autobiography so strange that there is nothing like it in the whole of world literature."[38] It helps a little that in *The Point of View*, Kierkegaard does grant that the explanation given concerning the aesthetic writing

---

35. In "Kierkegaard's Theology," in Lippitt and Pattison, *Oxford Handbook of Kierkegaard*, 292, Sylvia Walsh goes to Kierkegaard's journals where he describes himself as "personally and religiously a penitent" and makes the point that he is one "who flies to grace" inasmuch as "the one who presents this picture must first and foremost humble himself under it, confess that he, even though he himself is struggling within himself to approach this picture, is very far from being that" (JP, 6:6317). See also Bruce H. Kirmmse, "'I Am Not a Christian'—A 'Sublime Lie'? Or: 'Without Authority,' Playing Desdemona to Christendom's Othello," in *Anthropology and Authority*, ed. Poul Houe, Gordon D. Marino, and Sven Hakon Rossel (Amsterdam: Rodopi, 2000).
36. Søren Kierkegaard, *Concluding Unscientific Postscript to "Philosophical Fragments,"* ed. and trans. Howard V. Hong and Edna H. Hong (Princeton: Princeton University Press, 1992), 1:626 (hereafter cited as CUP).
37. Garff, *Søren Kierkegaard*, 552. Garff notes indecisiveness in the very structure of the work: "Its 'Epilogue' is not even its last word, but serves as a prologue to a subsequent 'Conclusion' which turns out not to be a conclusion because it is succeeded by 'Two Notes,' which are themselves preceded by a new 'preface,' after which follows more writing, followed by an additional 'Postscript,' the true postscript of which is yet another 'Postscript' that urgently pleads for 'just one more word.'"
38. Emanuel Hirsch, *Kierkegaard-studien* (Gütersloh: C. Bertelsmann, 1933), 357, cited in David R. Law, "A Cacophony of Voices: The Multiple Authors and Readers of Kierkegaard's *The Point of View for My Work as an Author*," in *The Point of View*, vol. 22 of IKC, ed. Robert L. Perkins (Macon, GA: Mercer University Press, 2010), 12–47.

as a deception "concedes [*indrømmer*] a little too much along the line of consciousness."³⁹ He pairs that overemphasis on consciousness with occasional references to God as the author.⁴⁰

Given limitations of space for this volume, perhaps it is best to place this puzzle of pseudonymity in the larger literary context of Kierkegaard's thinking about direct and indirect communication. While there's considerable complexity in his use of the term, it's clear that indirect communication is what is needed for ethical-religious communication. Noel Adams nicely summarizes the *Postscript*'s crucial distinction between a doctrine/teaching/theory (*Laere*) and an existence-communication (*Existence-Meddelelse*): "A doctrine can be communicated directly (and thus is an item of knowledge that can be understood), but . . . an existence-communication cannot (and thus is not an item of knowledge that can be understood)."⁴¹ Kierkegaard's concern is what it takes to become a Christian and that is not a doctrine to be taught. In 1846, in the *Postscript*, Johannes Climacus drives home relentlessly that "precisely because Christianity is not a doctrine, it holds true, as developed previously, that there is an enormous difference between knowing what Christianity is and being a Christian."⁴² And how does one become a Christian? It entails the passion of choosing. As Anti-Climacus would put it in *Practice in Christianity* in 1849 in commenting on John 12:32 ("And I, when I am lifted up from the earth, will draw all to myself."): "Christ also first and foremost wants to help every human being to become a self, requires this of him first and foremost, requires that he, by repenting, become a self, in order then to draw him to himself. He wants to draw the human being to himself, but in order truly to draw him to himself he wants to draw him only as a free being to himself, that is, through a choice."⁴³

Julia Watkin drives home the point that "the one communicating

---

39. PV, 77.
40. See Law, "Cacophony of Voices," 31–34.
41. Noel S. Adams, "Kierkegaard's Conception of Indirect Communication in 'The Dialectic of Ethical and Ethical Religious Communication' of 1847," *Søren Kierkegaard Newsletter* (August 2006): 10–15 (12). See also Alastair Hannay, "Something on Hermeneutics and Communication in Kierkegaard After All," *Søren Kierkegaard Newsletter* (September 2001): 8–14, for the sense of "imparting" carried by the term translated as communication (*Meddelelse*).
42. CUP, 1:380.

what the choice is also needs to step back to make room for the other person to make a real choice."[44] One way of stepping back for an author is pseudonymity and offering a "first and last declaration" of no responsibility for the pseudonyms. The aesthetic, ethical, and religious possibilities in the authorship are real possibilities, and the pseudonyms take away Kierkegaard's presence, which could interfere with his reader's choosing truly for himself. Another way, according to Anti-Climacus in *Practice in Christianity*, is to place "qualitative opposites in a unity" as with jest and earnestness, or attack and defense.[45] In 1848, lest one suppose from the second authorship that Magister Kierkegaard has suddenly been converted away from the aesthetic and ethical-religious writings of the first period, he publishes a purely aesthetic piece, *The Crisis and a Crisis in the Life of an Actress*, by the author Inter et Inter. Together the two authorships offer real alternatives, inviting the reader's passionate choosing. Noel Adams points out that in this there is "a kind of deception that is an integral part of the relationship between the communicator [*Meddeler*] and the receiver [*Modtager*]." He cites the *Journals* where Kierkegaard speaks of "deceiving into the truth"[46] and observes that "the duplexity of the deception in Christianity, of course, is the God-man's incognito."[47] Much more on the incognito follows as we turn to *The Sickness unto Death*.

    I am suggesting that Kierkegaard's use of pseudonymity was not simply adopting a literary strategy familiar from the Romanticism of the period, but a method rooted in the content of his message requiring indirect communication. But as that message seemed to be ignored, he found it necessary to speak more directly formally, while still preserving and even sharpening the challenging material otherness of his message, which still represents indirect communication.[48]

43. Søren Kierkegaard, *Practice in Christianity*, ed. and trans. Howard V. Hong and Edna H. Hong (Princeton: Princeton University Press, 1991), 160 (hereafter cited as PC).
44. Watkin, *Historical Dictionary*, 128.
45. PC, 133.
46. JP, 1:653:24, p. 288.
47. Adams, "Kierkegaard's Conception," 13.
48. See JP, 6:6786 where Kierkegaard defends his use of indirect communication, applying that term to Anti-Climacus's *Practice in Christianity*.

INTRODUCTION: A BIOGRAPHICAL SKETCH

The Kirkekamp: Who Is a Witness to the Truth?

In this second authorship, some of Kierkegaard's most influential works are to be found. I have mentioned the "semi-pseudonymous" works of Anti-Climacus and the signed *Works of Love* (1847) and *Christian Discourses* (1848); and then further, "upbuilding" discourses (1850–51) and *For Self-Examination* (1851). Finally there erupts the vituperative attack on the Danish state church, an attack so radical that some interpreters have questioned Kierkegaard's sanity at the time. Bruce Kirmmse makes a compelling case that "Kierkegaard's final, 'radical' political views, which inform his attack on the Church and which traditional interpretations find so unaccountable and unprecedented, are the fruit of at least a decade of political thinking and writing, a decade which straddles both sides of 1846."[49]

The attack was triggered by Hans Lassen Martensen's sermon at Mynster's funeral. The incendiary words were these: "From this man, whose precious memory fills our hearts, our thoughts are led back to the whole series of witnesses to the truth, stretching across the ages, from the days of the Apostles up to our own times. . . . Our departed teacher also served as a link in this holy chain of witnesses to the truth, to the honor of God Our Father."[50] That was more than Kierkegaard could bear, given the mild Romanticism of Mynster's preaching, but he waited thirteen months before responding. The response took the form of a series of articles published in *Faedrelandet* (The Fatherland) (1854–55) and culminated in the nine issues of the appropriately titled polemic *Øjeblikket* (The Moment, The Instant). On September 28, having exhausted his financial and physical resources, he collapsed on the streets of Copenhagen. He died in the hospital November 11 after having refused to see his brother Peter and infamously refusing to receive the sacrament from any ordained representative of the church.[51] It's important to recognize that even in this last turbulent

---

49. Kirmmse, "I Am Not a Christian," 4–5.
50. Garff, *Søren Kierkegaard*, 729.
51. Hannay, *Kierkegaard*, 411–18, writes movingly of these sad final weeks and of the verse Kierkegaard chose for his tombstone. The verse speaks of the whole fight being done and of resting and speaking, "unceasingly, unceasingly" "with my Jesus."

year, Kierkegaard could strike a quite different tone in publishing *The Unchangeableness of God*, to which I will refer in the final portion of this book.[52]

Out of this dizzying wealth of authorship, the reader of this book is invited to proceed to an analysis and commentary on *The Sickness unto Death*. Why this book? Well, this Mapping the Tradition series aspires to offer a guide to "pivotal thinkers in Christian history," with particular attention to "the lasting significance of that thinker for the history of Christian theology." SUD arguably represents the clearest statement of Kierkegaard's "take" on Christianity.[53] In a much-cited journal reference, Kierkegaard says: "Johannes Climacus and Anti-Climacus have several things in common, but the difference is that whereas Johannes Climacus places himself so low that he even says himself that he is not a Christian, one seems to be able to detect in Anti-Climacus that he regards himself to be a Christian on an extraordinarily high level. . . . I would place myself higher than Johannes Climacus, lower than Anti-Climacus."[54] Johannes Climacus offers the *Fragments* as a thought project. He is writing from outside the faith, wondering if "a historical point of departure can be given for

---

52. In September of 1855—some scant two months before his death—when he published this sermon (which he had preached back in May of 1851), he added a brief preface dated May 5, Kierkegaard's birthday of course. The text is James 1:17-21, "my first, my beloved text," on which he based three of his upbuilding discourses. See Garff, *Søren Kierkegaard*, 674.
53. See JP, 6:6361, where Kierkegaard says that in SUD, "it was granted to me to illuminate Christianity on a scale greater than I ever had dreamed possible; crucial categories are directly disclosed there. Consequently, it must be published." But see also JP, 6:6519, where he writes, "[T]he position of [*Three*] *Discourses at the Communion on Fridays* (1849) is once and for all designated as the fulcrum of the authorship." In her introduction to her translation of *Discourses at the Communion on Fridays* (Bloomington: Indiana University Press, 2011), Sylvia Walsh makes much of this emphasis, stressing the veronymous character of the discourses and also contrasts SUD's intensification of despair to the Communion Discourses' emphasis on a more positive intensification in the consciousness and life of the person coming to the altar after confession of sin. In JP, 6:6519, Kierkegaard speaks of these three discourses as being "parallel to Anti-Climacus." In any case, it is difficult to overstate the importance of SUD in the theological reception of Kierkegaard.
54. JP, 6:6433. See also JP, 6:6337, 6238. Scholars disagree about the meaning of "anti-." The Hongs caution us by writing, "It does not mean 'against.' It is an old form of 'ante' (before), as in 'anticipate,' and 'before' also denotes a relation of rank, as in 'before me' in the First Commandment." But Robert L. Perkins, the editor of the International Kierkegaard Commentary series, in introducing Anti-Climacus's other work, PC, writes: "Summing up, Kierkegaard initially intended 'Anti-Climacus' to be *against* Climacus, back toward the aesthetic. When the new pseudonym was finally used in *The Sickness unto Death* and later in *Practice in Christianity*, Anti-Climacus is still against Climacus, but in the opposite direction: he represents the decidedly Christian. Finally, 'Anti' continues to mean against. Relation of rank requires difference."

an eternal consciousness." Regardless of what we make of Kierkegaard locating himself below Anti-Climacus, SUD is written from within the faith. Lest that location suggest satisfied security, Anti-Climacus will remind us that the believer always faces the possibility of offense.[55] But it is the decisive Christian claims that carry that possibility; the claims are there for our study. From that precarious position, the book offers a perspective on many other Kierkegaardian treatments of themes important to Christian thought. Moreover, as for "lasting significance . . . for the history of Christian theology," part 2 of this book will show the crucial impact of *The Sickness unto Death* and, more broadly, of the claims in the other portions of the literature that this book illumines.

So, let us turn to *The Sickness unto Death* itself. A heads-up note may be helpful here. In the next two chapters, I offer a combination of exposition and analysis familiar to readers of commentaries. A glance at SUD's four-page table of contents may leave one dizzy and discouraged. Anti-Climacus offers an abundance of delicate distinctions, particularly in the first part's presentation of despair. His structure is not more complex than his subject matter: despair/sin as "the sickness unto death." In this short book, chapters 1 and 2 stay very close to the text, but do not offer a discrete comment on every one of the three dozen pieces composing this structure. Textual exposition is somewhat selective in order to lift out controlling themes for theological analysis.[56] My hope and expectation is that my readers will have SUD's text at hand and be called back into those profound pages repeatedly.

---

55. I have discussed this dialectic in Paul R. Sponheim, "God's Changelessness: The Triumph of Grace in Law and Gospel as 'Archimedean Point,'" in *"The Moment" and Late Writings*, vol. 23 of IKC, ed. Robert L. Perkins (Macon, GA: Mercer University Press, 2009), 101–28.
56. I have reproduced only the major headings of SUD's highly detailed structure. The headings I have introduced for commentary and analysis begin with **Com.:**

PART I

The Sickness unto Death: A Christian Psychological Exposition for Upbuilding and Awakening by Anti-Climacus: Analysis and Commentary

As we turn to this challenging and complex work, I offer a very brief overview of the journey ahead.

Anti-Climacus writes of what it is and how it is to exist "before God," given that there is an "infinite qualitative difference" between the Creator and the creature. There's no choice about being in some relationship with God, in the becoming self that is a given from/by the "Constituting Power." But there is life-determining choosing to be done about how one relates to God, for there's a calling in what's given for the human self. To choose to be wrongly related to God is to be in despair, whether or not one acknowledges that openly or feels it inwardly. That is the sickness unto death. The first part of this "Christian psychological exposition" offers a detailed analysis of the various forms to be found in the variegated territory of despair. In being related to the eternal God, the creaturely self finds the proper measure for assessing life's afflictions. All other problems and perils pale before despair, which, as ever present, is indeed the sickness "unto" death.

This becoming self is a relation as a duality of the temporal and the eternal, the finite and the infinite. But the self's narrative is the story of a third element—a "positive third"—as the self relates itself to itself, choosing how the elements of the self will come together. Thus, despair can be analyzed in terms of an imbalance in the constituting elements: freedom and necessity, infinitude and finitude. Or the self's despair can be analyzed in terms of the degree of consciousness to be found in the self's relating to itself and to the Constituting Power. Varying degrees of consciousness characterize the self's choosing either not to be the self it is being called to be or choosing to be a self other than that calling.

The second part, "Despair Is Sin," advances the analysis through the explicit judgment that this "misrelation" to God is sin, which is always against God. Again, the growing consciousness of the self marks a despairing deepening of the sinful condition. Anti-Climacus depicts this development in terms of the Trinity. As constituted, one exists "before God," and one is invited to live "on the most intimate terms with God." But the self may find that news too good to be true and in weakness or in strength be offended and go its own way. That going astray is not a matter of ignorance, but is rooted in a willed choosing. Anti-Climacus offers a sharp critique of his beloved Socrates, who is here understood to fail to recognize that one can know the good and yet not choose it. Moreover, the pseudonym tightens the knot of judgment by an appeal to the doctrine of hereditary sin. The intensification in consciousness and sin continues before God, who came to be born, suffer, and die for this self. Finally, there is the sin against the Holy Spirit, as in dismissing Christianity or as in saying that one has no opinion about the gospel that has been truly preached to them.

Thus a grim account awaits us, but throughout Anti-Climacus's message for "upbuilding and awakening," there are pointed references to the saving action of God toward the despairing creatures. There too, one is before a God who is marked by an "infinite qualitative difference" from the creatures. For the creatures, this radical God is risking the possibility of offense. Yet all the same, in no way does God differ from the creature more than in forgiving sins. In that difference there lies the hope that one may come to be grounded transparently in God after all, which is the definition of faith.

PART I: THE SICKNESS UNTO DEATH

Preface

Kierkegaard was on the verge of publishing this book under his own name, but at the last minute, Anti-Climacus appeared as the author.[1] As we have noted in the biographical sketch, Kierkegaard did not regard himself as "a Christian on an extraordinarily high level,"[2] the ranking Anti-Climacus receives from him. As Johannes Climacus in 1846, Kierkegaard had already made the point that while he did not claim to be a Christian, he could present Christian claims and use them as a measuring stick in relationship to what was going on in Danish Christendom.[3] Kierkegaard will not bind Anti-Climacus's presentation of those claims to his own flawed example, though the pseudonym does identify the direction of his striving and S. Kierkegaard appears on the title page as "editor," the one who "gives out" (*udgivet*) the message. There is a claim, a calling, in that message. Johannes Climacus offers his readers a "thought project," but "Anti-Climacus is thetical."[4] A truth claim is at stake in the pages of SUD.

The claim is presented in a "Christian psychological exposition." This is not the first time that the word psychological appears in a pseudonym's title. Back in 1844, in *The Concept of Anxiety*, Vigilius Haufniensis had offered "a simple psychologically orienting deliberation on the dogmatic issue of hereditary sin." There we are told that when psychology deals with sin, the "mood becomes that of persistent observation, like the fearlessness of a secret agent."[5] Thus Vigilius is "the watchman of Copenhagen." He is fearless in his observance of Copenhagen, but he lacks "earnestness [*Alvor*] expressed in courageous resistance."[6] Nonetheless, his book has a direction in mind. Its last sentence is, "As soon as psychology has finished with anxiety, it is to be delivered to dogmatics."[7] In Anti-Climacus, the

---

1. The journals provide an indication of Kierkegaard's earlier pondering of this pseudonym. See Robert L. Perkins, introduction to *Practice in Christianity*, vol. 20 of IKC, ed. Robert L. Perkins (Macon, GA: Mercer University Press, 2004), 1–9.
2. JP, 6:6433.
3. CUP, 1:271–74, 366–67, 466.
4. JP, 6:6439.
5. CA, 15.
6. Ibid.

delivery has arrived. The first part of SUD is richly theological, but its category is despair as the sickness unto death. The second part completes the delivery already in its three-word title, "Despair Is Sin." That's unambiguously theological talk. It will be clear in the analysis to follow that each part speaks to the other in this "Christian psychological exposition."

The title page for SUD employs varying font sizes and selective use of bold face. Now in a smaller (down two steps) font size but reclaiming the bold face of **Sickness unto Death** we find the words "**for upbuilding and awakening**."[8] That gets us to a crucial point in Anti-Climacus's preface. He writes:

> Many may find the form of this "exposition" strange; it may seem to them too rigorous to be upbuilding and too upbuilding to be rigorously scholarly. . . . From the Christian point of view, everything, indeed everything, ought to serve for upbuilding. . . . It is precisely Christianity's relation to life (in contrast to a scholarly distance from life) or the ethical aspect of Christianity that is upbuilding. . . . It is Christian heroism—a rarity, to be sure—to venture wholly to become oneself, an individual human being, this specific individual human being, alone before God.[9]

The "discourses," signed by Kierkegaard, carry "upbuilding" in their titles. In each preface, Kierkegaard stresses that what he offers is "'not sermons,' because its author has no authority *to preach*." But the discourses are located somewhere short of SUD in the progression of Kierkegaard's authorship, for that sentence continues by saying the discourses are "'upbuilding discourses,' not discourses for upbuilding, because the speaker does not claim to be a *teacher*."[10] In other words, the positive, direct communication of doctrine is absent from the discourses; they are not Christian dogmatics, but as dialectical exercises they indirectly invite the reader into the place of active ethical construction of the relation of the self. He seeks the effect of upbuilding for his reader but eschews the authoritative or

---

7. CA, 162.
8. Alastair Hannay prefers "Edification" to "Upbuilding." "Upbuilding" carries the literal force of "*opbyggelse*." Anti-Climacus writes this book is to build up and wake up (*Opvækelse*) his reader.
9. SUD, 5.
10. EUD, 5.

authoritarian role of the professor. Kierkegaard cared about the words he chose and the directive purposefulness of "for" seemed excessive for him: "The category 'for upbuilding,'" Kierkegaard wrote in a journal entry pertaining to *The Sickness unto Death*, "is more than my category, the poet-category: upbuilding."[11]

Now Anti-Climacus makes the point that from the Christian point of view, everything ought to serve for upbuilding.[12] The Christian claim carries a calling, for human life is a "venture," calling for passionate choice by each individual in becoming oneself before God. The self is not simply given; something has to happen that involves "prodigious strenuousness" and "prodigious responsibility." In a journal entry, Kierkegaard captured how the flowing temporality of human life into an uncertain future calls for this strenuous venturing in the midst of ambiguity:

> Philosophy is perfectly right in saying that life must be understood backward. But then one forgets the other clause—that it must be lived forward. The more one thinks through this clause, the more one concludes that life in temporality never becomes properly understandable, simply because never at any time does one get perfect repose to take a stance—backward.[13]

Throughout his authorship, Kierkegaard spoke variously of the telos of this venture. He can call the self, "which is freedom," the most abstract and the most concrete of all,[14] to "will one thing."[15] We spoke of the self's passionate choosing in freedom. But that doesn't get the self to a "done deal." There's no resting on one's laurels here. In several of his writings, Kierkegaard calls for "repetition." What's involved in that?

---

11. SUD, xxi, citing JP, 6:6431. See the opening pages of the next chapter for my discussion of Kierkegaard's understanding of the "poetical." In her introduction to *Discourses for the Communion*, Sylvia Walsh provides a very clear statement of Kierkegaard's complex understanding of the several distinctions he makes regarding these writings.
12. So the Hongs include the other veronymous writings as "for upbuilding," even though they do not carry the phrase in their titles. They point out that the phrase "for awakening" is used only for the two works by Anti-Climacus.
13. JP, 1:1030.
14. Søren Kierkegaard, *Either/Or*, ed. and trans. Howard V. Hong and Edna H. Hong (Princeton: Princeton University Press, 1992), 2:214 (hereafter cited as E/O).
15. See George B. Connell, *To Be One Thing: Personal Unity in Kierkegaard's Thought* (Macon, GA: Mercer University Press, 1985). Cf. James Giles, ed., *Kierkegaard on Freedom* (New York: Palgrave, 2000).

Well, given the successiveness of life, "the task of the self is not only to realize its potential but also to repeat this realization continually."[16] That will happen if there is a principled continuity through the times of decision in a person's life such that a kind of "contemporaneity" is attained. Johannes Climacus put it this way in his *Postscript*:

> In the individual the point is to ennoble the successive in contemporaneity. To have been young, then to have grown older, and then finally to die is a mediocre existence, for the animal also has that merit. But to unite the elements of life in contemporaneity, that is precisely the task.[17]

George Connell notes how the theme of contemporaneity is ultimately a christological category:

> By believing in, by becoming contemporaneous with, by following and imitating Christ, the self repeats this incarnation within itself. God's gracious act of redemption, when accepted, heals the inner wound of sin and allows the self to relate to itself properly and truly, to exist as it was created to exist: simultaneously finite and infinite, temporal and eternal.[18]

This is serious stuff and calls for earnestness. Already here in the preface, Anti-Climacus sends a shot across the bow of the vessel carrying the professor lecturing away serenely in "scholarly distance from life." It's that detached professor who might find SUD "too upbuilding to be rigorously scholarly," even as the naive religious enthusiast might find the "thetical" structure of the exposition "too rigorous to be upbuilding." The procedure in SUD is as it should be, passionate and precise. This venture "before God" is perilous. Things do not go smoothly. We are by a sickbed here and, indeed, in it. Anti-Climacus is writing about life-and-death matters. The preface closes by saying "the cure is simply to die, to die to the world." That may sound simple, but that prescription is preceded by the countering contained in a somber diagnostic warning we'll have occasion to remember more than once in the pages to follow:

---

16. Connell, *To Be One Thing*, 114.
17. CUP, 1:312.
18. Connell, *To Be One Thing*, 185–86.

PART I: THE SICKNESS UNTO DEATH

Just one more comment, no doubt unnecessary, but nevertheless I will make it: once and for all may I point out that in the whole book, as the title indeed declares, despair is interpreted as a sickness, not as a cure. Despair is indeed that dialectical.[19]

"Dialectical"—two things coming together though they counter each other.[20] The reader of The Sickness unto Death is going to get very familiar with that term. For example, we'll see repeatedly how predicament and promise coexist and even challenge each other in this perilous human venture. Anti-Climacus cannot even tell us what a self is without invoking "dialectic." Given the dialectical, things will seem more complicated, but that doesn't undercut the thetical character of the book. Kierkegaard scholarship has learned to speak of the "thought form of the paradoxical."[21] We are not traveling with Alice in Wonderland, trying to "believe six impossible things before breakfast." As Jason Mahn puts it with Emily Dickinson, Anti-Climacus will aspire to "tell all the truth but tell it slant."[22] Just one more point for now: Sylvia Walsh has well argued that Kierkegaard's writing is

---

19. SUD, 5–6.
20. Watkin, *Historical Dictionary*, 65, provides a concise suggestion of the various ways in which Kierkegaard uses this term. She suggests that his use differs from that of Georg Wilhelm Friedrich Hegel, "who conceives *dialectic* to be the ongoing and opposing movements in the world-historical process. For Kierkegaard, there is still a sense of something opposing something else, but in this case it is in terms of one's taking a questioning and critical stance, striving to see all possible angles in a situation or with a problem, especially seeing what counts against one's own view." Curtis L. Thompson has pointed out to me that in *The Phenomenology of Spirit*, Hegel employs the notion of dialectic at times in ways comparable to Kierkegaard.
21. See Henning Schröer, *Die Denkform der Paradoxalität als Theologisches Problem* (Göttingen: Vandenhoeck & Ruprecht, 1960), 11–28, 76, 131. Note the distinction between the thought form and its products, paradoxes. Schröer emphasizes that the fundamental paradox in Kierkegaard's thought is ontological, a matter of being. I will argue that there is a yet more crucial paradox for Anti-Climacus, one that calls for the language of faith.
22. Jason A. Mahn, *Fortunate Fallibility: Kierkegaard and the Power of Sin* (New York: Oxford University Press, 2011), 129. In explicating Anti-Climacus's claim that "humanity is bound to sin by their own volition—even if that volition cannot be reduced to an individual's 'personal' choice," Mahn even appeals to Niels Bohr's complementarity principle, which recognizes that a subatomic entity can be taken to behave like a particle or a wave, but never both at once. (Lee C. Barrett makes the same appeal in *Eros and Self-Emptying: The Intersections of Augustine and Kierkegaard* [Grand Rapids: Eerdmans, 2013], 395–96 in interpreting the theological plurality of Kierkegaard's writings.) Mahn's exploration of how Kierkegaard plays a "pivotal role in the modern tendency to understand sin in relation to the fissures of human freedom and self-consciousness" leads him to evoke *Felix Fragilitas* in *The Concept of Anxiety*, *Felix Fallibilitas* in *The Sickness unto Death*, and *Felix Offensatio* in *Practice in Christianity*. He closes with a hopeful *Felicitas*, but the book positions the Christian on Easter Eve between cross and resurrection. Mahn connects with "Luther's understanding of *communicatio idiomatum*, whereby God through Christ (and not only through the humanity of Jesus) suffers and dies" (Mahn, *Fortunate Fallibility*, 192).

characterized by an "inverse dialectic," "whereby the positive is always recognized through the negative, which is its essential form."[23] As an example, consider the assertion of Johannes Climacus that "the subjective thinker . . . is continually just as negative as positive, for his positivity consists in the continued inward deepening in which he is cognizant of the negative."[24]

Introduction

If in a page-and-a-half preface Anti-Climacus sets "earnestness" (*Alvor*) as the tone of his book, he needs just over two more pages to introduce his reader to two of the main themes of his work. The large backdrop of *Sickness unto Death* is the notion of the qualitative difference between God and creatures. While the phrase as such does not occur yet, the crucial difference between the eternal and the temporal is decisively expressed here and represents the perspective that undergirds the book's title. Throughout his authorship, he has Georg Wilhelm Friedrich Hegel, the Danish Hegelians, and the distinction-blurring passion for unity in his sights. Already back in 1843 in *Either/Or*, the book Kierkegaard regarded as the beginning of the authorship, we have this on the first page of the preface: "It may at times have occurred to you, dear reader, to doubt somewhat the accuracy of that familiar philosophical thesis that the outer is the inner and the inner is the outer."[25] Kierkegaard did have that doubt in double measure, writing in his journal that the principle of contradiction applies in life and thought.[26] In his *Science of Logic*, Hegel had asserted that the principle of contradiction had been repudiated, and some Danish Hegelians carried

---

23. Walsh, "Kierkegaard's Theology," 194. Cf. ibid., 305: "Kierkegaard views suffering as an inverse sign of God's grace and love, which is just as rigorous as it is lenient in dealing with those who are willing to venture all by entering into an absolute relationship with the divine."
24. CUP, 1:84.
25. E/O, 1:3.
26. See my fuller discussion of Kierkegaard's "systematic impulse" in his "critique of the [Hegelian] system" in Sponheim, *Kierkegaard on Christ*, 17–28. Hans Lassen Martensen carried into Denmark Hegel's assertion that the principle of contradiction has been overcome. J. P. Mynster was on the other side of this Danish controversy on the principle of contradiction. Kierkegaard studied Adolf Trendelenburg's critiques of Hegel. See Arnold B. Come, *Trendelenburg's Influence on Kierkegaard's Modal Categories* (Montreal: Inter Editions, 1991).

PART I: THE SICKNESS UNTO DEATH

this claim forward in arguing that rationalism and supernaturalism had been abrogated as absolute points of view. But Kierkegaard writes in 1843 that "tautology is and remains still the highest principle, the highest maxim of thought,"[27] and that principle bears an ethical burden in the very title of the work, *Either/Or*. So, too, the eternal is not the temporal, nor the temporal the eternal. But they are together, dialectically, in human life.

The recognition of the eternal provides the measuring stick for assessing the problems of human life. What is our worst enemy? Anti-Climacus answers: "Humanly speaking, death is the last of all, and, humanly speaking, there is hope only as long as there is life."[28] The Christ who raised Lazarus makes clear to the Christian that death and all the lesser tribulations of the temporal pale before a sickness that threatens us on the scale of the eternal. Anti-Climacus writes:

> Christianly understood, however, death is by no means the last of all: in fact, it is only a minor event within that which is all, an eternal life.... Nevertheless, Christianity has in turn discovered a miserable condition that man as such does not know exists. This miserable condition is the sickness unto death.[29]

There's the book's title taken from John 11:4. We will note only one further warning. The last paragraph of the introduction asserts that "only the Christian knows what is meant by the sickness unto death."[30] We note the explicitly Christian language employed here. The preface and the introduction after all serve the entirety of SUD. Watch for the explication of this Christian epistemological claim later in the assertion that only through a revelation from God can the sickness finally be understood.[31] On to the algebra of the spirit.[32]

---

27. E/O, 1:38.
28. SUD, 7.
29. SUD, 7–8.
30. SUD, 8.
31. SUD, 95–96.
32. JP, 5:6137.

1

The Sickness unto Death Is Despair

A. Despair Is the Sickness unto Death

Com.: The Algebra of the Spirit

We do well to begin by quoting the tripartite structure that will orient the reader throughout the entirety of this chapter.

> DESPAIR IS A SICKNESS OF THE SPIRIT, OF THE SELF, AND ACCORDINGLY CAN TAKE THREE FORMS: IN DESPAIR NOT TO BE CONSCIOUS OF HAVING A SELF (NOT DESPAIR IN THE STRICT SENSE); IN DESPAIR NOT TO WILL TO BE ONESELF; IN DESPAIR TO WILL TO BE ONESELF.[1]

If despair is a sickness of the self, what's a self? The next two pages in SUD are densely packed with crucial themes. We start with this:

> A human being is spirit. But what is spirit? Spirit is the self. But what is the self? The self is a relation that relates itself to itself or is the relation's relating itself to itself in the relation; the self is not the relation but is the relation's relating itself to itself. A human being is a synthesis of the infinite and the finite, of the temporal and the eternal, or freedom and necessity, in short, a synthesis. A synthesis is a relation between two.

---

1. SUD, 13.

> Considered in this way, a human being is still not a self.... If, however, the relation relates itself to itself, this relation is the positive third, and this is the self.[2]

There are two key points here: (1) the self is a synthesis, a relation, and (2) that relation is a relation that "relates itself to itself." It is a "positive third," involving potential and actual causality. As to the first, we are prepared for the notion that the self is a synthesis by the earlier contrast between the temporal and the eternal. That point was also made by Anti-Climacus in the introduction with the identification of the worst sickness threatening the self as lying on the level of the eternal. Certainly already in this specification of the terms of the synthesis as involving the eternal, we get a foretaste of the high status Anti-Climacus ascribes to the human self. Yet this human belonging with the eternal is not a matter of some sort of personal possession to which one might casually appeal when one finds the temporal fading. Anthropological dualisms have certainly seemed to offer that recourse. But "the third" resists that resolution and the trouble with the third is not a passing matter. Anti-Climacus ends this first section by writing of how the self "cannot rid himself of his self" and closes with this dialectical challenge:

> To have a self, to be a self, is the greatest concession, an infinite concession, given to man, but it is also eternity's claim upon him.[3]

There's a claim here and a calling. Gift and task come together in the constituting of the relation. One gets a sense of the biblical dialectic of the creation of humanity in the image of God as involving both

---

2. Ibid. There is scholarly disagreement about how best to translate the reflexive Danish construction *"forholder sig."* Arnold B. Come, in his intensive study of SUD, *Kierkegaard as Humanist: Discovering My Self* (Montreal: McGill-Queen's University Press, 1995), 8–9, omits the reflexive pronoun in English, arguing that the movement here "is not transitively forward toward an object but reflexively backward in reference to some hidden action of the relation within itself. To say that 'the relation relates itself to itself' could too easily be understood (in English) as positing two objective entities or selves that are being interrelated." Alastair Hannay essentially does likewise in his translation of *The Sickness unto Death* (London: Penguin, 1989), 43, reading Anti-Climacus to be saying "the relation relates to itself." He worries about an English reader supposing that the talk is about two selves, an actual self and a true self. Yet we must recognize that in the relating there is the reality of difference within the complex unity of the self-relating self.
3. SUD, 21.

endowment and telos. The sense of *imago dei* as relationship emerges as Anti-Climacus continues his "dialectical algebra" of the spirit.[4]

In the statement of the synthesis, we find the pairings of finite and infinite, the temporal and the eternal, and, interestingly, freedom and necessity. That third pair is especially interesting because less than twenty pages later, we are told that "freedom is the dialectical aspect of the categories of *possibility* and necessity."[5] It's that dialectical pairing of possibility and necessity in freedom that is used in the exposition of the forms of despair without consciousness of having a self. Arnold Come has offered perhaps the best interpretive suggestion at this point:

> Possibility becomes freedom only when the basic duality of infinitude/finitude and possibility/necessity becomes pervaded and modified by the individual's experience of temporality/eternity. Only at this point of full self-consciousness does the demand and the task of the self as freedom come into view.[6]

That drives us to the second point, the "positive third." As a relation between two as with the physical and psychical, a human becoming is not yet a self. So Anti-Climacus would have his reader understand that the basic constituent elements of the self are indeed "given," but the self as such is not thereby given.[7] Selfhood is not given, it is a calling, a task that can be met only as the synthesis/relation "relates itself to itself." As I mentioned, with this recognition of the relation relating to itself, Anti-Climacus separates himself from dichotomous views in which the way to health is often found to reside in one or the other of the poles of the spiritual/physical duality. Kierkegaard cannot be securely deposited in continental rationalism or British empiricism. People of faith have often found the greater temptation to be to join Descartes in chanting "*cogito ergo sum*" (I think, therefore I am).

---

4. JP, 5:6137.
5. SUD, 29; my emphasis.
6. Come, *Kierkegaard as Humanist*, 115. Cf. ibid., 42.
7. Arne Grøn, "The Human Synthesis," in Houe et al., *Anthropology and Authority*, 27–32 (31), aptly refers to the human being at this point as an "intermediate being," adding that "[m]an is a synthesis in the sense that he is already an aggregate, 'strangely put together,' but he is also a synthesis in the normative sense that he has to achieve identity with himself."

Christians have been tempted by a Platonist privileging of the nonmaterial in which the real hope for the self lies in the nonphysical element that promises a life above this struggle in the mortal coil of flesh. It is as if we can hope we will join Glaucon in emerging from Plato's cave. Does not Christian eschatological hope—calling us to remember that if the earthly tent we live in is destroyed, we have "a house not made with hands, eternal in the heavens" (2 Cor 5:1)—point in Plato's direction? Does not our hope lie in the nonmaterial part of us, presumably our reasoning capacity? "Despair Is Sin" will definitely respond in the negative to Plato (and Socrates, so beloved of Kierkegaard).

In his emphasis on consciousness, Anti-Climacus may seem to privilege the mental, but the hope for healing does not lie in the abandonment of the physical. Any such privileging of the pole of consciousness offers no guarantee of human fulfillment. Neither the mental nor the physical poles of the relation would get us into the territory of the spirit by itself. With Anti-Climacus's trichotomous understanding, the "third" (the becoming self relating itself to itself) provides the foothold for a posture of transcendence, where the spirit has some genuine freedom of perspective in relation to both poles of the relation. There is freedom in that relating and peril aplenty, for in the misuse of the third's freedom lies the root of despair.[8] In the self's despair, freedom is active. And yet there is hope. Despair is the sickness unto death, and yet in despair, the third's freedom is truly trading in the territory of the spirit, where healing can happen.

How can healing come about in the face of the self's sickness? Well, this given relation must choose what relationship to itself as a synthesis of two it wills to have. But the relation does not create itself. This becoming self has yet another relation as third, actually the most

---

8. Afflictions of the relation as a relation of two do not qualify as despair, for the becoming self's freedom is not fully active. Perhaps in that distinction, we get a sense for how Anti-Climacus might have us distinguish depression from despair. In depression, it is a relation of two. This suggests a response to Mary Louise Bringle's interrogative title *Despair: Sickness or Sin? Hopelessness and Healing in the Christian Life* (Nashville: Abingdon, 1990). Her own response to her question is a nicely dialectical "Yes." She writes of how "the person who dares to despair possesses a tensile spirit which can learn to brave the even more radical venture of hoping" (ibid., 174).

fundamental relation. And that calls for a third comment, requiring another quotation:

> If the relation that relates itself to itself has been established by another, then the relation is indeed the third, but this relation, the third, is yet again a relation and relates itself to that which established the entire relation.... If a human self had itself established itself, then there could be only one form: not to will to be oneself, to will to do away with oneself, but there could not be the form: in despair to will to be oneself. This second formulation is specifically the expression for the complete dependence of the relation (of the self), the expression for the inability of the self to arrive at or to be in equilibrium and rest by itself, but only, in relating itself to itself, by relating itself to that which has established the entire relation.[9]

This is clearly God-talk. Here Anti-Climacus does not yet use the explicitly Christian language of his second section, where despair is identified as sin. But in this presentation of the relation being established by another, we hear Anti-Climacus's theology of creation at work. It is clear already in "The Sickness unto Death Is Despair" that God's *opus proprium* (proper work), "which is to give and which is seen most clearly in the Gospel, is already operative in Creation and is expressed in the primary fact of life."[10]

The relation is established with an end in mind. If the positive third of the relating resists the Creator's calling, there will be despair in the form of "misrelation," whether that is by way of falling back from the calling or by willing to relate to itself in a selfhood that does not heed the Creator's calling. So Anti-Climacus can say that, in a way, "all despair ultimately can be traced back to" defiance, even though that term is often used by Anti-Climacus to refer only to the second form, willing to be oneself.[11] In the healing of despair, the relation finds

---

9. SUD, 13–14.
10. Gustaf Wingren, *Creation and Law*, trans. Ross Mackenzie (Philadelphia: Muhlenberg, 1961), 38. For a treatment of Kierkegaard's "theology of creation" in a veronymous writing comparable to SUD, part 1, see George Pattison, "Philosophy and Dogma: The Testimony of an Upbuilding Discourse," in *Ethics, Love, and Faith in Kierkegaard*, ed. Edward F. Mooney (Bloomington: Indiana University Press, 2008), 161.
11. SUD, 14. Later, Anti-Climacus adds that the despair of willing to be oneself "can be traced back to the first, in despair not to will to be oneself, just as we previously resolved the [first] form ... into the [second] form" (SUD, 20).

"equilibrium and rest" even in its passionate becoming. Indeed, of that state, Anti-Climacus says that "the self rests transparently in the power that established it."[12]

"Transparently"—it is hard to know what that means, but surely it includes trusting the constituting one in fully conscious faith. George Pattison has mined the upbuilding discourses to offer a parallel framework for transparency. He writes: "[T]he process of becoming as nothing, of becoming still and transparent and allowing the storms of doubt and rebellion to subside into a smooth reflecting surface, is not a simple reversion to a first immediacy: it is not a 'natural' or spontaneous process, but one that requires us to choose."[13] We'll be getting a more explicitly theological framing of this in chapter 2 in our exposition of the themes of "before God" and having God as one's "measure" (*Maalestok* [rule, standard]).[14] Perhaps at this point we may reach for first-order religious language and say that in this relationship of transparency, one recognizes that one cannot hide from God and that one need not try to hide from God.[15]

So how is this sickness of despair "*unto* death"? As Anti-Climacus closes this section, he writes of the despairing self's inability to die. This person cannot bear to be himself and wants to be rid of himself. That is impossible, for the "dying of despair continually converts itself into a living."[16] The self would tear itself away from the Constituting Power, but "the power is stronger and forces him to be the self he does not want to be."[17] Such is the sickness unto death.

---

12. SUD, 14.
13. George Pattison, *Kierkegaard's Upbuilding Discourses: Philosophy, Literature and Theology* (London: Routledge, 2002), 101.
14. SUD, 70–87.
15. John D. Glenn Jr. ("The Definition of the Self and the Structure of Kierkegaard's Work," in *The Sickness unto Death*, vol. 19 of IKC, ed. Robert L. Perkins [Macon, GA: Mercer University Press, 1987], 5–21) finds the three stages of human existence in the opening formula of SUD: the given relation as the aesthetic, the relation relating itself to itself as the ethical, and the self seeking or resisting the Constituting Power as the religious.
16. SUD, 18.
17. SUD, 20.

B. The Universality of This Sickness (Despair)

Com.: Despair Common and Rare

The becoming self is most clearly delineated in the following two sections of "The Sickness unto Death Is Despair": in the exposition of the universality of despair (section B) and in the morphology of despair (section C). Here two remarkable assertions are made. First, Anti-Climacus broadens and deepens his diagnosis, writing that "[t]he common view, which assumes that everyone who does not think or feel he is in despair is not or that only he who says he is in despair is, is totally false."[18] Clearly there is a broadening here, but equally important is the deepening point that despair reveals an objective truth about the human condition, regardless of varying degrees of consciousness and denial of despair. The diagnosis points to something far deeper than what we casually observe about each other. But when it comes to the degrees of intensity in this condition, the bluntly titled part two "Despair Is Sin" finds Anti-Climacus asking whether sin does not become a great rarity.[19] The way forward to getting a grip on that dialectic may be to recall that "Despair Is Sin" also insistently drives home the point that the opposite of sin is faith.[20] Consider the question the gospel writer has Jesus of Nazareth ask: "When the Son of man comes, will he find faith on earth?" (Luke 18:8). If true faith is not to be found on the earth, is not despair universally the human condition? Anti-Climacus writes of how, as spirit, the human condition is always critical. We do not speak of physical health as always critical. But there is simply no immediate health for the becoming spirit.[21] In "The Sickness unto Death Is Despair," it is clear that any hope for health points to the future with a challenge to the self's freedom. Amelioration of the self's condition seems an uphill journey. In

---

18. SUD, 26. I take the phrase "Common and Rare" from Mahn, *Fortunate Fallibility*, 107–10. He points out that *Almindelighed* might be translated as "customary," not "universal." See his observation that "the central hospital in Copenhagen, for example, was called the Almindeligt (General) Hospital" (ibid., 226n19).
19. SUD, 100–104.
20. SUD, 82.
21. SUD, 25.

"Despair Is Sin," Anti-Climacus deepens and anchors this diagnosis by appealing to the paradox of "hereditary sin."[22] Anti-Climacus is fully aware that this appeal may seem a strange "explanation" of the spirit's critical condition, but that's how paradox works after all.

Kierkegaard seems to have seen the great majority of his Danish contemporaries as in despair with hardly any consciousness of their condition. Faith requires the intensification of the self-constituting consciousness of being before God. So if that intensifying consciousness is rare, despair is indeed rare. Yet if the intended telos of faith for human becoming is hardly even envisioned, that yields a condition of despair. The gap between the call and the condition carries consequences. But the comfortable man on the street queries "*unconscious* despair?" Yes, you see, despair is dexterous in its deployment of itself. It is good at hiding. It can so live in a person that no one detects it. Indeed, the person themselves may not be aware of it.[23] So despair may well be common, universal even; but the consciousness of despair is rare.

In a second startling assertion, Anti-Climacus repairs again to the dialectical character of despair. He writes:

> Precisely because the sickness of despair is totally dialectical, it is the worst misfortune never to have had that sickness; it is a true godsend to get it, even if it is the most dangerous of illnesses, if one does not want to be cured of it. Generally it is regarded as fortunate to be cured of a sickness; the sickness itself is the misfortune. . . . The person who without affectation says that he is in despair is still a little closer, is dialectically closer, to being cured than all those who are not regarded as such and who do not regard themselves as being in despair.[24]

If one moves toward health by becoming conscious of this condition that seems to universally be a virtual given of being a creature, does that make the Creator responsible for what will come to be identified as sin later in the text? Anti-Climacus insists throughout SUD that it does not. Here he writes: "If the synthesis were the misrelation, then despair

---

22. SUD, 93.
23. SUD, 27.
24. SUD, 26.

would not exist at all, then despair would be something that lies in human nature as such. . . . No, no, despairing lies in man himself."[25] "Despair Is Sin" will bring to us the theme of human responsibility for sin in its critique of Socrates. Let us remember the warning in those last words of the preface: "Despair is interpreted as a sickness, not as a cure." Remembering that, we turn to the startling variety of forms this sickness may take.

C. The Forms of This Sickness (Despair)

Com.: The Morphology of Despair

A. DESPAIR CONSIDERED WITHOUT REGARD TO ITS BEING CONSCIOUS OR NOT, CONSEQUENTLY ONLY WITH REGARD TO THE CONSTITUENTS OF THE SYNTHESIS. . . .[26]

Anti-Climacus is writing of what we may call the polarization of the constituents of the synthesis. The dialectical character of the synthesis entails that any form of despair can only be understood "by reflecting upon its opposite."[27] The constituents are surely together, but they are a volatile mixture. Thus regarding the constituents of the self as a synthesis, he can say "each constituent is [er] its opposite."[28] But he will also speak of each being "the limiting aspect" (*det Begrændsende*) of the other and of each form of the polarization "lacking" (*at mangle*) its opposing form. Thus he writes of "Infinitude's Despair Is to Lack Finitude," and "Finitude's Despair Is to Lack Infinitude" and comparably "Possibility's Despair Is to Lack Necessity" and "Necessity's Despair Is to Lack Possibility."[29]

There are profound anthropological insights in the mining of this polarization. Let's take the first pair. True health for the human spirit lies in a process of moving away from the limitations of one's givenness and then coming back to oneself in a finitizing process. In the despair

---

25. SUD, 16.
26. SUD, 29.
27. SUD, 30.
28. SUD, 33.
29. SUD, 29–42.

of infinitude, the imagination moves fantastically away from itself in feeling, knowing, and will, but never manages to get back to itself. Fantastic feeling yields a kind of abstract sentimentality increasingly separating itself from actual human beings. In knowing turned fantastic, a vast amount of knowledge is acquired without the needed increase in self-knowledge. In infinitude's despair, willing potentiates itself in purpose and determination but loses touch with the "personally present and contemporary."[30]

Finitude's despair, on the other hand, involves reductionism or narrowness. Anti-Climacus speaks of this as a person having "emasculated oneself in a spiritual sense." There is a certain angularity in the relation as given, but what is needed is that the synthesis "be ground into shape, not that it is to be ground down smooth."[31] He notes that the person thus despairing can "very well live on in temporality" and be fully absorbed in all the temporal goals. Such a person has mortgaged himself to the world but has no self before God. He warns here about the despair involved in not believing in oneself and instead finding it "far easier and safer to be like the others, to become a copy, a number, a mass man."[32] Here, without the explicitly Christian language of the next chapter, Anti-Climacus is echoing the emphasis on the single individual that anchored Climacus's ridicule in the *Postscript* of N. F. S. Grundtvig's appeal to congregations confessing the same creed through eighteen centuries:

> It is Christianity itself that attaches an enormous importance to the individual subject; it wants to be involved with him, him alone, and thus with each one individually. It is in a way an un-Christian use of eighteen centuries to intend with them to entice the single individual into Christianity or to frighten him into it: he still does not enter into it. And if he does enter into it, he does so whether he has eighteen centuries for him or against him.[33]

The emphasis on genuine individuality is characteristic of Kierkegaard

---

30. SUD, 32.
31. SUD, 33.
32. SUD, 34.
33. CUP, 1:49.

of course and is often emphasized in his reception in both praise and criticism, but it is important to recognize that other selves are part of the self's becoming. Thus the "other" functions as part of the self's necessity and possibility, to take the next pairing. Pia Søltoft helpfully distinguishes Kierkegaard from "a strictly dialogical position, in which the Self is created only in relation to the Other." In Kierkegaard's "more moderate dialogical position," the self is not created, but "comes to itself" in this relation. In this position, "the dialectical moment guarantees an underlying relation between the Self and the Other which protects the Self against isolation without disrupting its subjectivity and uniqueness."[34]

The "Or" of E/O carries a strong emphasis on the crucial importance of the "other" in the venture of the self. The marriage service carries this concern through the public commitment found there. The ceremony "binds the new marriage in the great body of the human race. It thereby provides the universal, the purely human."[35] Thus, the "ethical view of marriage . . . does not show how a pair of very specific people can become happy because of their extraordinariness but how every married couple can become happy. It sees the relationship as the absolute."[36] The role of the other is not restricted to marriage. A little earlier we read about the individual: "If he thinks that the art is to begin like a Robinson Crusoe, he remains an adventurer all his life."[37] Kierkegaard wrote of "a social, a civic self," as Robert L. Perkins, the editor of the *International Kierkegaard Commentary*, recognizes in introducing the volume on *The Sickness unto Death* by emphasizing that in the newer research, scholars share the assumption "that Kierkegaard's thought has great importance for social philosophy and even constitutes a major critique of modernity."[38] More to come on that in the second half of this book.

---

34. Pia Søltoft, "Anthropology and Ethics: The Connection between Subjectivity and Intersubjectivity as the Basis of a Kierkegaardian Anthropology," in Houe et al., *Anthropology and Authority*, 41–48 (47).
35. E/O, 2:88–89.
36. E/O, 2:305.
37. E/O, 2:263.
38. Robert L. Perkins, introduction to *The Sickness unto Death*, vol. 19 of IKC, ed. Robert L. Perkins (Macon, GA: Mercer University Press, 1987), 1.

Then consider the second pairing, possibility/necessity. With the despair of possibility, while what is needed is a sort of movement in place, this person has failed to incorporate necessity with its location and so "more and more becomes possible because nothing becomes actual."[39] In this form of despair, "[w]hat is missing is essentially the power to obey, to submit to the necessity in one's life, to what may be called one's limitations."[40] The self flounders around in possibility. Anti-Climacus distinguishes one form of this despair as that of desiring or craving and another form as that of hope/fear or anxiety. In the first case, the person despairs because "[i]nstead of taking the possibility back into necessity, he chases after possibility—and at last cannot find his way back to himself."[41] In the second, "the individual pursues one of anxiety's possibilities, which finally leads him away from himself."[42]

Similarly, necessity's despair also comes in different forms. Anti-Climacus writes of the determinist/fatalist for whom everything has become necessary. The self is suffocated here. When smelling salts are needed for the self, then the word is "get possibility, get possibility."[43] Twentieth-century Yale Kierkegaard scholar Paul L. Holmer drilled generations of Kierkegaard students in the distinction between cognitive "possibles" and ethical "possibles." The former get their reference in virtue of an act of the thinker; the reference of the latter is to the interest and passion of a person. Holmer stressed that Kierkegaard "put these ethical possibles into linguistic form without making them tools of cognition."[44] In the twenty-first century, scholars Curtis Thompson and Joyce Cuff have caught the spirit of Kierkegaard in writing: "Possibility is employed creatively to empower, lure, move, entice, persuade, inveigle, draw, inspire, motivate, stir, encourage, enthuse, arouse, cajole, tease, tantalize, pull, invite and attract the creation into the future."[45]

---

39. SUD, 36.
40. Ibid.
41. SUD, 37.
42. Ibid.
43. SUD, 38–39.
44. Paul L. Holmer, "On Understanding Kierkegaard," in *A Kierkegaard Critique*, ed. Howard A. Johnson and Niels Thulstrup (New York: Harper, 1962), 40–53 (46–47).
45. Joyce M. Cuff and Curtis L. Thompson, *God and Nature: A Scientist and a Theologian Conversing on*

In relation to the despair of necessity, we get one of Anti-Climacus's most striking formulations: "What is decisive is that with God everything is possible."[46] Shall we read this as saying that with every situation of givenness with God, there is always some possibility? That makes hopeful sense. Or is something beyond that at stake in possibility? Anti-Climacus says that "for God everything is possible in *every* moment."[47] How does the believer hold to that conviction without losing recognition of his own necessity? That question will be with us to this book's ending. What is not in question is "the battle of *faith*, battling, madly, if you will, for possibility, because possibility is the only salvation." The call is for a person who "leaves it entirely to God how he is to be helped,"[48] clinging with his teeth to possibility.

Another form of necessity's despair is found in "the philistine-bourgeois mentality, that is triviality."[49] This person is "bereft of imagination" and "lives within a certain trivial compendium of experiences as to how things go, what is possible, what usually happens." He "leads possibility around imprisoned in the cage of probability."[50] Determinism and fatalism possess enough imagination to despair of possibility, but even that is lacking with the philistine-bourgeois mentality. Kierkegaard likely thought he saw much of this "spiritlessness" as he walked the streets of Copenhagen.

B. DESPAIR AS DEFINED BY CONSCIOUSNESS

Now Anti-Climacus has brought us to despair properly understood. Of the one who does not know that they are in despair, he says of this lack of consciousness, "it is almost a dialectical issue whether it is justifiable to call such a state despair."[51] That question arises because

---

the *Divine Promise of Possibility* (New York: Continuum, 2012), 3. They place a special stress on the ethical significance of "possibilizing," which "assists the other human being to become free."
46. SUD, 38.
47. SUD, 39–40; my emphasis.
48. SUD, 39.
49. SUD, 41.
50. Ibid.
51. SUD, 42.

he has begun his description of what one may call a "morphology of despair" with this claim:

> Generally speaking, consciousness—that is, self-consciousness—is decisive with regard to the self. The more consciousness, the more self; the more consciousness, the more will; the more will, the more self.[52]

Accordingly, the degree of despair's intensity varies with the degree of conscious awareness of the self's situation. Kierkegaard has a way of giving the reader a sentence that could easily be a chapter. Thus here, in an introductory paragraph for this section, Anti-Climacus identifies the devil's despair as the most intensive despair, for as sheer spirit the devil's unqualified consciousness has no obscurity that can serve as a mitigating excuse. We seek such excuses readily and speak of unfavorable circumstances that repress our basically moral nature. There's always some preexisting condition that takes us off the hook. Or, only half-humorously, we say the devil made me do it. In chapter 2, I'll write of how in Kierkegaard's view sin "presupposes itself." But in the devil's case, the defiance possible for sheer spirit closes the door to such self-exculpating infinite regress. Anti-Climacus is not delivering a lecture on the ultimate origin of evil; he is evoking a possible repentance over his reader's own despairing defiance. One recalls Adam's excuse in Eden: "She gave me fruit of the tree, and I ate" (Gen 3:12b).

Then Anti-Climacus begins his discussion of degrees of consciousness by describing despair that is ignorant of being despair, suggesting the notion of culpable ignorance. He writes of people who "intended to be spirit" but who settle for a "psychical-physical synthesis" and prefer to live in the basement.[53] There's a pointed reference to Hegelian hubris, which constructs "a huge building, a system, a system embracing the whole of existence, world history" but then lives in a shed alongside the palace. The only concern this doghouse dweller has is to "complete the system."[54] He cites Vigilius

---

52. SUD, 29.
53. SUD, 43.
54. SUD, 43–44.

THE SICKNESS UNTO DEATH IS DESPAIR

Haufniensis's *The Concept of Anxiety*, pointing out the despair that lies beneath the apparent sense of security rooted in ignorance. He finds this form of despair to characterize paganism, including "paganism in Christendom."[55]

Next, Anti-Climacus launches into despair proper, where there is some consciousness of one's condition. He ponders whether perfect clarity about one's despairing condition "might not simply wrench a person out of despair,"[56] but does not develop that pondering. He promises a later treatment of this question, but that treatment was never written in any fullness. In any case, conscious despair displays the forms of "not to will to be oneself" and of "to will to be oneself." He introduces a potentially highly fruitful distinction in despair between weakness (not to will to be oneself) and strength (to will to be oneself), and illustrates the difference with a famous—and infamous—gender-based metaphorical application, the feminine and the masculine.[57] He then gives seventeen pages to discriminating analysis of the forms of the despair of weakness, the despair of not willing to be oneself. We'll cite here the basic distinction:

> No despair is entirely free of defiance; indeed, the very phrase "not to will to be" implies defiance. On the other hand, even despair's most extreme defiance is never really free of some weakness. So the distinction is only relative. The one form is, so to speak, feminine despair, the other, masculine despair.[58]

At the low end of consciousness, "despair over the earthly or over something earthly is the most common form of despair."[59] In the very lowest form of this level, the person is in despair "to will to be someone else, to wish for a new self."[60] There's an advance in consciousness and consequent intensity when one no longer despairs over a particular

---

55. SUD, 45.
56. SUD, 47.
57. SUD, 49–50. One must mention Anti-Climacus's long footnote on those pages. In that note, he acknowledges that women "may have forms of masculine despair and, conversely, that men may have forms of feminine despair."
58. SUD, 49.
59. SUD, 56–57.
60. SUD, 53.

earthly happening that hits one ("a stroke of bad luck, perhaps it will pass"; the loss of a job, a lover, etc.) and reaches despair over the earthly as such. This can take the form of withdrawing into some inward sense of self, secure from the vagaries of external events. Or, that inward turn possibly fading, it can find the person turning outward, immersing himself in a "real" and "active" life as "a dynamic and enterprising man, a father and citizen, perhaps even an important man."[61] This form of despair does not favor one age over another; the youth despairs over the future, which holds something he is not willing to take upon himself. The "adult despairs over the past," over something that she "has not succeeded in forgetting . . . completely."[62] Both live in despair.

Let's turn back to the gender-related metaphorical application of the distinction between despair in weakness and in strength. Anti-Climacus speaks of women as representing "devotedness" in their nature, and men "reflection." There is a troublesome potential in these linkages. Thus Haufniensis develops the linkage of the male and the reflective with a contrast to the woman as more sensuous. We sense here the possible consequence of what we cited earlier: the portentous emphasis on "the more consciousness, the more self."[63] The next step is the introduction of the female "ethically under her ideal aspect, which is procreation."[64] We may find ourselves on the road to saying, "Venus is essentially just as beautiful when she is represented as sleeping, possibly more so, yet the sleeping state is the expression for the absence of spirit."[65] But we should note that at this point in SUD, Anti-Climacus says that women *and men* are called to devotion in the relationship to God, "where the distinction of man-woman vanishes."[66] Yet he closes the long footnote by saying, "it is probably true that in most cases the woman actually relates to God only through the man."[67]

61. SUD, 56.
62. SUD, 59.
63. SUD, 29.
64. CA, 65.
65. Ibid.
66. SUD, 50.
67. Ibid. We will look in part 2 at feminist ranges of reception of such passages, so I'll settle here for

THE SICKNESS UNTO DEATH IS DESPAIR

One can construe these one-sided assertions as phenomenological observations of culturally conditioned differences, then and still now. How many women have been pushed further into self-denigrating despair as they listened to the preacher berating human prideful defiance of God? In looking at the feminist reception of Kierkegaard in the second half of this book, we will find women digging beneath the offensive surfaces to find important insights on the nature of sexuality in relation to faith, as well as pointed criticism. All in all, some of Kierkegaard's remarks about the female gender probably cannot be extricated from the sexism of the period.

The despair further intensifies as there is a shift from despairing *in* weakness to despairing *over* one's weakness.[68] At this point, Anti-Climacus introduces the phenomenon of "inclosing reserve" (*Indesluttedhed* [shut-in-ness]).[69] This "closed-up" or "shut-in" person may long for solitude and fears being "led too far out."[70] When the inner tumult becomes too much to bear, he may "seek oblivion in sensuality, perhaps in dissolute living."[71] A real danger for this person is suicide. There are subtle distinctions to be noted in this process of intensification. Prepositions matter to Anti-Climacus. Consider the care at work in a footnote clarifying this final form of the despair in weakness, "despair of the eternal or over oneself":

> It is linguistically correct to say: to despair *over* [o v e r] the earthly (the occasion), *of* [o m] the eternal, but *over* [o v e r] oneself. . . . We despair *over* [o v e r] that which binds us in despair—over a misfortune, over the earthly, over a capital loss, etc.—but we despair *of* [o m] that which, rightly understood, releases us from despair: of the eternal, of salvation, of our own strength, etc. With respect to the self, we say both: to despair *over* [o v e r] and *of* [o m] oneself, because the self is doubly dialectical. (60–61)[72]

So this person despairs "over" himself that he makes so much of the

---

saying that a concise and discriminating orientation is available in Sylvia Walsh, "On 'Feminine' and 'Masculine' Forms of Despair," in Perkins, *The Sickness unto Death*, 129–34.
68. SUD, 61.
69. SUD, 63. Vigilius Haufniensis wrote expansively of this in 1844 in CA, 123–35.
70. SUD, 64.
71. SUD, 66.
72. SUD, 60–61.

earthly. He berates himself over his weakness, but does not turn to faith, humbling himself in his weakness.

"Then comes defiance, which is really despair through the aid of the eternal, the despairing misuse of the eternal within the self to will in despair to be oneself."[73] Again despair displays its versatility, for there are both more passive and more active forms of this despair "severing itself from any relation to a power that has established it."[74] As Haufniensis put the matter, here "unfreedom [freely] makes itself a prisoner,"[75] closing itself up within itself. Genuine freedom lies in communicating, but the closed-in self will have none of it. The height of defiance is reached in the "demonic." Here there is a kind of reversal in defiance of the Constituting Power as the self "in hatred toward existence, it wills to be itself, wills to be itself in accordance with its misery."[76] More on that in a moment. But as we come to the end of this chapter's road through the multitudinous switchbacks of despair, as a suggestion toward a summary, consider Alastair Hannay's observation of how Kierkegaard's understanding differs from a Hegelian reading where despair finds its place on the way to true knowledge. Hannay proposes that the Hegelian model could be applied to SUD in that there is a "negative" development of the kind in which the nature of what one is aiming at becomes ever clearer, "but the crucial difference is that in Kierkegaard what becomes clearer is not that we *are* the truth but how much more is needed if we are to *be* it—to be the selves we are."[77] One hears echoing here the words of Paul to the Romans (3:21): the law and the prophets "bear witness to" (RSV) or "attest" (NRSV) the righteousness of God, but they do not themselves "manifest" (RSV) or "disclose" (NRSV) that redemptive word.

---

73. SUD, 67.
74. SUD, 68.
75. CA, 124.
76. SUD, 73.
77. Alastair Hannay, "Kierkegaard and the Variety of Despair," in *The Cambridge Companion to Kierkegaard*, ed. Alastair Hannay and Gordon D. Marino (Cambridge: Cambridge University Press, 1998), 335.

Com.: The Error's Mutiny

Anti-Climacus closes "The Sickness unto Death Is Despair" with a startling example. When he began the dark discussion of defiant despair—which, unlike weakness, draws on the eternal in the self—he voiced a countering word:

> The despair that is the thoroughfare to faith comes also through the aid of the eternal; through the aid of the eternal the self has the courage to lose itself in order to win itself.[78]

Thus, Jason Mahn seems to be on target in writing that Anti-Climacus may describe "the despair of infinity and possibility in honorific terms—[for] while such despair is on the wrong track, it might be on the 'proper' wrong track—that is, able through its failure to be set aright."[79] Mahn very pointedly distinguishes his appropriation of the *felix culpa* from that of the early German Romantic avant-garde poets' version of the fortunate fall, "which does not express a drama of salvation but characterized the internally divided nature of the human as such."[80] Now, in the last paragraph, Anti-Climacus writes of how the self at its height, in defiance, is "rebelling against all existence," is feeling "that it has obtained evidence against it, against its goodness." The self does not want to hear "any consolation eternity has for him ... [for] this very consolation would be his undoing."[81] Then the final words about the mutiny against the Creator:

> Figuratively speaking, it is as if an error slipped into an author's writing and the error became conscious of itself as an error—perhaps it actually was not a mistake but in a much higher sense an essential part of the whole production—and now this error wants to mutiny against the author, out of hatred toward him, forbidding him to correct it and in maniacal defiance saying to him: No, I refuse to be erased; I will stand as a witness against you, a witness that you are a second-rate author.[82]

---

78. SUD, 67.
79. Mahn, *Fortunate Fallibility*, 121.
80. Ibid., 97.
81. SUD, 73–74.
82. SUD, 74.

What on earth can we make of this? Is Anti-Climacus participating in the Easter Eve service, crying out "O happy fault [*felix culpa*] which merited such and so great a redeemer!"? One can read him as edging toward that precipice.[83] Yet one remembers the "once and for all" warning of the preface that "despair is interpreted as a sickness, not as a cure"[84] and remembers as well, that SUD insists on human responsibility in the sickness of despair/sin. Mahn calls for us to read "sin backward from the special revelation of Christ rather than forward from the idea of a primal unity."[85] Arnold Come pleads that Anti-Climacus is here poised for the second half of his work and the dialectical with its theological affirmation of the inevitability of, and yet responsibility in, sin.[86] Anti-Climacus does indeed ponder how the Creator's love must risk the possibility of offense.[87] And yet does that give us despair as "an essential part of the whole production"? It does seem telling that with the error's mutiny, we are at the transition point in the study of the sickness unto death. Anti-Climacus ended that puzzling warning of the preface with these five words: "Despair is indeed that dialectical."[88] Let's see what dark light the next chapter may shed on this enigma.

---

83. See Mahn's delicate discussion in *Fortunate Fallibility*, especially chapter 3.
84. SUD, 6.
85. Mahn, *Fortunate Fallibility*, 211.
86. Come, *Kierkegaard as Humanist*, 140–44.
87. SUD, 126.
88. SUD, 7.

2

Despair Is Sin

A. Despair Is Sin

Com.: The Logic of Intensification I: Before God

Anti-Climacus doesn't beat around the bush. This "thetical" author makes a blunt assertion in his three-word title, and is no less direct in the first paragraph of his exposition:

> Sin is: *before God, or with the conception of God, in despair not to will to be oneself, or in despair to will to be oneself.* Thus sin is intensified weakness or intensified defiance: sin is the intensification of despair. The emphasis is on *before God,* or with a conception of God; it is the conception of God that makes sin dialectically, ethically, and religiously what lawyers call "aggravated" despair.[1]

Before launching into his discussion of the varying ways in which despair becomes sin, Anti-Climacus writes of "the most dialectical frontier between despair and sin," namely a "poet-existence" verging on the religious. The poet sins by "relating to the good and the true through the imagination instead of being that—that is, existentially

---

1. SUD, 77.

striving to be that," not merely imagining the good and the true but actually exemplifying it. He longs for God in despairing anguish and "yet he loves the anguish and will not give it up."[2] He is functioning with a conception of God in his anguished longing and "feels obscurely that what is required of him is that he should let go of this agony—but this he cannot do."[3] The poet may actually allow himself—again, "perhaps unconsciously,"—"to poetize God as somewhat different from what God is, a bit more like the fond father who indulges his child's every wish far too much."[4] This lamenting judgment of the poet is interesting given Kierkegaard's frequent reference to himself as a "poet of the religious." Despite Anti-Climacus's criticism of the poet for his failure to bring his yearning into action, Kierkegaard clearly valued the poetical. In his journals, he writes of his "attempt to introduce Christianity into Christendom." However, he cannot finish that sentence without adding, "but, please note, 'poetically, without authority,' for, as I have always maintained, I am no apostle, I am a poetic-dialectical genius, personally and religiously a penitent."[5] Recall the biographical sketch's discussion of "indirect communication" and the concern to appropriate the Socratic indirectness to leave "the reader alone with the work, free from extraneous interest in the author's personality and personal life."[6] Thus in 1849 he writes in his journal, "The fact that I cannot give the full truth in portraying myself signifies that essentially I am a poet—and here I shall remain."[7] Thus Kierkegaard valued and yet struggled with the poetical, and one final journal reference on this point presents the complex mix: "It is very proper that the maieutic be used in Christendom, simply because the majority actually live in the fancy that they are Christians. But since Christianity still is Christianity, the one who uses the maieutic must

2. Ibid.
3. The Hongs cite this journal reference in their supplement to SUD, 154–55.
4. SUD, 78.
5. JP, 6:6317.
6. This is how the Hongs summarize the maieutic matter in their introduction to PV, xi. Recall from chapter 1, pp. 4–5nn64–68 Kierkegaard's distinctions between preaching (sermons), teaching (discourses "for upbuilding"), and "Upbuilding Discourses" (the poetical).
7. JP, 6:6327, p. 109. See David R. Law, "The Point of View for My Work as an Author," in Perkins, *The Point of View*, 12–47.

become a witness."⁸ He does observe in ending the draft note that in his despairing longing for the religious, the poet has "the first element of faith," but "only" that. Yet striving to be a Christian—that he surely was.

Continuity between the two parts of SUD is carried in the theme of intensification, the notion employed already throughout the first half in distinguishing the potentiation in various forms of despair. Now in the second half, we will find a comparable intensification in an unobtrusively Trinitarian formulation. I say "unobtrusive" because Anti-Climacus does not lecture on the doctrine of the Trinity, but phenomenologically explains the work of God in relationship to human existence. That calls on him as a Christian to speak of the human consciousness of God as Father, Son, and Holy Spirit, in the intensification of the creature's condition. "The Sickness unto Death Is Despair" made the point that the key to intensification lies in the degree of consciousness of the self as a "positive third."

So what's different here? The self is consciously *"before God"* and Anti-Climacus amplifies the point about consciousness, writing *"before God* or with a conception of God." That makes a decisive difference in consciousness. Certainly one hears here an echo of Martin Luther's *coram Deo*. While Luther is not specifically cited in SUD, one could point out frequent points of resonance with Luther as this chapter progresses.⁹ This potentiation of the becoming self corresponds to the conscious relating or "misrelating" of the positive third toward God, who is the constituting power. Here we have at work already in this

---

8. JP, 2:1957.
9. Mahn, *Fortunate Fallibility*, offers frequent references to such Lutheran themes as the Christian being simultaneously saint and sinner, and perfectly free lord of all, subject to none (*coram Deo*) and "perfectly dutiful" servant of all, subject to all (*coram hominibus*). As we get into the Apostles Creed's second article concerns below, Luther's Heidelberg Disputation will echo through Anti-Climacus's paragraphs. See also Simon D. Podmore, *Kierkegaard and the Self Before God: Anatomy of the Abyss* (Bloomington: Indiana University Press, 2011). Podmore also dwells on the Luther connection and is especially tracking "the infinite qualitative difference" and the vision of the self before God. See also vol. 49 of the *Søren Kierkegaard Newsletter* from the Hong Kierkegaard Library at St. Olaf College. In this issue, Mahn and Podmore review each other's books appreciatively. At the end of this section, drawing on the Apostles' Creed's first article in recognizing the intensifying consciousness of sin as the motivating force in the acceptance of Christianity, we'll take fuller note of Kierkegaard's relation to Luther. This is a much-commented-on relationship, as we'll sample in an extended footnote. See below, p. 59n129.

part's first page the notion of the "infinite qualitative difference" between the Creator and creatures. Existing consciously, "directly before" (*lige over for*) that qualitatively different God, before the face of God, indeed face-to-face with God one might say, yields a corresponding qualitative intensification of the self. Anti-Climacus immediately brings to bear the notion of criterion, claiming that "the criterion for the self is always: that directly before which it is a self, but this in turn is the definition of 'criterion.'"[10] This crucial notion of criterion certainly reflects a deeply relational dimension of human existence, putting a large question mark beside the frequent attempts to read Kierkegaard as elevating and isolating the individual.

There's a gift in existing before God, but a task as well. Note the wordplay in the Danish:

> Just as only entities of the same kind can be added, so everything is qualitatively that by which it is measured, and that which is its qualitative criterion [*Maalestok*] is ethically its goal [*Maal*].[11]

Consider, then, the intensification the human self experiences in existing "before God":

First we get Anti-Climacus's exultant praise of the gift thus given:

> The point is that the previously considered gradation in the consciousness of the self is within the category of the human self, or the self whose criterion is man. But this self takes on a new quality and qualification by being a self directly before God. This self is no longer the merely human self but is what I, hoping not to be misinterpreted, would call the theological self, the self directly before [*lige over for*] God. And what infinite reality [*Realitet*] the self gains by being conscious of existing before God, by becoming a human self whose criterion is God![12]

There's good news here. The self venturing toward and into selfhood in relating to itself here finds a potentiating relationship in being related

---

10. SUD, 79.
11. Ibid.
12. Ibid. Pattison, *Kierkegaard's Upbuilding Discourses*, 97, aligns Anti-Climacus's notion of God as criterion to Immanuel Kant's regulative ideals, writing that "'Measure,' here is to be taken in the sense of the criterion that enables us to evaluate situations we encounter in the world, a criterion that is not the result of any particular experience but, rather, is independent of and prior to all particular experiences and precisely for that reason able to help make sense of experience."

to a being who is unlike all creaturely beings. The depth of eternity enters into the relationship, yielding an intensification of the self so related. Given that, there's simply more self here. The "other" giving the self its measure is none other than the Creator. This is a matter of being, and as such, the difference is qualitative. Thus Kierkegaard certainly speaks of God in terms that entail what American philosopher Charles Hartshorne has called "categorical supremacy." He writes:

> The superiority of deity to all others cannot (in accordance with established word usage) be expressed by indefinite descriptions, such as "immensely good," "very powerful," or even "best" or "most powerful," but must be a superiority of principle, a definite conceptual divergence from every other being, actual or so much as possible.[13]

How shall one more precisely formulate this difference of category? A formulation that Kierkegaard used as early as 1841 in his dissertation on *The Concept of Irony* is that of "being in and for itself."[14] The writings of Johannes Climacus (1844, 1846) derive their dialectical power from another framework highlighting ontological difference, the sheer otherness of an eternal happiness and historical happenings. Four days later, in that same month of June 1844 in which *Philosophical Fragments* appeared, Vigilius Haufniensis, in *The Concept of Anxiety*, would further develop a concept of time in which events were not leveled out in a flatland, where no events rise up in distinctive importance. He wrote of how in such a single linear sense of time, the past is no longer available as a thing in itself but in a "simple continuity with the future (with this the concepts of conversion, atonement, and redemption are lost)." Moreover, the future does not stand out distinctly "but in a simple continuity with the present (thereby the concepts of resurrection and judgment are destroyed)."[15] Haufniensis is not abandoning the flow of time from the past through the present into the future, but he knows

---

13. Charles Hartshorne and William L. Reese, eds., *Philosophers Speak of God* (Chicago: University of Chicago Press, 1953), 7.
14. See Arnold B. Come, *Kierkegaard as Theologian: Recovering My Self* (Montreal: McGill-Queen's University Press, 1997), 70–75. Come points out how Kierkegaard derived the formulation from Hegel but actually attributes the notion to Socrates "as reported in Plato's *Phaedo*" (ibid., 75, 78–79).
15. CA, 90.

that there are meaning-packed moments in time's flowing stream. They have to do with the eternal's interruptive presence in life. For Christians, those events in their distinctiveness are crucial and come together to form a narrative, a gospel that is rooted in the Creator's will.

The sense of qualitative difference was evident already in Anti-Climacus's preface, pointing out how the real sickness unto death trivializes all the misfortunes that befall a creaturely life. A year later Anti-Climacus would write: "[W]hat truly can be said to *draw to itself* must first and foremost be something in itself or must be a something that is in itself. That which is not in itself cannot possibly draw to *itself*."[16] A few pages earlier in PC, Anti-Climacus has ridiculed the "undialectical" presentation of Christian matters that "rhetorically lays out everything, even the paradox, in a direct superlative, so that to be God becomes a direct superlative of what it is to be a human being."[17] Earlier in PC, he had set Christ's inviting welcome "Come here to me, all you who labor and are burdened, I will give you rest" (Matt 11:28) in a setting of a seriousness that bespeaks the absolute: "Halt now! But before what is one to halt? Before that which at the same moment infinitely changes everything."[18]

To support these varying formulations' common ontological thrust, Kierkegaard has the traditional divine predicates ready to deploy but always with a dialectical twist. Thus Climacus in CUP writes that God is omnipresent and as such "is cognizable precisely by his being invisible."[19] And in writing of God's omnipotence in his signed *Christian Discourses*, Kierkegaard exults over the fact that God not only creates out of nothing but "lovingly makes the created being something in relation to himself."[20] Climacus can state the qualitative difference very sharply in these ontological terms:

---

16. PC, 158.
17. PC, 104.
18. PC, 23.
19. CUP, 1:245.
20. Søren Kierkegaard, *Christian Discourses: The Crisis and a Crisis in the Life of an Actress*, ed. and trans. Howard V. Hong and Edna H. Hong (Princeton: Princeton University Press, 1997), 128 (hereafter cited as CD).

> God does not think, he creates; God does not exist [*existere*], he is eternal. A human being thinks and exists, and existence [*Existens*] separates thinking and being, holds them apart from each other in succession.[21]

A similar ontological distinction between God and the human seems to be sounding in the characterization of God as infinite subjectivity. In the journals he writes:

> God is pure subjectivity, sheer unmitigated subjectivity, and intrinsically has no trace at all of the objective as such, since everything with such objectivity comes thereby within the realm of relativities.[22]

This formulation certainly differentiates God from human life, where relativities are part of the givenness of the self. But as the passage continues, it gives this subjectivity a different quality:

> God is infinite majesty in such a way that nothing in and for itself can concern [God] but only insofar as it pleases [God's] majesty.... Whether something concerns [God] does not derive from the object but from [God's] pleasure—[God] is infinite subjectivity.

This language strains some of the particular ontological formulations Climacus offers to express the qualitative difference. We come to terms here with the fact that Kierkegaard, like Luther before him, holds a voluntarist conception of God and God's action. The willed action of God comes precisely from the depth of God's own choosing. Kierkegaard's theology of creation does not merely speak of creation out of nothing; it bears witness to the very nature of God, for nothing at all causes God to create. It is God's good pleasure to do so. That action seems to issue forth from a "redoubling" in God, where God, as it were, consults God and decides to create. Something like thinking seems to be involved here, the pondering of a possibility. But the will plays the decisive role. One is tempted to think of Genesis's puzzling plural, "Let *us* make humankind in *our* image" (Gen 1:26; my emphasis). Arnold Come remarks, "It is crucial to note that this line of distinction (between what God is and is not) is not only *ontological* (a matter of

21. CUP, 1:332.
22. JP, 3:2570.

independent, transcendent being-in-and-for-oneself) but also *ethical.*"[23] He adds that in such references in Kierkegaard, the being of the eternal is described as righteousness.

Come is right that Kierkegaard will not settle simply for an ontological distinction, though a difference in being persists in what is added. But as we proceed in the second part of SUD we will see that even this decisive formulation of the dialectical difference in being between Creator and creature will pale before a difference that can only be formulated in religious terms. Moreover, the becoming that creating entails in God does not square easily with the language of a God who in "pure, unmitigated subjectivity" does not "exist" in genuine relationships. One could hear this corrective advance coming in 1848 in the veronymous *Christian Discourses* where Kierkegaard writes:

> Oh, wonderful omnipotence and love! A human being cannot bear to have his "creations" be something in relation to himself; they are supposed to be nothing, and therefore he calls them, and with disdain, "creations." But God, who creates from nothing, omnipotently takes from nothing and says, "Become"; he lovingly adds, "Become something even in relation to me." What wonderful love; even his omnipotence is in the power of love.[24]

David Gouwens has put well the point that for Kierkegaard "omnipotence, again, is not a curb to creaturely freedom, but its support."[25] In any case, consider how Anti-Climacus writes vividly of the potentiation of the self in having God as criterion, as measuring stick:

> Christianity teaches that . . . this individual human being exists *before God* . . . may speak with God any time he wants to, assured of being heard by him—in short, this person is invited to live on the most intimate terms with God! . . . Truly, if there is anything to lose one's mind over, this is it![26]

---

23. Come, *Kierkegaard as Theologian*, 78. In this section, I am indebted to Come's detailed discussion of two concepts ("being-in-and-for-itself" and "reduplication") and two analogies ("infinite subjectivity" and "personhood").
24. CD, 127.
25. David J. Gouwens, *Kierkegaard as Religious Thinker* (Cambridge: Cambridge University Press, 1966), 195. He lifts up as well the theme that to make a being free, omnipotence is required. Søren Kierkegaard, *Eighteen Upbuilding Discourses*, ed. and trans. Howard V. Hong and Edna H. Hong (Princeton: Princeton University Press, 1990), 61. Cf. JP, 2:1251.

Com.: Making the End Fast: Against Apologetics and Socrates?

"Losing one's mind," well perhaps. But this teaching more ominously carries the risk that the hearer will be offended. In *Practice in Christianity*, Anti-Climacus devotes his crucial central section to reflection on Christ's dialectical word of peril and promise: "Blessed is he who is not offended at me" (Matt 11:6). Already here in SUD, he peppers the text with talk of the possibility of offense that the believer must bear. But note that he asks about the offended one: "But why is he offended? Because it is too high for him, because his mind cannot grasp it, because he cannot attain bold confidence in the face of it."[27] One might say, colloquially, that the news is too good to be true. So faith is required here. Indeed, "faith itself [is] the only facticity."[28] One cannot avoid offense by simply employing the powers of reason for, while mind is one element in the relation-as-given, faith is the spirit's venture and comes about only through the positive third relating itself to itself as the Constituting Power intends. Faith does have to do with doctrinal propositions, the dimension that is classically phrased as the "*fides quae creditor*," the faith which we believe. Anti-Climacus is more finding his focus in the passion of faith, the "*fides qua creditor*," the faith *by* which we believe. Were his concern the former, the "what" of Christianity, perhaps a better teaching plan might suffice. But Anti-Climacus is after the spirit and seeks to evoke response on the order of the "how" of Christian trust, the "*fides qua creditur*."[29]

Accordingly, Anti-Climacus launches into withering derision over the prospects of apologetics. The apologist is "Judas No. 2: he, too, betrays with a kiss," for:

> To defend something is always to disparage it. . . . As for Christianity! Well, he who defends it has never believed it. If he believes, then the

---

26. SUD, 85.
27. SUD, 85–86.
28. SUD, 85.
29. In the terms of classic Lutheran distinctions, Anti-Climacus is focused not on knowledge (*notitia*) or assent (*assensus*) but on trust (*fiducia*). We'll later face the question of whether saving *fiducia* can prevail even in the absence of the cognitive elements.

enthusiasm of faith is not a defense—no, it is attack and victory; a believer is a victor.[30]

Then a little later he is no less sarcastic in his criticism. Imagine a lover. "[D]o you not think he would find it loathsome to speak in such a manner that he would try to demonstrate by means of three reasons that there is something to being in love[?]"[31]

Existing before God is a gift from the Creator that offers good news in the intensifying of the self's venture, but it also carries the reality "as a corollary that a person's sin should be of concern to God."[32] So with the gift there is a task. Faith is called for but offense is possible, and thus Anti-Climacus moves to an exposition of the nature of sin, the opposite of faith.[33] If virtue were the opposite of faith, as he finds commonly assumed, he would not make the move to which he now proceeds. He turns to critiquing his beloved Socrates.

It is hard to overestimate the importance for Kierkegaard of the example set by the simple wise man of Athens. Even here he writes "Socrates, Socrates, Socrates! Yes, we may well call your name three times."[34] Socrates called on the Athenians to truly know themselves and he himself professed "a God-fearing ignorance,"[35] walking around Athens asking questions. We'll come back to his praise of Socrates, but the crucial problem with Socrates is that he defined sin as ignorance. Accordingly, the human condition is that truth is available for each of us in each of us, but needs to be drawn out, as Socrates did by his probing questioning. This understanding of the Socratic maieutic method lay behind the juxtaposition Johannes Climacus posited between the Socratic and his own project of thought (*Fragments* or the *Postscript*, if the hypothesis be clothed in "historical dress") in which not merely the truth but the condition for receiving the truth must be given by the teacher. In this second case, the teacher acquires a

---

30. SUD, 87.
31. SUD, 103.
32. SUD, 83.
33. SUD, 82.
34. SUD, 92.
35. SUD, 99.

decisive significance; a "historical point of departure for an eternal happiness" is given.

Now Anti-Climacus draws out the decisive difference concerning the human problematic. It is one thing to suppose that the problem, let us call it "sin," is due to ignorance. The solution then is good education. Drawn to the making of distinctions, Anti-Climacus points beyond the "original" ignorance of incapability to an ignorance that reflects a person's "efforts to obscure his knowing." "Then the sin . . . is not in the knowing but in the willing."[36] Here education, even the services of the most dexterous midwife, will not avail. He speaks very directly of the failings of the Socratic view, which

> lacks a dialectical determination appropriate to the transition from having understood something to doing it. In the transition Christianity begins; by taking this path it shows that sin is rooted in willing and arrives at the concept of defiance.[37]

The defiant sinner is not ignorant. He knows the good but chooses the evil. Yet defiance may not express itself forthrightly. Willing is dialectical and may not directly oppose the known good.[38] Delaying tactics are available: "We shall look at it tomorrow."[39] Gradually, knowing comes over to the side of willing. Anti-Climacus opines that "this is how perhaps the great majority of men live: they work gradually at eclipsing their ethical and ethical-religious comprehension."[40] But in all its subtlety, sin lies in the will of the individual. And that truth is "made fast by means of the paradox."

What's going on here? Is Anti-Climacus fastening the end of individual responsibility on sin by saying that we are all simply stuck in sin because of an action of an Adam we don't remember voting for? We tread again on the turf of the dialectical. It is indeed the case that in Anti-Climacus's sewing image, the end of the thread must be tightly

---

36. SUD, 88.
37. SUD, 93.
38. See the discussion of "dialectic" in chapter 1, pp. 9–10, footnotes 20 and 23. Julia Watkin and Sylvia Walsh clarify what happens when "two things come together though they counter each other."
39. SUD, 94.
40. Ibid.

tied in a knot lest the thread slip through the cloth. We are skillful at finding explanations or excuses for our acts of moral evil. Thus the thread slips through the cloth and we are not indicted. Here what is being made fast we find in the wrong choosing of the individual. It's that thread, the willed misuse of our freedom. In stressing human responsibility for moral evil, Anti-Climacus is separating himself decisively from Hegel, where evil finds its place in the Absolute Spirit's movement outward into objectification. In *The Phenomenology of Spirit*, Hegel wrote that "in the statement, that the Divine Being from the beginning empties Itself of Itself, that its objective existence becomes concentrated in Itself and becomes evil, it is not asserted but implied that *per se* this evil existence is *not* something alien to the Divine nature. Absolute Being would be merely an empty name if in very truth there were any other being external to it, if there were a 'fall' from it."[41]

In this emphasis on the individual's choice, Anti-Climacus echoes the psychological investigation of Vigilius Haufniensis in CA. The watchman of Copenhagen observes that

> innocence is lost only by guilt. Every man loses innocence essentially in the same way that Adam lost it. It is not in the interest of ethics to make all men except Adam into concerned and interested spectators of guiltiness, but not participants in guiltiness.[42]

The passage continues by saying:

> nor is it in the interest of dogmatics to make all men into interested and sympathetic spectators of the Atonement but not participants in the Atonement.[43]

We're coming to the atonement. But we note here that Haufniensis does also observe that "since the race does not begin anew with every individual, the sinfulness of the race does indeed acquire a history."[44]

---

41. Hegel, *Phenomenology of Mind*, 775. Hans Lassen Martensen specifically objected that evil was an "interruption" of the immanent development of the world. See my discussion in Sponheim, *Kierkegaard on Christ*, 58–65.
42. CA, 36; cf. 30, 60–61. We note that Haufniensis explicitly denies that his presentation is Pelagian (CA, 34, 37), for the freedom of the anxious self is not "an abstract *liberum arbitrium* [free will]," but "an entangled freedom" (CA, 49).
43. CA, 36.

We remember that Haufniensis told us in his last sentence that psychology goes only so far in its deliberations about anxiety (*angst*) and then delivers the topic to dogmatics. "*Angst*" is not "*fortvivlelse*," the sickness unto death. In *angst*'s innocence, there is peace and repose, but there is something else as well, and that something disturbs the tranquility. What is it? It is nothing, Haufniensis says, and so distinguishes anxiety from the specific fears that might be associated with "dread," an earlier translation of "*angst*." Anxiety senses the "sheer sense of *being able*."[45] What will emerge out of my freedom? Sin emerges out of the dizziness of anxiety by a leap. Who wouldn't become dizzy looking down into "the yawning abyss" of freedom? Anxious, the becoming spirit looks down into its own possibility and lays hold of finitude to support itself, abandoning true freedom where finitude plays its proper subordinate role. At that moment, each Adam falls into guilt. Haufniensis sees the gap: "Between these two moments lies the leap, which no science has explained and which no science can explain." And he knows his limits, writing, "Further than this, psychology cannot and will not go."[46] But what of dogmatics?

Back to Anti-Climacus. There is discontinuity between the two pseudonyms because anxiety is not sin. But there is a crucial continuity in the presence of the dialectical. Haufniensis writes that "anxiety is neither a category of necessity nor a category of freedom."[47] Anti-Climacus seems to say that despair is a category of necessity *and* freedom. He began in the first half of SUD by telling us that despair is not "something that lies in human nature as such."[48] His critique of Socrates asserts human responsibility in choosing; the wrongness of sin lies in the will—the individual's will—not the understanding. It is to make that seam of personal responsibility fast that the dogmatic seamstress fastens the end with the dogma of original sin.

How does this make the end fast? Can't we still slip away with

---

44. CA, 33.
45. CA, 45.
46. SUD, 61.
47. CA, 49.
48. SUD, 36.

delaying tactics or alibis? As Anti-Climacus draws toward the close of his work, he asserts that the "teaching about sin—that you and I are sinners . . . unconditionally splits up 'the crowd.'"[49] This emphasis on the individual sinner follows naturally from the descriptive analysis of the self. But in the second half of this book, we will see that this emphasis on the individual is often overplayed in the interpretation or appropriation of Kierkegaard. The Christian faith does not disappear in the subjectivity of the individual. Kierkegaard, for example, reacted strongly against the claim of his contemporary A. P. Adler that his personal religious experience constituted a direct divine revelation. In *The Book on Adler*, he wrote:

> The essentially Christian exists before any Christian exists; it must exist in order for one to become a Christian. It contains the qualification by which a test is made of whether someone has become a Christian; it maintains its objective continuance outside all believers, while it also is in the inwardness of the believer. In short, here there is no identity between the subjective and the objective. If the essentially Christian enters into the heart of ever so many believers, every believer realizes that it did not arise in his heart.[50]

Haufniensis's categories were the self and the race. So too for Anti-Climacus the thread of individual responsibility for sin is made fast by the doctrine of hereditary sin. How are these two to be held together? No wonder that he speaks of this as fastening the end "by means of the paradox."[51] No wonder that he writes: "The possibility of offense lies in this: there must be a revelation from God to teach man what sin is and how deeply it is rooted."[52] Clearly this emphasis on the individual's responsibility for sinful willing entails not the absence of something (as, say, knowledge) but the presence of a definite, in that sense "positive," action. Anti-Climacus asserts that this individual action cannot be comprehended, for "the secret of all comprehending

---

49. SUD, 121.
50. Søren Kierkegaard, *The Book on Adler*, ed. and trans. Howard V. Hong and Edna H. Hong (Princeton: Princeton University Press, 1995), 117–18. See also the essay by the pseudonym H. H. on "The Difference between a Genius and an Apostle."
51. SUD, 93.
52. SUD, 96.

is that this comprehending is itself higher than any position it posits."[53] The comprehending fits the action tidily within a system of understanding. But the individual's sinning stands out eccentrically; it has a rough edge that refuses to be smoothed down to fit the system. How often do we say, "I can't understand why I did that"? To fasten the end by knotting the thread with the dogma of hereditary sin doubles the difficulty dialectically. It is difficult to face up to sin. It is difficult to face up to my individual responsibility for sin. And now we are told that responsibility is rooted in something far deeper than my individuality. The end, as Anti-Climacus says, is made fast, but it is by means of a paradox. Thus he tells us that this business of sinning is "a paradox that must be believed."[54] Haufniensis put the paradox in three words, "Sin presupposes itself."[55] Is there nothing more to be said? There seems not to be. Unless one were to speak with Blaise Pascal of the strange notion of the fall:

> Nothing, to be sure, is more of a shock to us than such a doctrine, and yet without this mystery, which is the most incomprehensible of all, we should be incomprehensible to ourselves. The tangled knot of our condition acquired its twists and turns in that abyss; so that man is more inconceivable without the mystery than the mystery to man.[56]

Com.: The Pathetic and the Dialectical

We are edging here into a major issue in Kierkegaard interpretation. One could look back to the project of Johannes Climacus. "Religiousness B," the explicitly Christian emphasis on the paradox of the incarnation, is certainly not simply "Religiousness A," the human striving to relate "absolutely to the absolute and relatively to the relative."[57] Even the "essential" expression of "A," suffering, and the "decisive" expression, guilt, do not get us to the explicitly Christian. Thus in the "intermediate clause" between "A" and "B," Climacus

---

53. SUD, 97. In their commentary on SUD, the Hongs note hearing in Anti-Climacus's charge a reference to Martensen, whose *Den christelige Dogmatik* appeared in 1849.
54. SUD, 98.
55. CA, 62, 112.
56. Blaise Pascal, *Pensées* (New York: E. P. Dutton, 1958), 121n434.
57. CUP, 1:407.

expressly writes that "A" "is not the specifically Christian religiousness,"[58] which he calls here "the dialectical." But the next sentence adds, "On the other hand, the dialectical is decisive only insofar as it is joined together with the pathos-filled and gives rise to a new pathos."[59]

Another way to frame this relationship is to ask Climacus where truth is to be found. After devoting about forty pages to the "objective issue of the truth of Christianity [that appeals to scripture, the church, and the eighteen centuries]," Climacus gives some three hundred pages to "the subjective issue" of the relation of an existing individual to the truth of Christianity. In the title of the second chapter of the section, we have the much-quoted three words "Truth is subjectivity."[60] The "highest truth there is for an *existing* person" is defined thusly: "*An objective uncertainty, held fast through appropriation with the most passionate inwardness, is the truth.*"[61] Climacus also gives us the famous distinction between the person who "prays in truth to God although he is worshipping an idol" and the person who "prays in untruth to the true God and is therefore in truth worshipping an idol."[62]

Yet when we get to the much briefer "punch line" of the *Postscript*, we learn from Religiousness B that what "to exist" signifies for a person is "that by coming into existence he has become a sinner."[63] Earlier in this work, and in the *Fragments* as well,[64] Climacus stresses that, unlike

---

58. CUP, 1:555.
59. Ibid. In beginning his discussion of "the pathetic" and the "dialectical," Climacus offers this criticism of the age: "But since we have forgotten what it means to exist *sensu eminenti*, since we usually trace the pathos-filled to imagination and feeling and allow the dialectical to annul it instead of uniting both in the contemporaneity of existence, the pathos-filled in our philosophical nineteenth century has fallen into discredit and the dialectical has become passionless" (CUP, 1:385). Andrew J. Burgess has suggested that Luther's language of "*Simul Justus et Peccator*," "at the same time justified and a sinner," is "related to but not identical with" the way in which "religiousness B includes within itself the apparently incompatible religiousness A." I am indebted to Dr. Burgess for his paper "'Simul Justus' in Kierkegaard's Postscript" presented at an American Academy of Religion meeting at Luther Seminary, Saint Paul. This meeting took place in the 1990s, but I am unable to locate the exact date.
60. CUP, 1:189.
61. CUP, 1:203.
62. CUP, 1:201.
63. CUP, 1:583.
64. Søren Kierkegaard, *Philosophical Fragments / Johannes Climacus*, ed. and trans. Howard V. Hong and Edna H. Hong (Princeton: Princeton University Press, 1985), 15 (hereafter cited as PF).

for Socrates, "the subject cannot be untruth eternally . . . he must have become that in time."⁶⁵ We seem in a different universe here than that of Religiousness A, where even in a sense of the totality of one's guilt, "the subject's self-identity is preserved, and guilt-consciousness is [only] a change of the subject within the subject himself."⁶⁶ One thinks of people paradoxically enjoying their sense of guilt, for it's at least "my" guilt, after all. I do recognize myself there. In "B," subjectivity seems, in effect, to be untruth, and yet this passage in the "Appendix to B" speaks in its title of "the retroactive effect of the dialectical *on pathos leading to a sharpened Pathos.*"⁶⁷ Climacus seems to be saying "subjectivity is the truth, is untruth, and yet is the truth." What can we make of this?

Clearly, there is continuity to be recognized in the human venture before God. That is evident elsewhere in the authorship. In reviewing *Stages on Life's Way*—"collected, forwarded to the press and published by one Hilarius Bookbinder"—in "A Glance at Danish Literature," Kierkegaard has Climacus tell us that "there are three stages, an esthetic, an ethical, a religious. . . . But despite this tripartition the book is nevertheless an either/or. That is, the ethical and the religious stages have an essential relation to each other."⁶⁸ Johannes de Silentio in *Fear and Trembling* finds that Abraham with Isaac on Mount Moriah represents a "teleological suspension of the ethical." Can the ethical claim that calls out to all humankind somehow be "suspended" in an individual's relationship to the absolute? How can Abraham sacrificing Isaac not violate our commonsense ethical emphasis on fatherly love and care? But he also knows that "from this it does not follow that the ethical should be invalidated; rather, the ethical receives a completely different expression," one contrary to the conventional ethical.⁶⁹ De Silentio may say over and over again that he cannot understand Abraham, but he does know that Abraham lived in the relational

---

65. CUP, 1:207.
66. CUP, 1:584.
67. CUP, 1:581; my emphasis.
68. CUP, 1:294.
69. FT, 70.

continuity of God's promises and could address God with the familiar "*du*."[70] Now Anti-Climacus gives us a comparable sense of continuity in the human venture as he carries his earlier psychological analysis of despair into the intensification provided via Christian dogmatic teaching. So he writes:

> Sin is—after being taught by a revelation from God what sin is—before God in despair not to will to be oneself or in despair to will to be oneself. (96)[71]

Yet there is no simple continuity between the two parts, for in the second, there is a dialectical reversal in despair as a matter of fact. The weakness in not willing to be oneself, a sinner, becomes before God the defiance of the forgiveness of sins. The defiance in willing to be oneself becomes, before God, the weakness of the sinner who remains adamant in refusing the forgiveness of sins. It is, after all, God the creator who is the criterion, setting the true telos for the self. Thus in the reversal, one sees revealed again the qualitative difference between the Creator and the creatures.[72]

Anti-Climacus puts this all together for us in a summary paragraph, ending the twenty-three-page opening section with its judgment of despair as sin. In doing so, he reaches ahead to the Apostles' Creed's second article and the atonement. He asserts a double paradox, challenging human hubris in relation to both the disease and the medicine. "Speculation, which talks itself out of the paradoxes, snips off a little bit from both sides and thereby gets along more easily."[73] Human rationalistic insolence resists the revelation of despair as sin and the making of the end fast in the dogma of original sin. But, ironically, it rejects as well Christianity's word about God's action in the atonement to bring full healing in the elimination of sin.[74]

One remembers that even Vigilius Haufniensis, for all his emphasis on individual responsibility in his psychological observation, can

---

70. FT, 77.
71. SUD, 96.
72. SUD, 113.
73. SUD, 100.
74. Ibid.

almost casually remark about the innocent suffering of the one "who freely chose to carry all the sin of the world," "for Christ was more than an individual."[75] There's no dogmatic development of atonement theory in SUD, but the tenor fits Anti-Climacus's other work, PC, where there are strong indications of some combination of an objective, sacrificial theme and a *Christus Victor*-like liberation theme. In this later work, Anti-Climacus's witness to Jesus the Christ speaks of "the infinite importance his death has as a death of Atonement."[76] Earlier he writes: "[A]s soon as the true divine compassion appears in the world it is unconditionally the sacrifice."[77] There seems to be a kind of punctiliar determinacy about the efficacy of the cross, which is "infinitely more important and infinitely more decisive" than the dribbling indeterminacy of historical process to which one wrongly turns to judge the Christ by the "results" of his life.[78]

Yet response is called for in the "practice" (*indøvelse* [exercise, training, working out]) of Christianity. In PC's long third part, Anti-Climacus is relentless in his scathing criticism of those who would "admire" or "adore" the Christ. Christians are called to be "imitators" of the Christ. Kierkegaard owned a copy of Thomas à Kempis's work. For Anti-Climacus in PC, Christ is the "prototype" (*Forbilledet* [the picture ahead of one]), who "must in one sense be *behind* people, propelling forward, while in another sense he stands *ahead*, beckoning."[79] Anti-Climacus holds these two motifs closely together. In the prayer that opens that final section, he addresses "our Savior and Redeemer" and speaks thusly of the work of Christ to "rescue the redeemed": "This was your task, which you have completed and which you will complete until the end of time."[80] "Completed" and "will complete" keep challenging company in Kierkegaard's theology

---

75. CA, 38.
76. PC, 182–83.
77. PC, 60.
78. PC, 23.
79. PC, 238.
80. PC, 151. I have written of PC's testimony to the work of Christ in Paul R. Sponheim, "Relational Transcendence in Divine Agency," in Perkins, *Practice in Christianity*, 47–68.

of the Apostles' Creed's second article. Thus in the signed *Works of Love* he writes:

> It is true that the pronouncement of the forgiveness of sin is pronounced also to you but the pastor does not have the right to say to you that you have faith, and yet it is pronounced to you only if you believe.... See, this is the struggle of faith in which you can have an occasion to be tried and tested every day.[81]

In any case, in both his works, Anti-Climacus has shifted the emphasis from Christology to soteriology, and in PC there is a move toward sharing in the suffering of Christ through public witness. Or perhaps it is better to say that the focus in SUD is more on the impact the reality of the Christ and his suffering has on the understanding of God and what the invitation to faith entails vis-à-vis the human condition of despair.[82] Were we to follow out PC's theme of the challenge to the believer's life in the world, we would want to look at *Works of Love*, which the Hongs call a "mature, indicative, expressive Christian ethics of grace."[83] In the preface preceding each of the two long series, Kierkegaard writes of these deliberations: "They are *Christian deliberations*, therefore not about *love* but about *works of love*."[84] WL (1847), wedged in between the works of Johannes Climacus (1844, 1846) and Anti-Climacus (1849, 1850), voices a new melody, not familiar from the first three pseudonymous works at least. The Christian inwardness of faith, so crucial in those three semi-pseudonymous writings, yields outward action in veronymous WL. Kierkegaard writes of Christ: "But he did, after all, come to the world to become the prototype, to draw

---

81. Søren Kierkegaard, *Works of Love*, ed. and trans. Howard V. Hong and Edna H. Hong (Princeton: Princeton University Press, 1995), 379–80 (hereafter cited as WL). Cf. CUP, 1:584: "The believer expands the consciousness of sin to the whole race and at the same time does not know the whole race to be saved, inasmuch as the single individual's salvation indeed depends on his being brought into relation to that historical event, which precisely because it is historical cannot be everywhere at once but uses time in order to become known to human beings."
82. Gouwens, *Kierkegaard as Religious Thinker*, 146–47, objects to a reading of Kierkegaard that reduces Christology to soteriology and instead holds the person and work of Christ together: "In theological terms, Kierkegaard's understanding of Christ *extra nos* and of salvation *pro nobis* and *pro me* employs strikingly objective and realistic language, including forensic justification. The sacred history of the Redeemer's death—that it effects redemption—is not open to imitation, but has intrinsic meaning."
83. WL, xiii.
84. WL, 3, 207.

human beings to himself so that they might be like him and truly become his own."[85] PC has the echoing emphasis on the Christian's suffering in the world.

Here in SUD, Anti-Climacus is doing the upbuilding work of uncovering the nature of the human predicament and can only glance ahead in first-order speech of praise about God's decisive action in forgiving sins. One hears in his critique of "speculation," which "snips off a little bit" from the statement of both the disease and the healing, the rhythm of Paul in Romans 5: "Therefore, just as sin came into the world through one man, and death came through sin, and so death spread to all because all have sinned.... But the free gift is not like the trespass. For if the many died through the one man's trespass, much more surely have the grace of God and the free gift in the grace of the one man, Jesus Christ, abounded for the many" (Rom 5:12–15).

B. The Continuance of Sin

We are prepared for Anti-Climacus further expounding his understanding of sin by speaking of sin as "not a negation but a position,"[86] and by affirming the "continuance" of sin by writing that "sin grows every moment that one does not take leave of it."[87] Readers aware of the Lutheran understanding of sin will have reason to note that Anti-Climacus is not talking about particular sins, this peccadillo or that. He is talking about sin singular—the fact that "deep within itself sin has a consistency and in this consistency in evil itself it also has a certain strength."[88] Anti-Climacus speaks of how there is within the human spirit "an essential interior consistency."[89] In the "continuance of sin," the sinner finds "that the state of sin is what holds him together deep down where he has sunk, profanely strengthening him with its consistency."[90] That's the notion of sin that

---

85. WL, 264.
86. SUD, 96–100.
87. SUD, 106.
88. SUD, 106–7.
89. SUD, 107.
90. SUD, 108.

prevails throughout the dark descriptions in "Despair Is Sin." Perhaps it's this sense of captivity that leads some Christian thinkers to speak with Luther of the bondage of the will. The apostle Paul wrote that "whatever does not proceed from faith is sin" (Rom 14:23). Luther heard that word condemning all human efforts to claim righteousness and underlined it, writing that anything outside faith "must necessarily be sin."[91]

As one makes one's way slowly through these pages, there may arise a dawning feeling of "Yes, in his criticism of Socrates, he's got that right; my problem goes that deep. The end is made that fast." But perhaps we are not as well prepared for the expression of continuity that occurs as he writes of the dialectical contribution of the ignorant wise man of Athens:

> Let us never forget that it was out of veneration for God that he was ignorant, that as far as it was possible for a pagan he was on guard duty as a *judge* on the frontier between God and man, keeping watch so that the deep gulf of qualitative difference between them was maintained.[92]

Anti-Climacus calls for Christianity to be "precisely a Socratic, God-fearing ignorance" that guards the faith against speculation so that the gulf of qualitative difference is preserved as in the paradox and faith.[93] To know is to know how little you know.

Socrates served Kierkegaard throughout his life in writing. In his dissertation, Kierkegaard lauded the Socratic use of irony over against a culture in decline. At the end of the first authorship, Johannes Climacus praised Socrates who, in facing the question of immortality, did not dabble in proofs, but staked "his whole life on this 'if'; he dares to die, and with the passion of the infinite he has so ordered his whole life that it might be acceptable—*if* there is an immortality."[94] He's there again in 1847 in *Works of Love* in the veronymous writing of "The Work of Love in Praising Love."[95] Then, even in the final vitriolic

---

91. Martin Luther, *Martin Luther's Basic Theological Writings*, ed. Timothy F. Lull (Minneapolis: Fortress Press, 1989), 195.
92. SUD, 99. Cf. CUP, 1:202.
93. SUD, 99.
94. CUP, 1:201.

assault on the church in the name of Christianity, it was Socrates with whom Kierkegaard would speak "if only for a half hour."[96] Little wonder, that wish from Kierkegaard who could say: "The only analogy I have for myself is: Socrates; my task is a Socratic task, to revise the determination of what it is to be Christian."[97]

Perhaps there is, after all, a sense in which there is an apologetic element in Kierkegaard's formulation of the human venture.[98] This will be a dialectically dense apology working with the complexities typified by Anti-Climacus's theological anthropology but present elsewhere in the authorship as well. Johannes de Silentio cannot understand the faith of Abraham. He recognizes that "faith is a marvel [*Vidunder*]," but he finishes that sentence by saying, "yet no human being is excluded from it; for that which unites all human life is passion, and faith is a passion [*Lidenskab*]."[99] There's the word Anti-Climacus employs in the first part of SUD in speaking of "the passion of the understanding"[100] and in saying in the second part that "the more passion and imagination a person has . . . the closer he is in a certain sense (in possibility) to being able to believe."[101] Johannes Climacus knew the word passion outside the faith and knows as well that "the ultimate potentiation of every passion is always to will its own downfall, and so it is also the ultimate passion of the understanding [*Forstand*] to will the

---

95. In his study of the *Upbuilding Discourses*, George Pattison, *Kierkegaard's Upbuilding Discourses*, 215, finds this "reappearance of Socrates" to "hint at" the significance of the discourses for Kierkegaard's theological understanding, namely "that the transition to a more overtly Christological understanding of religiousness, with its concomitant requirement of witnessing to the truth publicly and sufferingly, is nevertheless, conceived within a framework erected on the ground of common human experience and understanding." Or in the words of this chapter, the "pathetic" and the "dialectical" are held together in the intensification Christianity brings.
96. Søren Kierkegaard, *"The Moment" and Late Writings*, ed. and trans. Howard V. Hong and Edna H. Hong (Princeton: Princeton University Press, 1998), 341 (hereafter cited as TM). Yet we know that it is not Socrates but Jesus who finds his place on Kierkegaard's tombstone through the choice of the hymn by H. A. Brorson, which envisions speaking "perpetually and perpetually" with "my Jesus." See Andrew J. Burgess, "Kierkegaard, Brorson, and Moravian Music," in Perkins, IKC, *Practice in Christianity*, 215.
97. TM, 343.
98. Thus I am uneasy with Mahn, *Fortunate Fallibility*, 64, writing that Haufniensis "critiques Hegel's interpretation of the Fall not because it is bad theodicy but because it *is* theodicy." Richard McCombs, *The Paradoxical Rationality of Søren Kierkegaard* (Bloomington: Indiana University Press, 2013), is helpful in clarifying the legitimation and limitation of Kierkegaard's appeal to reason.
99. FT, 67.
100. SUD, 39.
101. SUD, 86.

collision" with the paradox that is the "passion of thought."[102] So it is possible that "the paradox and the understanding meet in the mutual understanding of their difference, [and] then the encounter is a happy one."[103] Reaching back to Johannes de Silentio, we have his assertion that "faith is the highest passion in a person."[104] There's no "going further" than faith and "no standing still" in faith, for the believer's witness is, "I have my whole life in it."[105]

There's a word here to the Hegelians holding that "revealed religion" falls short of philosophy where the "*content*" of "Spirit as a whole" is known, no longer in figurative form.[106] Already in his early theological writings Hegel had the representational Christ prophesy: "When ye cease merely to see the divine in me and outside yourselves, then will the divine come to consciousness in you also because you have been with me from the beginning because our natures are one in love and in God."[107] For Johannes de Silentio, the principle of contradiction applies, and there's no getting beyond faith in relation to a God who is distinguished from creatures by an infinite qualitative difference, not least in that God's very relatedness to creatures.

"I have my whole life in it," wrote de Silentio. There's the *Lidenskab* of which Kierkegaard would write veronymously and pseudonymously. We've used Johannes Climacus's language in CUP to suggest how this passion joins with the "dialectical" in sketching what it means to become a Christian. In part 2 of this book, we'll see that much Kierkegaard scholarship subdivides over the distinction between the "how" of becoming a Christian and the "what" of Christianity. In his journals, Kierkegaard has a fascinating remark about how Climacus is being read:

> In all that is usually said about Johannes Climacus being purely subjective and so on, people have forgotten, in addition to everything else concrete

102. PF, 37.
103. PF, 49.
104. FT, 122.
105. FT, 123.
106. Georg Wilhelm Friedrich Hegel, *The Phenomenology of Spirit*, trans. J. B. Baillie (New York: Harper, 1967), 791.
107. Hegel, "Spirit of Christianity," 272.

about him, that in one of the last sections he shows that the curious thing is: that there is a "how" which has this quality, then if it is truly given, that the "what" is also given; and that it is the "how" of "faith." Here, quite certainly, inwardness at its maximum is shown to be objectivity again. And this is a turning of the principle of subjectivity which, so far as I know, has never before been so carried through or worked out.[108]

The passage he refers to seems to be one toward the end of CUP's "Conclusion":

> An orthodox defends Christianity with the most terrible passion; with perspiring face and the most worried gestures. . . . He does everything in the name of Jesus and uses Christ's name on every occasion as a sure sign that he is a Christian and is called to defend Christendom in our day—and he has no intimation of the little ironic secret that a person, just by describing the "how" of his inwardness, can indirectly indicate that he is a Christian without mentioning Christ's name.[109]

How perfect! Climacus begins the passage by ridiculing the apologist and ends in what I am calling here an "apology of sorts" by arguing that in the maximum intensity of the "how" the "what" is "indirectly" given. Yes, "indirectly." Recall what was said in the biographical sketch about Kierkegaard's use of "indirect communication" and of how pseudonymity served that method formally as did all his writing materially. Thus in the *Postscript*, Climacus will draw the subjective and objective together by saying that

> this "how" can fit only one thing, the absolute paradox. Therefore there is no vague talk that being a Christian means to accept and accept, and accept altogether differently . . . but *to have faith* is specifically qualified differently from all other appropriations and inwardness.[110]

So too, the "psychological" consideration of despair in the first part of SUD is incorporated materially in the "theological" reflection on sin in the second, with the motor moving the writing forward in and between both parts being the rhythm of the intensification of consciousness. Yet it is not a smooth progression. In veronymously writing of the life

---

108. JP, 4:4550.
109. CUP, 1:613.
110. CUP, 1:610–11.

of the Christian in *For Self-Examination* in 1851, Kierkegaard can sound a warning note to the enthusiasts of intensification, suggesting that the advance in consciousness involves epigenetic breaks in continuity:[111]

> This life-giving in the Spirit is not a *direct* heightening of the natural life in a person in *immediate* continuation from and connection with it—what blasphemy! How horrible to take Christianity in vain this way!—it is a new life.[112]

Moreover, we recall that Anti-Climacus in SUD's preface told us that the cure for this most terrible sickness "is simply to die, to die to the world."[113] How much continuity do we hear there?

One could see this same issue of the relationship between the "pathetic" and the "dialectical" in *Works of Love* as Kierkegaard discourses on self-love. What emerges most sharply is the emphasis on self-denial, "which is Christianity's essential form."[114] After all, "[t]he way to the essentially Christian goes through offense. . . . The offense guards the approach to the essentially Christian."[115] He is very critical of preferential love, "which selfishly can unite the two in a new self. The spirit's self, in contrast, takes away from myself . . . all self-love."[116] That would seem to close the door to the affirmation of self-love and turn the key emphatically in the lock.[117] Yet in reflecting on the second commandment, "You shall love your neighbor as yourself," he can write that the phrase "as yourself" "does not want to teach a person that he is not to love himself but rather wants to teach him proper self-

---

111. There would seem to be continuity even through the breaches in the self's becoming. Thus natural scientists speak of "punctuated equilibrium," referencing the "bursts of rapid speciation" in the fossil record. See Ian G. Barbour, *Religion in an Age of Science* (San Francisco: HarperCollins, 1990), 158. In *At Home in the Universe: The Search for Laws of Self-Organization and Complexity* (New York: Oxford University Press, 1995), Stuart Kauffman finds similar patterns in widely different levels of evolution.
112. Søren Kierkegaard, *For Self-Examination / Judge for Yourself!*, ed. and trans. Howard V. Hong and Edna H. Hong (Princeton: Princeton University Press, 1990), 76 (hereafter cited as FSE).
113. SUD, 6.
114. WL, 56.
115. WL, 59.
116. WL, 56.
117. See Amy Laura Hall, *Kierkegaard and the Treachery of Love* (Cambridge: Cambridge University Press, 2002), for a sustained reading of Kierkegaard that essentially holds out no hope for self-love.

love."[118] The dialectic continues throughout WL's nearly four hundred pages.[119]

To turn back to Johannes Climacus one more time on this major issue of continuity/discontinuity, it is important to note that Kierkegaard did not think of faith as a blind leap into the dark, lacking criteria.[120] Climacus, in giving the *Fragments*' project of thought its "historical dress," writes:

> Consequently the believing Christian both has and uses his understanding [*Forstand*], respects the universally human, does not explain someone's not becoming a Christian as a lack of understanding, but believes Christianity against the understanding and here uses the understanding—in order to see to it that he believes against the understanding. Therefore he cannot believe nonsense against the understanding, which one might fear, because the understanding will penetratingly perceive that it is nonsense . . . but he uses the understanding so much that through it he becomes aware of the incomprehensible (*det Uforstaaelige*), and now, believing, he relates himself to it against the understanding.[121]

We'll have much more to say later about the happening of faith in discussing interpretive alternatives that have surfaced in the reception of Kierkegaard.[122] We'll develop there M. Jamie Ferreira's emphasis on the leap as an act of the imagination, though willing (as intentional decision-making) is involved before and after the leap.[123] Here it must suffice to note that with Johannes Climacus we seem left with somehow saying both (1) that God "gives the condition" for knowing the truth and "gives the truth,"[124] and (2) that the human hearer "is indeed

---

118. WL, 18.
119. The best treatment of this complex matter that I know of is M. Jamie Ferreira's *Love's Grateful Striving* (Oxford: Oxford University Press, 2001).
120. To my knowledge, the phrase often associated with Kierkegaard, "the leap of faith," does not occur in the authorship.
121. CUP, 1:568.
122. See John J. Davenport and Anthony John Rudd, eds., *Kierkegaard after MacIntyre: Essays on Freedom, Narrative and Virtue* (Chicago: Open Court, 2001). Gordon D. Marino, "The Place of Reason in Kierkegaard's Ethics," in Davenport and Rudd, *Kierkegaard after MacIntyre*, 113-28, responds to MacIntyre's critique as it applies to the transition from the aesthetic to the ethical.
123. M. Jamie Ferreira, *Transforming Vision: Imagination and Will in Kierkegaardian Faith* (Oxford: Clarendon, 1991). Come, *Kierkegaard as Theologian*, 320-37, has a fairly full discussion of the various positions taken and includes his own reading that gives a greater role to will than Ferreira does.
124. PF, 15.

created, and, accordingly God must have given him the condition for understanding the truth."[125] Yet God must "remind" the learner that "he is untruth and is that through his own fault."[126] The hearer must somehow then act to receive the truth given. Climacus leaves us with a question: "Or is the matter made more difficult by this—that the non-being preceding the rebirth has more being than the non-being that precedes birth?"[127] Now Anti-Climacus tightens the knot by giving the truly despairing the dialectical word of grace.

How does Anti-Climacus understand the motivation for the move into faith? He is most explicit in PC in asking the question that has been likely building all through our presentation of the Christian understanding of despair: "But if the essentially Christian is something so terrifying and appalling, how in the world can anyone think of accepting Christianity?" He responds: "Very simply and, if you wish that also, very Lutheranly: only the consciousness of sin can force one, if I dare to put it that way (from the other side grace is the force), into this horror."[128] We have not found Anti-Climacus in SUD naming Luther as such, but his sin/grace dialectic reeks of the German reformer of the church. Kierkegaard was sharply critical of the Danish Lutheran misappropriation of Luther. Thus he writes in his *Journal*:

> Precisely in contrast to the exaggeration and deluded meritoriousness of the ascetic, Luther devoutly marked out a simple secularity in the good sense of the word. But here the contrast is the very point. Now Christianity has been completely homogenized with unadulterated secularism—and still we continue to appeal to Luther.[129]

---

125. Ibid.
126. Ibid.
127. PF, 20. See Come, *Kierkegaard as Theologian*, 323, for Climacus saying "faith is not an act of will" and that "faith is not a cognition but an act of freedom, an expression of willing."
128. PC, 67.
129. JP, 3:2513. For a sustained appreciation of Kierkegaard's appropriation of Luther's themes from the perspective of over forty years in congregational ministry, see Ronald F. Marshall, *Kierkegaard for the Church: Essays and Sermons* (Eugene, OR: Wipf & Stock, 2013). Already in the mid-twentieth century, Jaroslav Pelikan in *From Luther to Kierkegaard* (St. Louis: Concordia, 1950), 115, made the point that "Kierkegaard is the first major thinker after Luther to build it [an existential understanding of truth] into a working and critical philosophy." Now in the twenty-first century, Merold Westphal, "Kenosis and Offense: A Kierkegaardian Look at Divine Transcendence," in Perkins, *Practice in Christianity*, 19, writes, "Kierkegaard is in many respects simply a good Lutheran." Westphal draws especially on Luther's Heidelberg Disputation and its contrast between a theologian of glory and a theologian of the cross. For a pointed criticism of

What of Luther himself? Kierkegaard could be critical of Luther. In his journals he remarks, improbably, that Luther could be too soft on sinners. He charges that Luther did not recognize the specificity called for in his appeal to grace as juxtaposed to works. The appeal was a needed corrective in his context. Instead, he made the corrective normative, leaving the door open to the insidious cheap grace.[130] Yet he did not seem to be thus troubled when he wrote in *Judge for Yourself*, "Luther did not therefore abolish imitation nor did he do away with the voluntary, as pampered sentimentality would like to have us think about Luther. He affirmed imitation in the direction of witness to the truth."[131] On the other hand, at the end of his life, in the final issue of *The Moment*, he could write:

> It is of great importance to Protestantism in particular, to correct the enormous confusion Luther caused by inverting the relation and actually criticizing Christ by means of Paul, the Master by means of the follower. I, on the contrary, have not criticized the apostle, as if I myself were something. I, who am not even a Christian [not binding the ideal to his example], what I have done is to hold Christ's proclamation alongside the apostle's.[132]

But he could praise Luther "as the truest figure," second only to Jesus himself,[133] and as "the master of us all."[134] We probably cannot make Søren Kierkegaard say just a single thing about Martin Luther, but on the whole, Ronald Marshall is probably right in his summary statement that "whatever criticisms, then, Kierkegaard had of Luther, they were only 'little exceptions' (JP, 2:1922) to his otherwise compelling

---

Kierkegaard's reading of Luther, see Regin Prenter, "Luther and Lutheranism," in *Kierkegaard and the Great Traditions*, vol. 6 of *Bibliotheca Kierkegaardiana*, ed. Niels Thulstrup and Marie Mikulová Thulstrup (Copenhagen: Reitzel, 1981), 121–73. Prenter is troubled by Anti-Climacus's references to Christ as example for the Christian: "Kierkegaard transforms the gospel, the message of Christ the Redeemer, into a new law, still more severe than the law which requires perfect love for God and the neighbour" (Prenter, "Luther and Lutheranism," 145). One wonders how Prenter's Kierkegaard can be the Kierkegaard who wrote "The brightness of the law is fatal, that of the gospel infinitely salutary" (JP, 3:2533). For my own interpretation of Kierkegaard's emphasis on movement through terror and reassurance in Lutheran law/gospel categories, see Sponheim, "God's Changelessness," 101–28.

130. JP, 3:2556, 3:2682.
131. JFY, 193.
132. TM, 341.
133. JP, 3:2898.
134. JP, 3:2465.

argument against Christendom."[135] Similarly, in this book's closing section on Kierkegaard's legacy, we'll need to consider how Kierkegaard's passionate theological anthropology functions as a corrective in the present context.

In any case, with reference to PC's understanding of becoming a Christian, Anti-Climacus's acknowledgment of his Lutheran heritage seems straightforward enough. In the PC passage quoted on the Lutheran 'how,' it is crucial not to miss his parenthetical remark about the force from the other side being grace. Here Luther's sin/grace dialectic is certainly at work, as commentators have hastened to point out with regard to other of Kierkegaard's works.[136] In SUD, Anti-Climacus is not as explicitly asking and answering PC's question of why anyone could possibly accept Christianity, but in the rising intensification the self experiences, one may well say that one is building the consciousness and the accompanying energy for the leap.

As to the leap itself, perhaps faith as the opposite of sin also presupposes itself. In the very nature of the case, freedom cannot be explained by something other than freedom. The "other side" is indeed the God-ward side of the matter. The one who is without faith does not see that side: "[T]o him Christianity is a madness because it is incommensurate with any finite wherefore. But then what good is it? Answer: Be quiet, it is the absolute."[137] The understanding comes to a standstill at the absolute, writes Anti-Climacus. So why accept Christianity? "There is no 'why,' because there is an infinite 'why.'"[138] What of the suffering that comes from following Christ? If one knows Christ and loves him, one knows that "Christianity is not at all closer to heavy-mindedness [*Tungsind*] than to light-mindedness; they are both equally worldliness, equally far away, and both have just as much need of conversion."[139]

---

135. Marshall, *Kierkegaard for the Church*, 311. See his appendix, 308–12, for his critique of Christopher B. Barnett's evaluation that Kierkegaard is "a footnote to Luther."
136. See Lee C. Barrett, "The Paradox of Faith in Kierkegaard's *Philosophical Fragments*: Gift or Task?," in *"Philosophical Fragments" and "Johannes Climacus,"* vol. 7 of IKC, ed. Robert L. Perkins (Macon, GA: Mercer University Press, 1994), 261–84.
137. PC, 62.
138. PC, 120.
139. PC, 154.

All the same, we do well to resist a reverse rationalism, glorying in contradiction. We have noted that Kierkegaard, employing indirect communication, can speak of the one who comes to believe "being deceived into the truth." Yet the transcendent Christ in drawing all to himself "will not *entice* anyone to himself," for "to entice to oneself is falsely to draw to oneself."[140] The God-man may be a "sign of contradiction," but as a sign, "there must be something by which it draws attention to itself or to the contradiction. Thus the contradictory parts must not annul each other in such a way that the sign comes to mean nothing or in such a way that it becomes the opposite of a sign, an unconditional concealment."[141] As Anti-Climacus sees matters, God wills to be known and enables faith.

Perhaps what Anti-Climacus is up to in speaking of the choice faith represents is better understood in a Wittgensteinian understanding of "situated rationality." Anthony John Rudd writes that "Wittgenstein's philosophical therapy consists in returning concepts to the contexts in which they are actually used, where they have their life and their meaning."[142] To apply the point to this writing, where were we situated in our analysis and commentary on SUD? Well, we were speaking of Anti-Climacus's Trinitarian intensification of the self in the second half. We have thus far not made it much beyond the theology of the first article of the Apostles' Creed. But there is further intensification deriving from the relationships of which the second and third articles speak.

Com.: The Logic of Intensification II: Before Christ

Anti-Climacus has prepared the reader for what happens when the sinner confronts the message of the second article of the Apostles'

---

140. PC, 153.
141. PC, 125.
142. Anthony John Rudd, "On Straight and Crooked Readings: Why the *Postscript* Does Not Self-Destruct," in Houe et al., *Anthropology and Authority*, 124. See also Thomas Miles, "Ludwig Wittgenstein: Kierkegaard's Influence on the Origin of Analytic Philosophy," in *German and Scandinavian Philosophy*, tome 1 of *Kierkegaard's Influence on Philosophy*, vol. 11 of KRSRR, ed. Jon Stewart (Aldershot, UK: Ashgate, 2012), 209–41. More to come in part 2 on the merging of Kierkegaard and Wittgenstein in the work of such luminaries as Paul Holmer.

Creed. Already under the first article's rubric of SUD's "before God" creation theology, he writes of the sinner's resistance to the gracious action of God. That resistance can take subtle disguises. For example, there's an ambiguity about what appears to be sorrowful recognition of the seriousness of relapses into sin:

> Despair over sin is not averse to giving itself the appearance of being something good. . . . Such a person emphatically declares, perhaps in ever stronger terms, that this relapse plagues and torments him, brings him to despair, and he says "I will never forgive myself" . . . but now if God would forgive him this, well, he certainly could have the goodness to forgive himself. No, his despair over the sin is a far cry from being a qualification of the good, is a more intensive qualification of sin, the intensity of which is absorption in sin.[143]

This sorrowing soul savoring his repentance reminds us of George Bernard Shaw's oft-quoted line, "Forgiveness is a beggar's refuge; we must pay our debts."[144] Anti-Climacus speaks paradoxically (*doxa*, [against the opinion]), for he has learned with Haufniensis that ethics is "shipwrecked" on the rock of sin.[145] He is closer to Martin Luther's last word of confession, "We are beggars; that is true."[146]

But now Anti-Climacus explicitly raises the bid by speaking of how word of the coming of the Christ brings further intensification. What if the becoming self has Christ as the criterion?

> A self directly before Christ is a self intensified by the inordinate concession from God, intensified by the inordinate accent that falls upon it because God allowed himself to be born, become man, suffer, and die also for the sake of this self.[147]

In recognizing the qualitative difference between the Creator and creatures, we spoke of the difference as ontological, revealed sharply in the juxtaposition of the eternal and the temporal already in the preface. But now the sheer particularity of the Christ reveals a still

---

143. SUD, 111.
144. George Bernard Shaw, *Major Barbara* (New York: Brentano's, 1907), 152.
145. CA, 17.
146. Martin Luther, *Table Talk*, ed. and trans. Theodore C. Tappert, vol. 54 of *Luther's Works* (Philadelphia: Fortress Press, 1967), 476.
147. SUD, 113.

more significant difference. Anti-Climacus writes: "In no way is a man so different from God as in this, that he, and that means every man, is a sinner, and is that 'before God,' whereby the opposites are kept together."[148] He nicely makes the point that in this holding together, "the differences show up all the more sharply."[149] He is speaking of sin, and then goes on to write:

> Sin is the one and only predication about a human being that in no way, either *via negationis* [by denial] or *via eminentia* [by idealization], can be stated of God. To say of God (in the same sense as saying that he is not finite and, consequently, *via negationis*, that he is infinite) that he is not a sinner is blasphemy. . . . God is separated from man by the same chasmal qualitative abyss when he forgives sins. If by some kind of reverse adjustment the divine could be shifted over to the human, there is one way in which man could never in all eternity come to be like God: in forgiving sins.[150]

Wouldn't denying that God is a sinner simply be a piece of pious praise? Well, to say God is not a sinner is to speak in defiance of the most crucial will and work of God in relation to who we are, sinners. To deny that God is a sinner is to place sin and God within the same range of possibility. It is to retreat from what is revealed in the Christ, the forgiveness of sins. In this passage, Simon Podmore has found transforming efficacy for his interpretation of Kierkegaard. In the preface to his *Kierkegaard and the Self Before God: Anatomy of the Abyss*, he writes:

> I wish to begin by confessing that this project commenced under the belief that the meaning of Kierkegaard's "infinite, radical, qualitative difference" (*uendelig svælgende qualitativ Forskjell*) between humanity and God was essentially *sin*. Mercifully, it concluded with the conviction that the true meaning of the infinite qualitative difference between God and humanity is expressed through *forgiveness*.[151]

Anti-Climacus makes it clear that the forgiving God is known most

---

148. SUD, 121.
149. SUD, 122.
150. Ibid.
151. Podmore, *Kierkegaard and the Self*, xi.

clearly in the Christ. He is not talking about some kind of mystical Christ principle, for he critiques pointedly what he sees happening in a Danish state church where "the qualitative difference between God and man is pantheistically abolished."[152] There may be such generalizing talk about the God-man, but that represents a misappropriation of the teaching of the paradox of the divine and the human being together in one person, Jesus.[153] Anti-Climacus traces this to an anthropological error in which the category of the individual human being is sacrificed to "what Aristotle calls the animal category—the crowd."[154]

With this section's emphasis on the singularity of the God-man and recalling Anti-Climacus's questionable distinction between the masculine and the feminine, we should note that the term "man" is used here to translate the Danish "*Menneske,*" which is the generic human reference as distinguished from the male-specifying "*Mand.*" The singularity of this message, that the dialectically different God and humankind came together to form one specific person, carries the challenge of the paradox to the hearer once again. The incommensurability of this claim is indirect communication to a quintessential degree. Given this intensification, it is little wonder that Kierkegaard in his journals joined Pascal in the word that God is hid more deeply in the incarnation than in creation.[155] In PC this divine hiddenness in the Christ is driven home relative to the person of Christ, whereas in SUD Anti-Climacus seems to agree with Philip Melanchthon that "to know Christ is to know his benefits."[156]

The question may arise as to whether the ontological framing of the qualitative difference between Creator and every creature can accommodate the priority given here to God's forgiveness as marking the true difference. It's not easily done. What, for example, of God's alleged ontological impassibility, given the suffering God-man?

---

152. SUD, 117.
153. Ibid.
154. SUD, 118.
155. JP, 3:3110.
156. Philip Melanchthon, *The Loci Communes of Philip Melanchthon*, trans. Charles L. Hill (Boston: Meador, 1944), 68.

Already back in the *Fragments*, Johannes Climacus had strained for language to express the incarnational truth of how the ontologically other God could be united with the human in that one man. Climacus reaches for a parable to make his point. Is the incarnation like a king temporarily taking the form of a servant in order to win a maiden's love only to return triumphantly to the palace? No, the kenosis of God is not like that. Indeed,

> from the hour when by the omnipotent resolution of his omnipotent love he became a servant, he has himself become captive, so to speak, in his resolution and is now obliged to continue (to go on talking loosely) whether he wants to or not.[157]

This monarch in love has bound himself in a relationship. Climacus continues:

> He cannot betray his identity; unlike that noble king, he does not have the possibility of suddenly disclosing that he is, after all, the king—which is no perfection in the king (to have this possibility) but merely manifests his impotence and the impotence of his resolution, that he actually is incapable of becoming what he wanted to become.[158]

Climacus, writing from outside the faith, has used the ontological expression of the qualitative difference as his orienting framework and struggles ("so to speak," "to go on talking loosely") to articulate the love that drives God's kenotic choice. Anti-Climacus, writing from decisively within the faith, knows that the primary human problem is not finitude but sin, and God's saving response is forthrightly stated in terms of forgiveness and the atonement. In *Practice*, Anti-Climacus, in pondering the God-man as "the most profound incognito or the most impenetrable unrecognizability that is possible," echoes the theme of God's binding God's self:

> But it is his will, his free decision, and therefore it is an omnipotently maintained incognito. Indeed, by allowing himself to be born he has in a certain sense bound himself once and for all.[159]

---

157. PF, 55. Note the double use of "omnipotent."
158. Ibid.
159. PC, 131. On the kenosis theme, see Barrett, *Eros and Emptying*; David R. Law, *Kierkegaard's Kenotic*

Moreover, if Anti-Climacus does indeed see sin and not finitude as the primary human predicament, the issue becomes not simply christological but downright soteriological with a reactive force for the doctrine of God. In SUD, Anti-Climacus makes his decisive point about forgiveness as the key infinite qualitative difference directly but without specifically engaging the impact on the concept of God's ontological otherness. Perhaps he felt freer writing in his journals:

> They say that God is unchangeable, the Atonement teaches that God has become changed—but the whole thing is an anthropopathetic conception which cannot stand up under reflection. . . . What the Atonement expresses is . . . that God has remained unchanged while men changed, or it *proclaims* to men altered-in-sin that God has remained unchanged.[160]

Or this: does human sin somehow qualify God's love?

> No, God is not impressed; he changes nothing. Yet believe that it is out of love that he wills what he wills. He himself suffers infinitely in this, but he does not change. Yes, he suffers in love more than you do, but he does not change. . . . In all this he suffers infinitely more than you do, even when it is you who distress him by new sin—but he does not change.[161]

What we have to come to terms with in these closing sections of SUD is the fact that Kierkegaard was at the root a Christian author for whom the gospel message must decisively shape faith's reflection about God. For him, it is indeed the case that God is most clearly revealed in the suffering and death of the crucified Jesus. His doctrine of God will be a theology of the cross. That's the theology that will carry a Christian pastor into the pulpit. Kierkegaard's last publication was of a sermon he had preached back in May of 1851. The opening prayer speaks of God's changelessness, but note the dipolar content of the notion:

> You Changeless One, who nothing changes! You who are changeless in

---

Christology (Oxford: Oxford University Press, 2013); Tim Rose, *Kierkegaard's Christocentric Theology* (Aldershot, UK: Ashgate, 2001), 111–14; and Gouwens, *Kierkegaard as Religious Thinker*, 169, for an emphasis on how the kenosis involved a willingness to suffer not simply on the part of the human will, but by the divine will. I have discussed this theme in PC in Sponheim, "Relational Transcendence."
160. JP, 2:1348.
161. JP, 3:2554.

love, who just for our own good do not let yourself change.... You are not like a human being. If he is to maintain a mere measure of changelessness, he must not have too much that can move him, and must not let himself be moved too much. But everything moves you, and in infinite love. Even what we human beings call a trifle and unmoved pass by, the sparrow's need, that moves you, what we so often scarcely pay attention to, a human sigh, that moves you, Infinite Love. But nothing changes you, you Changeless One!"[162]

Very well, but we creatures must face the reality of change. Given the gospel message articulated in "Despair Is Sin" and the understanding of the human condition presented in "The Sickness unto Death Is Despair," Anti-Climacus understands each individual to face a choice, either to believe or to be offended. He says that God has only one more thing to say: "judgment is at hand."[163]

Com.: The Logic of Intensification III: Sin against the Holy Spirit

There awaits Anti-Climacus the third-person expression of the Trinitarian dialectic of intensification. While despairing over the forgiveness of sins is a definite position and not solely a retreat in relation to God's offer of mercy, yet deeper is "offensive war," the "sin against the Holy Spirit."[164] Since the Holy Spirit is understood biblically to emphasize glorifying Christ (John 16:14), the focus here is on response to God's invitation in the Christ. In this sin, one renounces Christianity as untrue. Anti-Climacus specifically mentions denying Christ "either docetically or rationalistically."[165] One takes the action of dismissing Christianity. In these final pages, Anti-Climacus reminds the reader again that "the possibility of offense is the dialectical element in everything Christian."[166] Here the dialectic is at the heart of the matter.

---

162. TM, 268. Kirmmse, *Kierkegaard in Golden Age*, 521, perceptively suggests that at this time, early September 1855, it may have been particularly important to Kierkegaard to stress God's unchangingness in the face of the fact that in this revolutionary time, "all else in Denmark was changing." He adds that the timing of the publication makes the point that the attack on Christendom "was not mere destructiveness . . . but rested upon a base which SK felt to be constructive."
163. SUD, 122.
164. SUD, 125.
165. SUD, 131.
166. SUD, 125.

He has pointed out endlessly the Christian emphasis on the "infinite qualitative difference" separating God and the human being. Just when we have that difference straight, we are told that "in Christianity God makes himself man (the God-man)."[167] Is that not so offensive that any person "who still preserves his understanding must come to the verdict that only a god bereft of understanding could concoct such a teaching"?[168]

To clarify this deepest offense, Anti-Climacus reviews the forms of offense. Its lowest expression is to remain neutral about Christ. He grants that the "mediocre" preaching of Christianity present in Denmark may not have given some hearers the real challenge to decide. But "[i]f Christ is proclaimed to you, then it is offense to say: 'I do not want to have any opinion about it.'"[169] With the proclaimed word comes the admonition to the hearer: "You shall have an opinion about Christ." The work of the Holy Spirit making Christ known eliminates neutrality for the hearer. To claim to have no opinion about Christ is to sin against the Holy Spirit indeed. The next form of despairing offense knows this, knows that it cannot ignore Christ. But it stares "fixedly and exclusively" at the paradox, not making the movement of faith. Then comes the deepest offense, which in effect "makes Christ out to be an invention of the devil."[170]

Anti-Climacus ponders how God must suffer over the fact that his love-motivated sacrifice "could become the greatest unhappiness for ... the beloved."[171] Either of two things could happen for that God. God's love could fall into brooding over mournful feelings and give up the incarnating act. "Or love would conquer, and he would venture the act out of love."[172] God would complete the act in "the joyousness of love" but not without tears. And so Anti-Climacus hears John testifying that the Christ comes forth, saying "The Father and I are one" but also "blessed is he who takes no offense at me."[173]

---

167. SUD, 126.
168. Ibid.
169. SUD, 129.
170. SUD, 131.
171. SUD, 127.
172. Ibid.

DESPAIR IS SIN

These last pages of SUD are severely stated. One may well wonder if anyone is truly a believer. In a truly Kierkegaardian manner, one may wonder that about oneself. Is there no hope beyond that either/or of faith/offense? At times, indeed much of the time, Anti-Climacus seems to leave it there. He appropriates the language of Martin Luther at the Diet of Worms to ponder God's predicament:

> In Christianity God makes himself man (the God-man). But in this infinite love of his merciful grace he nevertheless makes one condition: he cannot do otherwise. Precisely this is Christ's grief, that "he cannot do otherwise"; he can debase himself, take the form of a servant, suffer, die for men, invite all to come to him, offer up every day of his life, every hour of the day, and offer up his life—but he cannot remove the possibility of offense. What a rare act of love, what unfathomable grief of love, that even God cannot remove the possibility that this act of love reverses itself for a person and becomes the most extreme misery—something that in another sense God does not want to do, cannot want to do.[174]

Arnold Come has commented on this powerful statement of divine risk and vulnerability by pointing out that the Creator's gift of freedom "exposes human beings to the possibility of failure in a context so unstable that failure is unavoidable." That surely seems true as far as it goes. But, given the deep and wide power of moral evil in this world, is it sufficient to end this portentous sentence with the calming assurance that this unavoidable failure "must be dealt with as part of the maturing process"?[175] Anti-Climacus's emphasis on the correlation between a rise in consciousness and a rise in despair/sin seems to call for a recognition of the clear-eyed evil in which we willingly do what

---

173. SUD, 128.
174. SUD, 126. Timothy Polk, *The Biblical Kierkegaard: Reading by the Rule of Faith* (Macon, GA: Mercer University Press, 1997), thus argues that for Kierkegaard, the rule stipulates that all of scripture is to be read in the light of the love of God and points to the love of God when so read.
175. Come, *Kierkegaard as Theologian*, 191. Come closes *Kierkegaard as Theologian*, 368–74, with a postlude, looking back to an American Academy of Religion meeting where I raised this question: "Does the language and concept of my self as a 'failure' do justice to Kierkegaard's stress (in *Sickness*) on sin as defiance, or on sin as what might be called 'clear-eyed evil'?" I am convinced by Come's argument for the continuity between the two halves of SUD, but I still wonder if Anti-Climacus's critique of Socrates does not call for language stronger than "discovering my self" (*Kierkegaard as Humanist* with a focus on the first part of SUD) and "recovering my self" (*Kierkegaard as Theologian* with a focus on the second part). I'll take this up again in this book's final section on Kierkegaard's legacy.

we know is wrong. That was the main point in his critique of Socrates. Remember again that the opposite of sin is faith. This is the sin against the Holy Spirit that, hearing the message of forgiveness, one turns away saying, "I have no opinion," for that amounts to saying, "I will not trust the word of forgiveness." But the bar seems raised so high in the dialectic of offense/faith. Who can meet it? Is there nothing more to be said?

What about the cry of Mark's father seeking healing for his sick child? What if one's own heart cries out "I believe; help my unbelief!" (Mark 9:24)? In his final footnote, Anti-Climacus seems to open the door a crack in commending a prayer that in part reads, "I thank you for requiring only faith, and I pray that you will continue to increase it."[176] If we put that together with another note some pages earlier, perhaps the crack widens. There he writes of how the pagan who despairs over his sin may be "dialectically understood as pointing toward faith. The existence of this dialectic must never be forgotten (even though this book deals only with despair as sickness); in fact, it is implied in despair's also being the first element in faith."[177] One could also point out that Vigilius Haufniensis closes another sobering book, a book that has earned Kierkegaard the cheerful moniker "the gloomy Dane," with a last chapter entitled "Anxiety as Saving through Faith."[178] Ever dialectical, despite citing these hopeful notes as we close our commentary on SUD, one must note that Anti-Climacus can speak of how "ethically the more intensive form of despair is further from salvation than the lesser form."[179]

In speaking of the hopeful take on despair, are we talking again about the claim that the error's mutiny is mistaken? Is "rebelling against all existence" as the Creator's doing wrong because "perhaps it actually was not a mistake but in a much higher sense an essential part of the whole production"?[180] Well, perhaps the prayer and the

---

176. SUD, 129.
177. SUD, 116.
178. CA, 155–62.
179. SUD, 101.
180. SUD, 73–74.

footnote's dialectical understanding of despair as pointing toward faith are talking about God. They may be pointing us back to a much-studied *Journal* entry from 1846. Kierkegaard wrote:

> He to whom I owe absolutely everything, although he still absolutely controls everything, has in fact made me independent. If in creating man God himself lost a little of his power, then precisely what he could not do would be to make man independent.[181]

Or perhaps in the prayer and the evocation of the dialectical, Anti-Climacus is pointing ahead a year to *Practice in Christianity*. There again Anti-Climacus is forcing up the requirement for being a Christian "to a supreme ideality." He is calling for "a personal admission and confession." But the thrice-repeated preface ends by explaining that he does that "so that I might learn not only to resort to *grace* but to resort to it in relation to the use of *grace*."[182] Just a couple of paragraphs back we put together two words that challenge the believer who clings to the faith that "with God all things are possible." There we put the word "cannot" with the word "God" in writing that in God's infinite love "he cannot remove the possibility of offense."[183] But if God's omnipotence is "under the power of his love,"[184] perhaps there is a resorting to grace even in the dialectical passion of offense. So George Pattison raises the question of "whether God is free to love in the face of no matter what objection to or refusal of his love."[185] Pattison believes "the answer of *The Sickness unto Death* is, it seems, clear: there is nothing that God cannot forgive, and there is nothing and nobody that is beyond the scope of God's love."[186] Perhaps Anti-Climacus had in mind already in 1849 *Practice in Christianity*'s 1850 resort to grace in the [mis?]use of grace. Thus he closes SUD with the definition of faith, speaking of

---

181. JP, 2:1251.
182. PC, 7, 73, 149.
183. SUD, 126.
184. CD, 127.
185. George Pattison, "Lev Shestov: Kierkegaard in the Ox of Phalaris," in *Kierkegaard and Existentialism*, vol. 9 of KRSRR, ed. Jon Stewart (Aldershot, UK: Ashgate, 2011), 355–73 (370).
186. Ibid. Pattison is responding to Shestov's suggestion that God is bound by the necessity of God's immutability, which Shestov interprets as representing the ethical with its "You Shall," so that Kierkegaard does not manage to follow Abraham in transcending the ethical in faith. Pattison is saying, "Well, perhaps he does."

the self so relating itself to itself and willing to be itself that it "rests transparently in the power that established it."[187]

---

187. SUD, 131.

PART II

The Theological Reception and Legacy

3

The Theological Reception of Kierkegaard

Søren Kierkegaard has been read and researched around the world. The sheer breadth of his reception is staggering and defies description in a single volume. We shall limit ourselves as far as possible to the explicitly theological reception, and even there we shall need to be selective. Jon Stewart of the Søren Kierkegaard Research Centre in Copenhagen has edited three substantial tomes for *Kierkegaard's Influence on Theology*, the tenth volume in the *Kierkegaard Research: Sources, Reception and Resources* series—something more than eight hundred pages of text and bibliography. We'll be looking at people who can arguably be considered the most influential theological receivers for this vertigo-inducing production. Our emphasis will be on Christian theology, the second-order reflection in the service of the first-order reality of faith in the God believed to be revealed in the person and work of Jesus the Christ. There's a limiting selection by profession and confession there, so we'll not be writing of Woody Allen's films or of the novels of Walker Percy or John Updike, though one cannot deny the efficacy of such figures for faith.

Our discussion will locate itself chronologically in the terms of reception by centuries. But there are two questions to be asked about that ordering: (1) what is reception? and (2) what is a century? Heiko Schulz tackles the first question with exemplary thoroughness by distinguishing "six basic types and/or attitudes of reception: reception without production; production without reception; unproductive reception; productive reception; receptive production; mixed types or borderline cases."[1] We will focus on just two of the six: "[A] genuinely *productive reception* is characterized by the central role that author A's [Kierkegaard's] work takes on in author B's work vis-à-vis type, content, and genesis—even if explicit or implicit traces of the former are only recognizable in isolated passages of the latter. The term *receptive production* has been coined to designate the most frequent and prominent type of reception: author B referring to author A by means of explicitly and directly addressing the latter's work, if only to a limited extent."[2]

There are issues of selection even when employing the deceptively simplifying notion of chronology. For example, when we are considering theological developments, it's not all that clear when the nineteenth century ends. Does the substantive start of the theology of the twentieth century really only occur in 1922 when Karl Barth's second edition of his commentary on Romans is published? Moreover, holding rigidly to a century-by-century progression in our discussion and referring to the twentieth century as the "theological high-water mark" may obscure the fact that, for example, "no complete work of the Danish philosopher had been translated into Bulgarian until 1991." Then began a flourishing such that Kierkegaard has been "one of the most translated philosophical authors" in the last twenty-five years in that country.[3] We'll loosely follow the flow of time while trying to

---

1. Heiko Schulz, "Germany and Austria: A Modest Head Start: The German Reception of Kierkegaard," in *Northern and Western Europe*, tome 1 of *Kierkegaard's International Reception*, vol. 8 of KRSRR, ed. Jon Stewart (Aldershot, UK: Ashgate, 2009), 307–419 (308). Habib C. Malik in *Receiving Søren Kierkegaard: The Early Impact and Transmission of His Thought* (Washington, DC: Catholic University of America Press, 1997) gets at some of this complexity in distinguishing "non-reception," "glimmerings of an early reception," "misreception," "suppression," and "serious reception."
2. Schulz, "Germany and Austria," 309.
3. Desislava Töpfer-Stoyanova, "Bulgaria: The Long Way from Indirect Acquaintance to Original Translation," in *Southern, Central and Eastern Europe*, tome 2 of *Kierkegaard's International Reception*, vol. 8 of KRSRR, ed. Jon Stewart (Aldershot, UK: Ashgate, 2009), 285–99 (285).

recognize the fits and starts of the particular in theological reception. Remembering the peculiarity of the particular we arrive at our first heading.

The Nineteenth Century: Danish Is a Minor Language

Scholars pondering the reception of Kierkegaard often comment on how delayed and indirect his influence seems to have been. Thus if we begin with Kierkegaard's own century, we find ourselves quite limited geographically, talking first of all about the Scandinavian reception and then the German. At the end of the nineteenth century, we find Kierkegaard coming to be known elsewhere principally through the lens provided by three Scandinavian authors—Georg Brandes, Harald Høffding, and—surely indirectly—Henrik Ibsen. This is not true without exception. In France, for example, there was secondary reference to the *Kirkekamp* in 1856, and a French translation of *The Difference between a Genius and an Apostle* appeared in 1886.[4] We know that late in the century in Russia there was Peter Emmanuel Hansen translating Kierkegaard for Leo Tolstoy.[5] If we extend the century for a decade, we have Miguel de Unamuno in Spain receiving the first three volumes of the first Danish Edition of Kierkegaard's collected works.[6] Much earlier, if we look across the waters, we find Linka Keyser Preus reading Kierkegaard in the parsonage in Spring Prairie, Wisconsin, and writing of him in her diary in 1845.[7] It is surely the case that Kierkegaard's writings found their place in many Scandinavian-American prairie parsonages in the last half of the century. But that's again the point: the story of Kierkegaard's theological reception has Scandinavia for its setting for a half century, for Danish is a minor language.

---

4. See Jon Stewart, "France: Kierkegaard as a Forerunner of Existentialism and Poststructuralism," in Stewart, *Northern and Western Europe*, 442–74.
5. Darya Loungina, "Russia: Kierkegaard's Reception through Tsarism, Communism and Liberation," in Stewart, *Southern, Central and Eastern Europe*, 247–48.
6. Dolors Perarnau Vidal and Óscar Parcero Oubiña, "Spain: The Old and New Kierkegaard Reception in Spain," in Stewart, *Southern, Central and Eastern Europe*, 18–29.
7. See Malik's account, *Receiving Søren Kierkegaard*, 72–76.

Norwegian Pietism and Henrik Ibsen

The most animated Scandinavian reception may have been in Norway and very directly involves voices from Norwegian Pietism: Gustav Adolph Lammers (1802–1878) and Gisle Christian Johnson (1822–1894). Another Norwegian voice that became a powerful influence in Kierkegaard's reception was that of Henrik Ibsen, though the historical case for Kierkegaard's direct influence on Ibsen is somewhat conjectural. Norwegian Pietism, tracing back to Hans Nielsen Hauge (1771–1824), had a history of supporting lay preaching and entailed a troubled relationship to the state church. In the 1850s, Kierkegaard's attack on the church in *Øjeblikket*, referred to as the *Kirkekamp*, spread like wildfire among the Pietistic revivalists. Habib Malik seems justified in saying, "Everywhere among Norwegian pietists, Kierkegaard was seen as a prophet."[8] Lammers's incendiary sermons quoted *Øjeblikket* liberally and gave explicit attention to the seventh issue, where infant baptism is the target. Kierkegaard's writings were known earlier in Norway; already in 1846 Henning Thue's reader, "used at all the higher levels in schools," included three writings of Kierkegaard's.[9] *Works of Love* (1847) was being read well before the attack literature of 1855. But *Øjeblikket* became a popularizing catalyst stimulating interest in his earlier works. That attraction did not fail to yield action on the ground: Lammers left the church on March 19, 1856, as did many young men in the 1850s.

Gisle Christian Johnson, twenty years younger than Lammers, came under Lammers's influence and became "perhaps the most important instigator" of the Pietist revival.[10] Johnson was a professor for many decades at the University of Christiania (now Oslo). The amount of

---

8. Ibid., 115.
9. Svein Aage Christoffersen, "Gisle Christian Johnson: The First Kierkegaardian in Theology?," in *Anglophone and Scandinavian Protestant Theology*, tome 2 of *Kierkegaard's Influence on Theology*, vol. 10 of KRSRR, ed. Jon Stewart (Aldershot, UK: Ashgate, 2012), 191–202 (196). It's fascinating to learn that Thue was present at Kierkegaard's oral defense of his thesis in 1841.
10. Paulus Svendsen, "Norwegian Literature," in *The Legacy and Interpretation of Kierkegaard*, vol. 8 of *Bibliotheca Kierkegaardiana*, ed. Niels Thulstrup and Marie Mikulová Thulstrup (Copenhagen: Reitzel, 1981), 9–39 (20). Svendsen takes us back to Hauge and his imprisonment for holding illegal revival meetings.

Kierkegaard's direct influence on Johnson is unclear, but he certainly resonated with the emphasis on commitment and the attack on complacency as well as with the stress on faith as an inward relationship to God. He seems to incorporate something of the notion of three stages on life's way. Yet Johnson's early enthusiasm for *Øjeblikket* cooled as he taught future pastors for the state church, and already in 1857 he wrote a piece critiquing Lammers and defending infant baptism. In closing the reference to Norwegian Pietism, it is worth noting that Lammers was a pastor in Skrien, Ibsen's birthplace. Paulus Svendsen points out that, unsurprisingly, several of Ibsen's relatives were involved in Lammers's revival.[11]

Is there a good case for a serious and substantial reception of Kierkegaard by Ibsen? The matter is complicated. The case for what Schulz calls "receptive production," entailing explicit and direct reference to Kierkegaard, is weak. But what of "productive reception," involving "type, content and genesis"? The reception is usually seen as involving particularly Ibsen's "middle period," the 1860s. In 1870 Ibsen wrote to one of his biographers, Peter Hanson, saying that with regard to Kierkegaard, he had "read only little and understood less."[12] Nonetheless, Kierkegaard was "in the air" in Norway in the 1860s. In little Grimstad (pop. c. 800), while working as an apothecary's apprentice, young Henrik was a member of a reading circle where another member, an elderly Scottish woman named Miss Crawford had read Kierkegaard.[13] We have already mentioned the fiery Norwegian preacher Gustav Adolph Lammers, who served in Skrien, where Ibsen's sister Hedvig was a member of Lammers's reading circle. Remembering

---

11. Ibid., 18.
12. Paulus Svendsen, "Norwegian Literature," 9-39, Kalle Sorainen, "Brøchner," in Thulstrup and Thulstrup, *Legacy and Interpretation*, 33. Cf. Malik, *Receiving Søren Kierkegaard*, 145n26, citing Henrik Ibsen, *Letters of Henrik Ibsen*, trans. J. Nilsen Laurvik and Mary Morison (New York: Duffield, 1908), 198–99. Malik notes that this is the third instance in which Ibsen uses a letter to deny significant influence from Kierkegaard.
13. Svendsen, "Norwegian Literature," Sorainen, "Brøchner," 34. This is perhaps the basis for Alastair Hannay's suggestion that Ibsen had acquired a copy of *Either/Or*. See Hannay, *Kierkegaard*, 428. For that acquisition, Hannay suggests a dating in the later 1840s and wonders if Ibsen had the book with him on his travels beginning in 1864.

Nordic pride and individualism, some scholars minimize Ibsen's denials in the light of "glaring" parallels in language and theme.[14]

So what are those parallels? The three plays usually referenced are *Love's Comedy* (1862), *Brand* (1866), and *Peer Gynt* (1867).[15] With the first, scholars have noticed the situation between two lovers and their subsequent disengagement. With *Peer Gynt*, Peer seems stuck in the aesthetic stage, given to compromise and lacking personal vision.[16] That is not the case with *Brand*, the play most often linked with Kierkegaard. There are parallels but with differences present in the pairings as well. Brand, like Abraham, has a son, Alf, whom he proceeds to sacrifice as he responds to a higher calling. Malik underlines, however, the difference: "In Brand's case this calling is not from God as for Abraham, but from Brand's own will. Brand actually loses Alf because he believes in himself, while Abraham gains Isaac because of his faith in God."[17] Certainly in the character of Brand we find the ethical stage's sense of an unwavering commitment to the call of conscience, but the move to the religious in Kierkegaard's understanding seems lacking. Ibsen identified the model for Brand, saying to his friend and biographer Henrik Jaeger that "it is all nonsense to say that Brand had anything to do with Kierkegaard. . . . A man who formed a sort of model for Brand was a Pastor Lammers."[18] Or he could find yet another model, writing to Peter Hansen, "Brand is myself in my best moments."[19] The conflict between Kierkegaard scholars on Ibsen's relationship to Kierkegaard is striking. Walter Lowrie asserts that Ibsen's play is "an example of illegitimate interpretation of Kierkegaard," but Bruce Kirmmse objects, affirming

---

14. Malik, *Receiving Søren Kierkegaard*, 146. In his 396-page study, Malik devotes a whole chapter to the case of Ibsen with the title "A Foray into Drama?"
15. Ibid., 160. Svendsen, "Norwegian Literature," Sorainen, "Brøchner," 33, looks back to 1859 and the poem "Paa Vudderne" (On the Heights) and finds there a struggle "to move from a purely aesthetic attitude of life to an ethical one."
16. Yet there is disagreement. Svendsen, Sorainen (ibid., 38) references an interpretation of the fourth act of *Peer Gynt* as reflecting German Romanticism's theme of poetic self-creation, while the fifth act finds Peer being poetically created by Solveig, corresponding to a Kierkegaardian understanding of the Christian view.
17. Malik, *Receiving Søren Kierkegaard*, 155.
18. Ibid., 151.
19. Ibid., 158.

Brand as "a powerful, sympathetic, and permissible version of the radical Kierkegaard of the attack on Christendom."[20]

Scholars have looked for and found apparent Kierkegaardian influence elsewhere—in *A Doll's House* (1879) in Nora's movement from the aesthetic to the religious, and in the critique of the culture's leveling and contempt for the "majority" in *An Enemy of the People* (1882). But the question of actual influence remains unclear. What is clear is that the widespread interest in Ibsen gave Kierkegaard's writings a kind of "free ride." In the reception story, we find Ibsen leading people to Kierkegaard again and again. It was true of scholars like Unamuno in Spain, learning Norwegian in the late 1890s to read Ibsen and coming to Kierkegaard, or like seventeen-year-old Hungarian Georg Lukács traveling in 1902 to visit the ailing dramatist in Christiania and carrying Kierkegaard back to his wide circle of friends and associates. Likely there was a comparably deep reception via Ibsen beyond the academy. Michael Meyer puts it well in writing that "*Brand* was . . . discussed and debated as no previous book had ever been in Scandinavia—including Kierkegaard, for *Brand* was written in more accessible and less abstract language."[21] Malik remarks perceptively about the historical context of the nineteenth-century European intellectual life, when liberalism and individualism were in ascendancy.[22]

Denmark: Rasmus Nielsen and Hans Brøchner

What about Denmark? As to the reception of Kierkegaard and his writings during his lifetime, this book's biographical sketch referred to his disappointment over the Danish response to this work. There were few reviews of his publications and few sales as well. Only *Either/Or* was a financial success. He was particularly disturbed by J. P. Mynster's apathetic non-response.[23] At his burial at Assistens Cemetery after the service at the Church of Our Lady, the *Kirkekamp* challenge sounded a

---

20. Kirmmse, *Kierkegaard in Golden Age*, 523n28, citing Walter Lowrie, *Kierkegaard* (London: Oxford University Press, 1938) 10.
21. Malik, *Receiving Søren Kierkegaard*, 164.
22. Ibid., 160.

final time when a young medical student named Henrik Lund emerged from the crowd at the grave site to protest "that the state Church had no right to bury someone and bury him as one of her own when she knew very well that while he lived he had dissociated himself from her totally."[24] The obituaries in the papers were mixed; one does not find anything in the church's response resembling the reform the deceased had sought.

In the remaining decades of the century, two books were published that came to be highly influential in Kierkegaard's reception in Scandinavia and internationally: Georg Brandes's *Søren Kierkegaard: En Kritisk Fremstilling i Grundrids* [. . . A Critical Exposition in Outline] in 1877 and Harald Høffding's *Søren Kierkegaard som Filosof* [. . . as Philosopher] in 1892. On the way to Brandes and Høffding, we will simply note the work of two other Danes, Rasmus Nielsen (1809-1884) and Hans Brøchner (1820-1875). Both men knew Kierkegaard personally and, for a time, were regarded as trusted friends. Nielsen, professor of moral philosophy at the University, was a keen supporter of Kierkegaard in 1846-47 and a close friend in 1848-50. He was deeply affected by the *Postscript*'s devastating critique of Hegelianism and moved toward a more person-centered position. There are many references to Nielsen in Kierkegaard's journals, and apparently Kierkegaard had for some time hoped that Nielsen could be relied on to publish his papers.[25] He cooled as Nielsen failed to grasp the subtlety of Kierkegaard's method of indirect communication.[26] Nonetheless, Nielsen defended Kierkegaard throughout the *Kirkekamp*, in one article calling Kierkegaard's protest "a good deed" by an author who has "willed one thing" throughout his writings. In a second article, Nielsen responded to Bishop Martensen, who had limited his response to a

---

23. The Hongs include Kierkegaard's reaction to his conversation with Mynster weeks after PC came out. See his JP references in their "Supplement" in PC, 356-58.
24. Malik, *Receiving Søren Kierkegaard*, 123. For a vivid account of the dramatic interruption, see Garff, *Søren Kierkegaard*, 797-99.
25. For a succinct description of Nielsen, see Watkin, *Historical Dictionary*, 179-81.
26. Malik, *Receiving Søren Kierkegaard*, 93-97, has a very helpful discussion of the relationship. He cites a journal reference (*Papirer*, X6 B 99, not translated in the Hong edition), where "Kierkegaard describes how, after a long period of coolness, Nielsen finally approached him and they became friends and began to take regular Thursday walks together."

single piece in which he accused Kierkegaard of having a "Christianity without church and without history."[27]

It was Rasmus Nielsen who gathered and annotated all of Kierkegaard's newspaper articles, including the twenty-one from the *Kirkekamp*. Nonetheless, despite his devoted service to Kierkegaard's legacy, he tended in his own voluminous publications to turn Kierkegaard's dialectical tension between faith and reason into a stark dualism. Hence he provoked in the 1860s what was known as the "*Tro og Viden*" [Faith and Knowledge] controversy. He exposed himself to the charge of self-contradiction by arguing that these "absolutely heterogeneous principles" could be combined in "one consciousness." The apparently self-contradictory character of this claim was quickly attacked from both sides. From the left, Darwin's *Origin of the Species* was published in 1859, and the rising recognition of evolutionary thought found expression in a decisive critique of Nielsen by Georg Brandes, of whom we will soon hear more. From the right, Bishop Martensen joined the criticism by deflating the opposition between faith and knowledge, holding instead to a Schleiermacherian unity of the two.[28] The point is that in their criticism, both Brandes and Martensen explicitly saw themselves to be in the process of "receiving" Kierkegaard, and we see how both failed to fathom his dialectical subtlety. As for Nielsen, he began to appeal to the notion of "mystery," abandoning the specificity of Kierkegaard's affirmation of paradox. He eventually emigrated to Gruntvigianism.

Another participant in the controversy, and one who perhaps did more justice to Kierkegaard's thought, was the Danish philosopher Hans Brøchner, a distant relative of Kierkegaard. For over twenty years, the two men would often meet in family gatherings. Deeply influenced by David Friedrich Strauss and Ludwig Feuerbach, Brøchner differed significantly from Kierkegaard but regarded him highly and wrote a moving obituary of him. Shortly after Kierkegaard's death, Brøchner wrote warmly of how on their long walks Kierkegaard's

---

27. Malik, *Receiving Søren Kierkegaard*, 90, 96.
28. Hans Lassen Martensen, *Om Tro og Viden, et Lejlighedsskrift* (Copenhagen: Reitzel, 1867).

"friendly disposition" inspired and encouraged him. Brøchner's "Reminisces," found in his posthumous papers in 1877 and apparently written in 1871-72, are a rich source of information about "Kierkegaard's appearance, eating habits, walks and views of certain contemporaries."[29] In the *"Tro og Viden"* controversy, Brøchner wrote several pieces attacking Nielsen. He recognized Kierkegaard in Nielsen but contended that Nielsen converted Kierkegaardian dialectical tension into absolute dualism and let Kierkegaard's emphasis on subjectivity slide into subjectivism.

Denmark and Beyond: Georg Brandes and Harald Høffding

The *"Tro og Viden"* controversy brings us at last to engage perhaps the major force in Kierkegaard's reception well into the twentieth century, Georg Brandes (1842-1927), literary critic, prolific author, and peripatetic lecturer. Of Jewish descent (though the family was not observant), he personally went through a turbulent time early on, including becoming a Christian in 1861. Back in 1860, he had written in his diary: "I must never forget Kierkegaard, for in a sense he is the only one."[30] He made his way voraciously through *Either/Or*, finding Judge William's ethical affirmations in *Or* convincing. Then, still in 1860, he read *The Moment*, *Fear and Trembling*, and *The Point of View*, as well as other of Kierkegaard's works. He specifically cites *The Sickness unto Death* where he found "a brain superior to [his] own."[31] Neither his own personal conversion nor the decisively Christian character of Kierkegaard's writings held up very well for Brandes. But his fascination with Kierkegaard did, though it began to take a decisively critical turn. He studied under both Rasmus Nielsen and Hans Brøchner, and gradually the latter won out, drawing Brandes toward nonconformist pantheism and eventually to an atheism drinking deeply of French and English positivism.

In 1877, he published the book already mentioned here, *Kritisk*

---

29. Malik, *Receiving Søren Kierkegaard*, 242. See also Kalle Sorainen, "Brøchner," 198-203 in Thulstrup and Thulstrup, Legacy and Interpretation.
30. F. J. Billeskov Jansen, "Brandes," in Thulstrup and Thulstrup, *Legacy and Interpretation*, 204-8 (204).
31. Malik, *Receiving Søren Kierkegaard*, 234.

Fremstilling i Grundrids, a beautifully written formulation of what has come to be known as the "biographical-psychological" approach. From Kierkegaard's biography, Brandes selected three key elements: the troubled relationship with his melancholic father, the turbulent and failed relationship with Regine, and his petulant reaction in the inward-turning controversy with the satirical paper *Corsair.* Psychologically, he found the twin rhythms of "reverence" and "contempt" working their way through these decisive moments and finding expression in the authorship. Of course, reverence will find its voice especially in *Practice in Christianity* with its call to the imitation of the suffering Christ, but reverence must give way finally to the contemptuous attack on the church in *Øjeblikket.* In Kierkegaard, then, we have "a genius who was on the verge of freeing himself from the last traces of religion's suffocating grip when he was tragically overtaken by death."[32]

Much attention has been devoted to a letter sent by Brandes to Friedrich Nietzsche in 1888 where he speaks of his book as "a sort of polemical pamphlet written to curb [*hemmen*] his [Kierkegaard's] influence."[33] Brandes's book elicited a diverse surge of response praising and attacking the author. In his sesquipedalian lecturing, Brandes's reputation preceded him, given his earlier writings. For example, looking to Norway again, we find already in 1876 the University authorities in Christiana denying Brandes access to the lecture hall for his announced lecture. (Brandes, not to be silenced, spoke to a large crowd in the student union.) The 1877 book solidified his fame and infamy. Without question, it became one of the most influential moments in Kierkegaard's international reception. Sometimes praise and attack are to be found together. Thus Aage Henriksen in *Methods and Results of Kierkegaard Studies in Scandinavia* comments that "Brandes does not seek the core of Søren Kierkegaard's nature, but its circumscribing orbit."[34] He speaks of it as a "semi-

---

32. Ibid., 253.
33. Ibid., 254.
34. Aage Henriksen, *Methods and Results of Kierkegaard Studies in Scandinavia* (Copenhagen: Ejnar Munksgaard, 1951), 27.

agitational" work.³⁵ Yet he can sum up this "poetical interpretation" as "translucent and refulgent crystal, a masterly and brilliant paraphrase of the history of a genius."³⁶ Howard Hong can speak of the "genetic fallacy."³⁷ Habib Malik can title his Brandes chapter "Criticism as Suppression." But Malik can see the irony in the fact that this "true child" of positivism should "end up serving, in spite of himself, as popularizer of the very same thinker he had intended to suppress."³⁸

We turn to the second name that stands out in the nineteenth-century reception, Harald Høffding. We'll be briefer, since the reading of Kierkegaard here seems like "same song, second verse." Given this book's commitment to read Kierkegaard as a "becoming" Christian theologian, that positivist take on the authorship, most especially in SUD, seems like a truncated melody. But without question, we meet in Høffding a figure whose international influence in making known this Danish "genius in a market town" is very considerable. For example, William James, American pragmatist and shaper of process philosopher A. N. Whitehead, invited Høffding to lecture at Harvard in 1904. One wonders what they talked about in Cambridge and when James hosted Høffding at his farm in New Hampshire. We do know that James called him "a good pluralist and irrationalist" and was particularly taken by Høffding's citing Kierkegaard's saying that "we must live forward, but we understand backward."³⁹ Høffding traveled widely, and one finds his name appearing constantly in the twentieth-century reception of Kierkegaard.

Høffding had studied under a man familiar to us now, Rasmus Nielsen, and defended Nielsen against Brandes's polemics toward Nielsen.⁴⁰ Yet in his own reading of Kierkegaard, Høffding takes off from a Brandesian positivist position, yielding a comparably reductionist understanding in which Kierkegaard at his death was on

---

35. Ibid., 28.
36. Ibid., 30.
37. Malik, *Receiving Søren Kierkegaard*, 280n253, citing an unpublished piece by Howard Hong. Malik finds Paul L. Holmer and Stephen Crites offering comparable criticisms.
38. Ibid., 279.
39. Ibid., 328–29.
40. Kalle Sorainen, "Høffding," in Thulstrup and Thulstrup, *Legacy and Interpretation*, 209–10.

his way to abandoning Christianity in favor of a free-thinking relativism.[41] Thus in the *Kirkekamp*'s battle against Martensen, Kierkegaard was externalizing his inner recognition that he himself was not a "witness to the truth." Høffding particularly emphasizes Kierkegaard's notion of personality and finds melancholy to be a determinative force in his life. Høffding sees this as yielding a subjectivism in which all absolutes must be abandoned. In any case, he argues, the New Testament's clear expectation of an imminent "second coming" of God at the world's end has been proven mistaken and there is no point in further futile waiting.[42]

We've written of reception in Scandinavia, particularly in Denmark and Norway, although Sweden could well have been mentioned. After all, as early as 1846, a Swedish poet and publicist named Patrick Sturzen-Becker was writing of Kierkegaard in his discussion of Danish literary figures. But Kierkegaard's works had to be translated into Swedish to reach a wide reading public, which was not the case in Norway. Actually, Sturzen-Becker did that translating with large sections from *Øjeblikket* in 1855. Somehow the conditions in Sweden were not ripe for anything resembling the Norwegian response to the *Kirkekamp*. There is a fascinating Kierkegaard misconnection with a famous Swedish writer and founder of the suffragette movement in Sweden, Frederika Brenner. She had met most of the leading Danish intellectuals and was particularly impressed with Martensen's dogmatics. She wrote Kierkegaard twice, unsuccessfully seeking a visit as a " recluse, like you."[43] She does receive scornful attention in his journals.

Brenner was responsible for the first appearance of the name Kierkegaard in the English language when her book *Lif in Norden* [Life in the North] was translated by an English Quaker woman named Mary Howitt. But one looks in vain for any fulsome nineteenth-century

---

41. Such positivism did not prevail unchallenged in Denmark. Malik, *Receiving Søren Kierkegaard*, 331–32, notes that Niels Bohr, the father of the quantum theory in physics, was one of Høffding's students. Our students do grow beyond and against us.
42. See Henriksen, *Methods and Results*, 37.
43. See Malik, *Receiving Søren Kierkegaard*, 54–60.

reception of Kierkegaard in English, though the translation of Brandes's 1877 book brought that truncated perception into view in the century's closing quarter. Across the waters, there was not only Linka Preus and her likes reading Kierkegaard in Norwegian American immigrant congregations in the 1840s. A half century later, there was a young professor of philosophy at the University of Minnesota, David F. Swenson, wandering into a used bookstore in Minneapolis and stumbling on a copy of PF in Danish. He stayed up all night reading PF, and the rest of his life was consumed by the process of translating Kierkegaard. In the 1880s, Kierkegaard was being briefly discussed in a survey of Scandinavian literature published in Chicago, and just up the road in Evanston, Illinois, Nels Simonsen was drawing on Kierkegaard in courses at Garrett Biblical Institute.[44] Elsewhere there were first flickerings of his name here and there, to the east in Slovakia (1865), Poland (1879), and Russia (1878).[45] But Danish is and surely was a minor language. That remains true beyond Europe as well, though Høffding, Brandes, and the alleged Ibsen connection drew some attention in Japan in the 1880s, and in 1895 Kanzo Uchimura wrote *How I Became a Christian*, a work that was translated into German, Finnish, Swedish, and Danish.[46]

But that language barrier began to be crossed already in the nineteenth-century in Germany, where we find serious efforts at translation and research preparing the way for the explosion of the twentieth century. Compared with the torrent of twentieth-century reception, the nineteenth may seem "unproductive" and deemed only "*pre*-reception," as Heiko Schulz puts it.[47] But it paved the way for the deep reception that followed, even if it also put some obstacles in the way that would require correction.

Kierkegaard's name came to be mentioned in Germany already during his lifetime but only a very few times. A notable case is an

---

44. Ibid., 315–16.
45. See KRSRR, Stewart, *Southern, Central and Eastern Europe*.
46. See Satoshi Nakazato, "Japan: Varied Images through Western Waves," in *The Near East, Asia, Australia and the Americas*, tome 3 of *Kierkegaard's International Reception*, vol. 8 of KRSRR, ed. Jon Stewart (Aldershot, UK: Ashgate, 2009), 149–74.
47. Schulz, "Germany and Austria," 310.

anonymous review of *Philosophical Fragments* in the very year of its publication. The review is elaborate and includes many of the major categories of Johannes Climacus. In 1847, a German-educated Dane by the name of A. F. Beck acknowledged that he was the author of the review. Beck had been present at Kierkegaard's defense of his dissertation in 1841 and continued to manifest deep interest in Kierkegaard's literary career even though he was otherwise writing in Danish and German several anti-theological pamphlets and articles. Here we see a theme that pervades the Kierkegaard reception: people are engaged by Kierkegaard's writings even though they do not go where he does with the matter at hand. Beck's 1842 review of *The Concept of Irony with Continual Reference to Socrates* was probably "the first printed mention" of Kierkegaard in the German language.[48] The detailed presentation of PF is particularly interesting because it receives a lengthy footnote in CUP where Climacus praises its excellence and then turns the dialectical corner to point out that, unlike PF, unfortunately "the report is didactic, purely and simply didactic."[49] Ironic indirect communication at work in lamenting precisely the lack of irony.

After Kierkegaard's death, the German reception is dominated by the *Kirkekamp*. Some selections from *Øjeblikket* were translated in 1856, and the dominance was evident throughout the 1860s. Reference should be made to the students of J. T. Beck at Tübingen: Albert Bärthold, Christoph Schrempf, and Hermann Gottsched. From 1872 onward, Bärthold translated many excerpts from Kierkegaard's pseudonymous and veronymous publications as well as authoring several secondary studies in which he emphasized the centrality of the notion of personality. Gottsched's pen reached well into the decisive turn in the twentieth century in Karl Barth's reading of Gottsched's edition (1905) of Kierkegaard's journals. But perhaps it was Schrempf (1860-1944) who had the greatest influence on the reception. While an author in his own right, Schrempf's efficacy is to be found primarily in his

---

48. See Malik, *Receiving Søren Kierkegaard*, 18-19.
49. CUP, 275.

translations. His first translations, of *Concept of Anxiety* and *Philosophical Fragments*, came out in 1890 and the marathon of translating ended in 1922 with the first complete edition of Kierkegaard's works. His translations are not highly regarded, and in his secondary works and prefaces and postscripts to his translations, we see the long arm of Georg Brandes at work. Against Kierkegaard, Schrempf argues that "Kierkegaard's own principle of subjectivity . . . both compels us to the attempt to draw a reliable picture of the historical Jesus *and* to the acknowledgment of his non-divine character as the actual outcome of this attempt."[50]

Where are the theologians in this reception or "pre-reception," to use Schulz's term? Apart from a few isolated examples like Joseph Jörg, eager to find the momentum of the *Kirkekamp* drawing Kierkegaard toward Rome, we look in vain for theological efficacy. Philosophers we can find: there's Wilhelm Dilthey (1833–1911), who read Høffding's 1892 book and went on to study Kierkegaard as carefully as could be done in Schrempf's German translations. There's Nietzsche, indicating to Brandes his intention to "take up the psychological problem of Kierkegaard."[51] There are the luminous literary figures like Rainer Maria Rilke (1875–1926), reading Kierkegaard already in 1901, and Franz Kafka (1883–1924), pondering in 1913 his life's parallel to Kierkegaard and Regine. But where are the theologians? We haven't written much of *The Sickness unto Death* in these pages, though we noted Brandes's feeling inferior to SUD's author, and we could have mentioned an occasional inefficacious writer like the Norwegian author Johan Christian Heuch (1883–1904), who wrote of Anti-Climacus's definition of faith[52] or the Dane J. C. M. Ørum, who in 1858 appealed to Martin Luther in his defense of Kierkegaard's attack on the church.[53] But in terms of significant efficacy, where are the theologians?

---

50. Schulz, "Germany and Austria," 317. Schulz points out that Schrempf was true to his word and in 1891 renounced his clerical vows and left the Lutheran church.
51. Malik, *Receiving Søren Kierkegaard*, 253–54.
52. Ibid., 175–78.
53. Ibid., 132.

One can ask that question more widely of the international reception of Kierkegaard in the nineteenth century. If we dribble into the first decades of the twentieth, we get some beginnings: Scottish theologians like H. R. Mackintosh (1870–1936) writing of Kierkegaard as early as 1902, and P. T. Forsyth (1848–1921) doing so in 1910. Back in Germany in that year of 1910, we have the launch of the journal *Der Brenner* and the circle that formed around it. Chief among the theological voices heard through this center of intellectual ferment was that of Theodor Haecker (1879–1945). He put Kierkegaard in the company of Augustine and Blaise Pascal and especially stressed CA and SUD. He found in Kierkegaard "the perfect antidote" for "all forms of idealism and positivism, of socialism and the new sociologism, and of the unchecked rise in Nietzsche's popularity."[54] Once again, we find an effort to discern in Kierkegaard's last years a move toward Rome. *Der Brenner* and Haecker were read by Martin Buber, Martin Heidegger, Edmund Husserl, and Karl Jaspers, central figures in the reception of Kierkegaard in this new century. Given our space limitations, it's past time to turn explicitly to that century.

The Twentieth Century: The Theological High-Water Mark?

The Bombshell: Barth, Brunner, and Bultmann

We closed our brief discussion of the reception in Kierkegaard's own century with the lamenting question, "Where are the theologians?" I am presenting Søren Kierkegaard as a world-class theologian, but he goes almost without notice in the theological world in his own century. Gary Dorrien hardly overstates matters when he writes that Kierkegaard "was arguably the greatest religious thinker of the nineteenth century, although he had no influence in the nineteenth century."[55] When the big names in the story are Georg Brandes and Harald Høffding, the theological pickings are pretty slim. That's certainly not the case in the twentieth century. Here the enigmatic

---

54. Ibid., 377.
55. Dorrien, *Kantian Reason*, 243.

Dane becomes a central figure in at least Protestant theology, particularly in the middle five decades. We'll have to settle for a few major set pieces, and the first surely must be Karl Barth (1886–1968). The decisive turn takes place in 1922 with Barth's publication of the second edition of his commentary on *The Epistle to the Romans*. Of course, there were the theological ponderings in the century's first decades, which we stretched the nineteenth century to include. But in terms of the spreading efficacy of Kierkegaard's writings, Barth marks the turning point. Again with Barth we observe the phenomenon we noted with Ibsen: there is considerable uncertainty as to how much Kierkegaard he had read, but the Dane gets a free ride on the coattails of the Swiss critic over against the theological establishment's Hegelian and Schleiermacherian regnant voices. Barthian appeals to Kierkegaard circulated widely in the theological seminaries, perhaps most among students who had actually not read much of Barth, not to mention Kierkegaard.

So, what had Barth read of Kierkegaard and what did he make of that reading? We know that already in 1909 he purchased *The Moment* in a German translation and that critique of the domestication of biblical Christianity came to dominate his appropriation of Kierkegaard. He also relied on Anti-Climacus's *Practice in Christianity*, though there is no explicit reference to *The Sickness unto Death*. He also cites a volume of selections from Kierkegaard's journals. It is thought that a reading of *Works of Love* is reflected in his understanding of the Christian's relationship to the neighbor as well as in his criticism of what he mistakenly takes to be Kierkegaard's total disjunction between agape and eros. His appeal to Kierkegaard was most prominent in his writing in the 1920s, and that appeal prevailed in the wider reception history even after Barth himself had pulled back from the dangerous existentialist subjectivism he came to believe Kierkegaard represented. The high-water mark for actual citation was that second edition of *Der Römerbrief*.

Dorrien may overstate matters a little in writing that "all of Kierkegaard's major theological concepts were there,"[56] but already in the preface Barth appeals to one theme we have highlighted in our analysis of *The Sickness unto Death*: the infinite qualitative difference. Barth writes: "[I]f I have a system, it is limited to a recognition of what Kierkegaard called the 'infinite qualitative distinction' between time and eternity. . . . 'God is in heaven and thou art on earth.'"[57] Barth had written of the "inner dialectic of the matter" in the words of the biblical text and, on that account, had been accused of imposing his own system on the text. In any case, Barth and his associates (including Emil Brunner and Rudolf Bultmann, of whom we shall speak shortly) came to be known as representing "dialectical theology."

In reading Romans, Barth saw in the coming of God's son on account of sin the "'Otherness' of God by which the whole realm of humanity is confronted and dissolved."[58] He cites Kierkegaard's witness to the "impenetrable incognito" of the divine and the human together in this one man.[59] His Danish predecessor had seen that when the profession of Christian faith becomes a direct communication and no longer shocks, it can neither inflict deep wounds nor heal them.[60] Barth wrote of the "terrible disturbance of The Moment . . . before God," while yet recognizing "the demand" of God that may shine through "a secondary act of human ethics."[61] He speaks of proclaiming the "eternal worth of each single one (Kierkegaard!) by announcing that his soul is lost before God and, in Him is dissolved—and saved."[62]

Barth could be critical of Kierkegaard already in the Romans commentary. Looking at Romans 12:17 ("Take thought for what is noble in the sight of all"), Barth says that "here Kierkegaard needs to be corrected from time to time by reference to Kant."[63] In any case, Kierkegaard's name appears much less frequently in the 1930s and on. Lee Barrett notes that "in the first volume of *Church Dogmatics*

---

56. Ibid., 468.
57. Karl Barth, preface to *The Epistle to the Romans*, trans. Edwyn C. Hoskyns, 2nd ed. (London: Oxford University Press, 1933).
58. Ibid., 278.
59. Ibid., 279.
60. Ibid., 98–99.
61. Ibid., 439–40.
62. Ibid., 116.
63. Ibid., 468.

that appeared in 1932 Barth asserted that Kierkegaard was partly responsible for the evolution of Christian subjectivism from Pietism to existentialism, a movement that was too fascinated with the inner life of the self."[64] In 1963 in an address in Copenhagen, Barth acknowledged the importance of Kierkegaard's incisive criticism of Christendom, but was troubled by the fact that Kierkegaard "has failed to express clearly that the gospel is the *joyous* message of God's YES to man."[65] Such accusations seem to suggest a deficient reading of Kierkegaard, whose own account of the joy of Christian existence could be robust, as in a journal entry from 1838:

> There is such a thing as an *indescribable joy* which glows through us as unaccountably as the Apostle's outburst is unexpected: "Rejoice, and again I say, Rejoice!"—Not a joy over this or that, but full jubilation, "with hearts, and souls, and voices": "I rejoice over my joy, of, in, by, at, on, through, with my joy"—a heavenly refrain, which cuts short, as it were, our ordinary song; a joy which cools and refreshes like a breeze, a gust of the trade wind which blows from the Grove of Mamre to the eternal mansions.[66]

The mature Barth seems to be uneasy with Kierkegaard's emphasis on human responsibility in the relationship with God. Perhaps a factor in that uneasiness was Barth's polemical interchange with Kierkegaard scholar Emanuel Hirsch, who later supported National Socialism and emphasized "a mode of existence based on self-surrender to God."[67] We remember that Barth was the principal author of the confessing church's Barmen Declaration and its assertion of the Lordship of Christ against Nazism. More basically, Lee Barrett may be correct in tracing the difference in terms of the law/gospel dialectic:

> Kierkegaard's pattern of presenting the Christian life reflected the Lutheran law-gospel sequence, for Kierkegaard did see gratitude for forgiveness as requiring a prior experience of profound guilt, a pervasive

---

64. Lee C. Barrett, "Karl Barth: The Dialectic of Attraction and Repulsion," in *German Protestant Theology*, tome 1 of *Kierkegaard's Influence on Theology*, vol. 10 of KRSRR, ed. Jon Stewart (Aldershot, UK: Ashgate, 2012), 1–42 (15).
65. Karl Barth, "Mein Verhältnis zu Søren Kierkegaard," *Orbis Litterarum* (1963): 97–100, 99; his emphasis. See Sponheim, *Kierkegaard on Christ*, 223n95, and Barrett, "Karl Barth," 16–19.
66. JP, 5:5324.
67. Barrett, "Karl Barth," 15.

moral and religious dissatisfaction with one's own self. . . . The mature Barth reversed this pattern and came to advocate a radically different gospel-law pattern.[68]

To sum up, we see in the early Barth a strong reception of the late Kierkegaard's critique of Christendom. He remained appreciative of that critique even as he moved away from what he perceived as the subtle works righteousness of a Pietism clothed in the proto-existentialism he believed he saw in Kierkegaard. His own summary word in 1963 puts it well: "I consider him to be a teacher whose school every theologian must enter once. Woe to him who misses it—provided only he does not remain in or return to it."[69] It remains the case that the Barthian reception of Kierkegaard, one-sided as it may have been, continued to be a factor in the Dane's reception, especially evident in the tendency to emphasize single-mindedly the discontinuity between the paradoxical Religiousness B and the immanent Religiousness A. In 1961, Barth was piping a different tune, putting the "pathetic" and the "dialectical" together in *The Humanity of God* where he writes, "It is when we look at Jesus Christ that we know decisively that God's deity does not exclude, but includes *His Humanity*. . . . In Him the fact is once for all established that God does not exist without man."[70] But the early Barth's decisive emphasis on discontinuity continued to be linked with Kierkegaard, obscuring the continuities that have been recognized more widely by such authors as Merold Westphal.

The maturing Barth's difficulty with human responsibility in the relationship to the wholly other God occasions a brief reference to two other theologians widely associated with the reception of Kierkegaard in and through the movement of dialectical theology. We have already mentioned Emil Brunner and Rudolf Bultmann. Brunner puts Barth and Bultmann together in writing of Luther's point that "God and faith belong together." He finds Bultmann sacrificing the former, and Barth the latter.[71] Well, without question, Brunner himself posits a human

---

68. Ibid., 32.
69. Ibid., 18.
70. Karl Barth, *The Humanity of God*, trans. Thomas Wieser and John Newton Thomas (Richmond, VA: John Knox, 1960), 49–50.

"point of contact" (*Anknüfungspunkt*), and that recognition Barth could not stomach, occasioning a parting of the ways between these two men who had worked as colleagues in the journal *Zwischen den Zeiten*. While Karl Barth may be the theologian responsible for Kierkegaard's name being mentioned the most often in twentieth-century reception, in Emil Brunner we meet a theologian who carried forward Kierkegaard's themes more faithfully throughout his voluminous authorship (691 items).[72]

Brunner appealed to the biblical theme of the human as created in the image of God, arguing that the formal image is not lost in the material devastation of the fall. Curtis Thompson elaborates that the formal image "is the *humanitas* with its two means of a capacity for words and responsibility."[73] Thus human beings possess "word-power" (*Wortmächtigkeit*), a power to receive God's word, the rational capacity to use and understand words.[74] So there is given a possibility for natural theology, and of course Barth's response to that was made with uncharacteristic brevity: *Nein!*[75] Brunner appropriated Kierkegaard's emphasis on the subjectivity of the individual, setting that in the context of community: "Precisely this is the church: a society which consists of qualitative individuals, that is to say, of those who under personal responsibility stand before God . . . the church, that is the society of all those who have ceased being the mass, because they have become individuals."[76] He seconded Vigilius Haufniensis's insistence in *The Concept of Anxiety* that Adam not be placed "outside the race," absolving the rest of us of responsibility for sin. He drew heavily on Kierkegaard's *Concluding Unscientific Postscript*, writing of the "Dialectical-Pathetic," as we have done. He drew heavily as well on "our" book, *The Sickness unto Death*, finding there a "dialectical psychology" related to Augustine and Dostoevsky and appreciating

---

71. See my discussion in Sponheim, *Kierkegaard on Christ*, 283n45.
72. Mark G. McKim, *Emil Brunner: A Bibliography* (Lanham, MD: Scarecrow, 1996).
73. Curtis L. Thompson, "Emil Brunner: Polemically Promoting Kierkegaard's Christian Philosophy of Existence," in Stewart, *German Protestant Theology*, 65–103 (71).
74. Ibid., 70.
75. See Karl Barth and Emil Brunner, eds., *Natural Theology: Comparing "Nature and Grace" by Professor Dr. Emil Brunner and the Reply "No!" by Dr. Karl Barth*, trans. Peter Fraenkel (London: Centenary, 1946).
76. Emil Brunner, "Søren Kierkegaard's Budskap," *Janus* (1939): 241.

particularly Kierkegaard's assertion that sin is not a negation but a position.⁷⁷

Brunner could be critical of Kierkegaard, objecting to Climacus's statement that, for later individuals, the bare assertion that God had become man was "more than enough." Perhaps such criticism reflects the fact that Brunner gave little attention to the pseudonymous character of many of the writings he was citing. In any case, he found Kierkegaard deficient on the doctrine of the church while yet defending him against Martensen's accusation that Kierkegaard had destroyed community. All in all, Thompson seems justified in his summary word: "Brunner was a leader among those giving Kierkegaard a serious reception. He was a very popular Christian author who was read far beyond the confines of his Swiss-German social location."⁷⁸

And what of Rudolf Bultmann? Well, he was in the dialectical theology mix early with Barth, Brunner, and others—Friedrich Gogarten (1886–1968) for example. It's clear that he came to read Kierkegaard about the time Barth did. When his father died, Bultmann took two volumes from his library—*Fear and Trembling* and *The Concept of Anxiety*. In 1923 he was reading Kierkegaard with his new colleague in Marburg, Martin Heidegger. There are sixty-two explicit references to Kierkegaard in Bultmann's writings, but Heiko Schulz remarks that, considering implicit reference, Kierkegaard is "almost omnipresent" there.⁷⁹ His favorite texts seem to be *Philosophical Fragments, Practice in Christianity*, and *Works of Love*. Schulz closes his commentary by identifying over twenty major concepts or ideas that the German and the Dane shared, ranging from the analysis of the human condition to the paradox of God's transcendence and immanence.⁸⁰

But what of Brunner's claim that in Luther's pairing of God and faith, Bultmann loses God? That may seem rather wrongheaded given the prominence of Jesus in Bultmann's writings. But what Jesus is

---

77. See Thompson, "Emil Brunner," 90–91.
78. Ibid., 99.
79. Heiko Schulz, "Rudolf Bultmann: Faith, Love and Self-Understanding," in KRSRR, Stewart, *German Protestant Theology*, 111.
80. Ibid., 114–15.

this? Well, it's clear that unlike Kierkegaard, it is a Jesus without any messianic consciousness. That's one key difference between these two theologians. Another, related to the first, is their context: Kierkegaard is addressing an enculturated church that falsely considers itself Christian, while Bultmann is defending Christianity in a secular post-enlightenment, even post-liberal, culture. Yet in a way, Bultmann's major project parallels the "thought project" of Johannes Climacus's *Fragments*: "Can a historical point of departure be given for an eternal consciousness?" For Bultmann it becomes the question of how the preaching of the historical Jesus can become truly the preached Christ of faith. The missing link is filled when kerygmatic preaching in the present moment actually meets "the eyes and ears of faith" in the listener.[81]

We recognize here the emphasis on the contemporaneity of Christ and the call to receptive human faith. Thus in his programmatic essay "New Testament and Mythology," Bultmann wrote: "I am deliberately renouncing any form of encounter with a phenomenon of past history, including an encounter with the Christ after the flesh, in order to encounter the Christ proclaimed in the kerygma, which confronts me in my historic situation."[82] So we are not talking about "a mythical process wrought outside of us and our world, or with an objective event turned by God to our advantage," but we are speaking of the call "to make the cross of Christ our own, to undergo crucifixion with him."[83] Or again, "If the event of Easter Day is in any sense an historical event additional to the event of the cross, it is nothing else than the rise of faith in the risen Lord since it was this faith which led to the apostolic preaching. The resurrection itself is not an event of past history."[84]

For many Christians, Bultmann's take on contemporaneity with

---

81. Ibid., 124.
82. Rudolf Bultmann, *Kerygma and Myth*, ed. Hans Werner Bartsch, trans. Reginald H. Fuller (New York: Harper & Row, 1961), 117.
83. Rudolf Bultmann, "The Primitive Christian Kerygma and the Historical Jesus," in *The Historical Jesus and the Kerygmatic Christ*, trans. Carl E. Braaten and Roy A. Harrisville (New York: Abingdon, 1964), 25.
84. Bultmann, *Kerygma and Myth*, 42.

Christ evoked questions like, "Can I join him in his affirmations but not in his negations?" For others, picking up on his concern to address secularity, there was the effort to go him one better, as in Schubert Ogden's *Christ without Myth*. Other readers heard here the call to re-mythicize Jesus.[85] But Schulz's summary statement on Bultmann seems on the mark: "Not only do his writings testify to one of the most substantial and original appropriations of Kierkegaard's thought ... they are an impressive document of the various ways in which Bultmann stimulated and in fact set the agenda for major debates within contemporary theology."[86]

Kierkegaard as the Father of Existentialism?

We surely need to look at other voices coming together in the loosely defined "Neo-Orthodoxy" represented by Barth, Brunner, and even Bultmann in his own reductionist way. Voices like Paul Tillich and the Niebuhr brothers on the American scene. But it seems appropriate first to pause to give at least cursory mention to another movement of thought regularly linked with dialectical theology: existentialism. In this case we are not dealing with an explicitly theological reception of Kierkegaard. Indeed, the incredible diversity of the Dane's reception is illustrated by the fact that in Martin Heidegger (1889–1976), Jean-Paul Sartre (1905–1980), Simone de Beauvoir (1908–1996), Albert Camus (1913–1960), and their compatriots we face an explicitly atheistic (mis)appropriation. Yet they belong to the theological reception of Kierkegaard in the middle half of the twentieth century because their appeal to Kierkegaard, real or simply supposed, accurate or not, functioned to sharpen a reading of Kierkegaard in which the decisively Christian Religiousness B of Johannes Climacus was severed from its role in the "pathetic-dialectical" faith we discussed in chapter 2. It was as if contact with the other "stages on life's way" might somehow contaminate the true faith: only Religiousness B can keep us safe from

---

85. I am thinking particularly of Ogden's teacher, University of Chicago professor Bernard Meland. See also Herbert C. Wolf's comparative study, *Kierkegaard and Bultmann: The Quest of the Historical Jesus* (Minneapolis: Augsburg, 1965).
86. Schulz, "Rudolf Bultmann," 136.

the Kierkegaard of the atheists. Or as if the second half of *The Sickness unto Death* could best be appropriated without the pulsing presence of the first half.

In any case, these four existentialists did interact with the Kierkegaard corpus and with SUD in particular. One can still find Anti-Climacus in Camus's *The Myth of Sisyphus* (1941). Back in 1932, Sartre was reading SUD in Jean Wahl's French translation. Unsurprisingly, perhaps the most-cited text is *The Concept of Anxiety*, where Vigilius Haufniensis offers his penetrating observations about anxiety without yet turning the matter over to dogmatics. Something of Kierkegaard is surely present in these writers. But one hears no full-throated acknowledgment of their debt to the Dane. Claudia Welz writes of how Kierkegaard is omnipresent in Sartre, but we find a scanty four references in *Being and Nothingness*.[87] Vincent McCarthy titles his chapter on Heidegger "Kierkegaard's Influence Hidden and in Full View."[88] What, then, of Kierkegaard *is* affirmed? Kierkegaard is claimed for his emphasis on the individuality of human life. Human freedom in its anxiety and anguish is brought into clearer relief by the descriptions of the watchman of Copenhagen. But otherwise there is scarce reference to the more systematic writings of Anti-Climacus. Heidegger can even find "there is more to be learned philosophically from his 'edifying' writings than from his theoretical ones—with the exception of his treatise on the concept of anxiety."[89]

And what of the theological substance of an Anti-Climacus? In a famous 1946 lecture, "Existentialism Is a Humanism," Sartre's three-word summary, "existence precedes essence," may serve us.[90] If existentialism may be thus defined, obviously Anti-Climacus—and I will say Kierkegaard—is no existentialist. But what then do the

---

87. Claudia Welz, "J. P. Sartre: Kierkegaard's Influence on His Theory of Nothingness," in KRSRR, Stewart, *Kierkegaard and Existentialism*, 323–46.
88. Vincent McCarthy, "Martin Heidegger: Kierkegaard's Influence Hidden and in Full View," in KRSRR, Vol. 9, *Kierkegaard and Existentialism*, ed. Jon Stewart (Aldershot, UK: Ashgate, 2011).
89. Martin Heidegger, *Being and Time*, trans. John Macquarrie and Edward Robinson (Oxford: Basil Blackwell, 1967), 494, division 2, section 45, note vi.
90. Jean-Paul Sartre, "Existentialism Is a Humanism," in *Existentialism from Dostoevsky to Sartre*, ed. Walter Kaufman, trans. Philip Maret (New York: Meridian, 1989), 287–311.

existentialists make of this notion of a "constituting Power"? In the final sentences of *Being and Nothingness* Sartre tells us:

> Every human reality is a passion in that it projects losing itself so as to found being and by the same stroke to constitute the In-itself which escapes contingency by being its own foundation, the *Ens causa sui*, which religions call God. Thus the passion of man is the reverse of that of Christ, for man loses himself as man in order that God may be born. But the idea of God is contradictory and we lose ourselves in vain. Man is a useless passion.[91]

There's no indication of Sartre having considered an alternative conception of deity, such as *Christian Discourses*' vision of a Creator whose "omnipotence is under the power of love." So we live in the anguish and anxiety of our freedom, faced with vertiginous choosing. Kierkegaard expresses that well enough. But we need to recognize "our choice—i.e., ourselves—as *'unjustifiable.'*"[92] As Heidegger puts it, "Kierkegaard makes it too easy on himself."[93]

The existentialists cannot all be painted with a single brush, of course—even these four. Thus Sartre's colleague and lover, Simone de Beauvoir, does not seem to find human passionate choosing useless. She could write *The Ethics of Ambiguity*, "which will refuse to deny *a priori* that separate existents can, at the same time, be bound to each other, that their individual freedoms can forge laws valid for all."[94] The individual man in his passionate choosing

> will understand that it is not a matter of being right in the eyes of a God, but of being right in his own eyes. . . . This rejection of any extrinsic justification also confirms the rejection of an original pessimism which we posited at the beginning. Since it is unjustifiable from without, to declare from without that it is unjustifiable is not to condemn it.[95]

Perhaps something of this teeth-clenched courage was reflected in the

---

91. Jean-Paul Sartre, *Being and Nothingness: An Essay on Phenomenological Ontology*, trans. Hazel E. Barnes (New York: Philosophical Library, 1956), 615.
92. Ibid., 464; his emphasis.
93. McCarthy, op. cit., 100.
94. Simone de Beauvoir, *The Ethics of Ambiguity*, trans. Bernard Frechtman (New York: Philosophical Library, 1948), 18.
95. Ibid., 14–15.

writings of Albert Camus, if not so much in his novels as in his essays carrying a prophetic ring of protest. A prime example is his reflections on the guillotine.[96]

The existentialists may differ, then, in what move each makes in response to their common rejection of Anti-Climacus's faith that with God all things are possible. But their severance of Kierkegaard's anthropological analysis from its theological grounding functioned to encourage a theological reading that left Religiousness B standing alone as a fideist medicine for despair. Perhaps that distortion was already reflected in what can mistakenly be taken to be a fulsome appropriation of the Dane's anthropology. Human freedom is understood by the existentialists in Kierkegaardian terms as entailing a radical individuality, but an individuality with little recognition of the human connectedness a doctrine of creation entailed for Anti-Climacus. As Heidegger put it: "The ownmost possibility is *non-relational* . . . [for] the non-relational character of death individualizes Dasein down to itself. . . . All Being-with Others will fail us when our ownmost potentiality-for-Being is the issue."[97]

American Appropriations: Paul Tillich, Reinhold Niebuhr, Colleges, and Commentaries

That anthropological narrowing is not present in the two final figures we will consider in the so-called Neo-Orthodox appropriation of Kierkegaard that dominated theology in the mid-twentieth century: Paul Tillich (1886–1965) and Reinhold Niebuhr (1892–1971). Speaking from the left edge of Neo-Orthodox terrain, Tillich seems to have received Kierkegaard over a roughly sixty-year period and yet actual citations are somewhat rare. As early as his student years in Halle (1905–7) and reaching into the third volume of his *Systematic Theology* (1963), he read SK, depending in the early years on the Schrempf German translations but coming later to draw on the English

---

96. Albert Camus, *Resistance, Rebellion and Death*, trans. Justin O'Brien (New York: Knopf, 1961), 173–235.
97. Heidegger, *Being and Time*, 308.

translations of David F. Swenson and Walter Lowrie. The writings of Johannes Climacus seem to have been significant for him, along with *Either/Or*, but what stands out most clearly is the reception represented by his statement that *The Concept of Anxiety* and *The Sickness unto Death* were two books that every theologian should read.[98] In the early years, he was influenced by his Marburg colleagues Bultmann and Heidegger and their appropriation of Climacus's emphasis on subjectivity. That theme of subjectivity also sounded strongly in Emanuel Hirsch, who became Tillich's friend despite their heated quarrel in print in 1933–34 that arose over Hirsch's pro-Nazi stand.[99] After Tillich left Germany under Nazi pressure and settled at Union Seminary in New York City, Anti-Climacus may have played a greater role as the immigrant connected with Rollo May and Robert Coles along with his Union colleague Reinhold Niebuhr.[100]

If the atheistic existentialists were somewhat one-sidedly stressing the theme of subjectivity in Kierkegaard, Tillich manifests a concern to ground the individual's choice ontologically. In his *Systematic Theology*, he strongly makes the point that "it is the mistake of Brunner in *The Mediator* that he makes the offense of logical rationality the criterion of Christian truth."[101] In the second volume, he points out that "Kierkegaard exaggerates when he says that it is sufficient for the Christian faith nakedly to assert that in the years 1–30 God sent his son."[102] Barrett remarks: "For Tillich, the paradox of the Incarnation

---

98. Lee C. Barrett, "Paul Tillich: An Ambivalent Appropriation," in KRSRR, Stewart, *German Protestant Theology*, 335–76 (353), citing Tillich's *Perspectives on 19th and 20th Century Protestant Theology*, ed. Carl Braaten, 2 vols. (London: Nisbet, 1953, 1957), 1:102.
99. Barrett, "Paul Tillich," 338.
100. It was Tillich who urged Coles to read Mississippi novelist Walker Percy, yielding Coles's appreciative *Walker Percy: An American Search* (1978). See Lewis A. Lawson, "Small Talk on the 'Melancholy Dane,'" in Thulstrup and Thulstrup, *Legacy and Interpretation*, 178–97 (196). Percy, stricken with pneumonia during his medical studies at Columbia University, had taken a year off and read Kierkegaard. That year off changed his sense of vocation radically. Percy talked about the "great bombshell" that occurred in his reading of SK and specifically cites *The Sickness unto Death* for the point that "the only way to be yourself is to be yourself transparently before God." See my discussion in Paul R. Sponheim, "America," in *Kierkegaard Research*, vol. 15 of *Bibliotheca Kierkegaardiana*, ed. Niels Thulstrup and Marie Mikulová Thulstrup (Copenhagen: Reitzel, 1987), 9–36 (24). This is a striking illustration of the incredible variety of ways Kierkegaard's influence spread.
101. Paul Tillich, *Systematic Theology* (Chicago: University of Chicago Press, 1951), 1:57.
102. Paul Tillich, *Systematic Theology* (Chicago: University of Chicago Press, 1957), 2:114.

is not primarily the union of the infinite and the finite . . . but rather the appearance of a non-estranged life under the conditions of finite existence."[103] What we see repeatedly is a Kierkegaard appropriated in the shadow of Friedrich Wilhelm Joseph Schelling (1775–1854). Gary Dorrien makes a good case that "Tillich held Kierkegaard and Marx together" as both recognizing that "truth was bound to the situation of the knower."[104] But that existentialist affirmation is set within an ontological or essentialist framework without losing touch with the individual's concreteness.

That dialectical balancing can be shown best by looking at Tillich's understanding of the ontological polarities and the application of that understanding in the highly successful *The Courage to Be*. In volume 2 of the *Systematic Theology*, he remarks that "the most impressive description of the situation of despair has been given by Kierkegaard in *Sickness unto Death*."[105] In volume 1 (1951), the most essentialist of Tillich's three volumes, he lays out the ontological polarities. That ontological grounding finds existentialist concreteness in *The Courage to Be*'s discerning description of the threats facing mid-twentieth-century human beings.

The polarities of which Tillich speaks are precisely ontological, for they "constitute the basic structure of being."[106] Tillich is claiming some logos to support the kairotic word. As ontological, the polarities qualify every being, not only history but also nature. And they are precisely polar as well. We recall Anti-Climacus writing of how "due to the dialectic inherent in the self as a synthesis . . . each constituent is [er] its opposite."[107] That echoes in Tillich's rendering: "Each pole is meaningful only in so far as it refers by implication to the opposite pole."[108] The person of faith may ask, "What of the being of God?" Tillich reaches for divine transcendence in writing, "The polar

---

103. Barrett, "Paul Tillich," 360. Barrett perceptively points out that the desired fuller content of the life of Christ is there to be appropriated in *Practice in Christianity* and *Christian Discourses*.
104. Dorrien, *Kantian Reason*, 494.
105. Tillich, *Systematic Theology*, 2:75.
106. Ibid., 1:165.
107. SUD, 30.
108. Tillich, *Systematic Theology*, 1:165.

character of the ontological elements is rooted in the divine life, but the divine life is not subject to this polarity."[109]

The *Systematic Theology* identifies the polarities as "three outstanding pairs of elements . . . : individuality and universality, dynamics and form, freedom and destiny."[110] In *The Courage to Be*, Tillich focuses on individuation and participation. The terminological parallel to Anti-Climacus is not exact, but the development of the "Courage to Be as a Part" and "The Courage to Be as Oneself" reminds the reader of *Sickness unto Death*'s presentation of despair through the dialectic of possibility and necessity. Standing on the shoulders of Kierkegaard and Heidegger as to "the analysis of human existence,"[111] Tillich describes both natural and pathological anxiety in the terms of three forms: fate and death, guilt and condemnation, and emptiness and meaninglessness. He sees each form dominating a particular historical period: the patristic, the medieval and Reformation, and the modern. Kierkegaard's pseudonyms make a fairly clean-cut distinction between the anxiety (*Angst*) experienced as a creature and the despair (*Fortvivelse*) known in sin. For Tillich, the transition seems almost a natural development resisting Reinhold Niebuhr's distinction between "inevitable" and "necessary" regarding the fall into sin, soon to be discussed. All the same, the updating of Anti-Climacus's analysis of the human predicament is brilliantly done, as in the showing of how the excesses of individualism and the vices of collectivism can strikingly coexist.

There is no question that Paul Tillich drank deeply of the streams flowing from Kierkegaard, albeit in a flask fashioned by Schelling. One sees that imbibing in his categorical distinction between penultimate and ultimate concern, reflecting Religiousness A's call to relate relatively to the relative and absolutely to the absolute. One is not

---

109. Ibid., 1:243. See ibid., 1:247, for how in God as "Being-Itself" one finds "both rest and becoming, both the static and the dynamic elements." See also Charles W. Kegley and Robert W. Bretall, eds., *The Theology of Paul Tillich* (New York: Macmillan, 1952), for process philosopher Charles Hartshorne's spirited effort to locate the dipolarity of Tillich's theology in "process-itself" correcting some incoherencies (164–95) and Tillich's vigorous response (339–40).
110. Tillich, *Systematic Theology*, 1:165.
111. Paul Tillich, *On the Boundary* (New York: Charles Scribner's Sons, 1966), 48.

surprised to find a theologian rooting kairos in logos urging that the stages on life's way be understood as structurally interdependent.[112] In a sense, their contextual agenda was sharply different, the later Kierkegaard especially concerned with distinguishing Christianity from Danish culture and the later Tillich claiming a method of "correlation" in which Christian responses represent answers to the deep questions of the culture. Perhaps Lee Barrett makes a good point in aligning Kierkegaard with Lutheran Pietism's emphasis on sin and forgiveness and Tillich with Lutheran orthodoxy's affirming of the *finitum capax infiniti* (the finite capable of bearing the infinite).[113]

No figure in the theological reception of Kierkegaard fulfilled Tillich's concern to connect with contemporary culture more fully than Reinhold Niebuhr. He may arguably be called the leading Protestant theologian of the twentieth century and functioned as a "public theologian" throughout the last half of that century and indeed into the twenty-first, if President Barack Obama's reading preferences are considered. Reinhold Niebuhr's reading of Kierkegaard is best viewed through the lens of his two-volume magnum opus, *The Nature and Destiny of Man*,[114] especially the first volume on human nature.[115] Here we find a mixture of exultant praise and puzzling criticism. Kierkegaard is "the greatest of Christian psychologists," whose "analysis of the relation of anxiety to sin is the profoundest in Christian thought."[116] Yet he is said to bring confusion to the understanding of the paradox of human freedom "by his identification of the self with the Absolute and with 'eternal personality.'"[117] Some interpreters have contrasted Reinhold Niebuhr's emphasis on social concerns with Kierkegaard's concern with the subjectivity of individuality.[118] Niebuhr

---

112. Paul Tillich, *Love, Power and Justice* (New York: Oxford University Press, 1960), 31.
113. Barrett, "Paul Tillich," 369–70.
114. Reinhold Niebuhr, *The Nature and Destiny of Man*, 2 vols. (New York: Scribner's Sons, 1941-43).
115. Volume 2 refers to Kierkegaard only three times. Perhaps the most interesting is the first (ibid., 2:39), where in speaking of how Jesus "transformed the Messianic expectation in the process of negating and fulfilling it," Kierkegaard is said to go too far in CUP's juxtaposing the absurdity of faith to all degrees of probability.
116. Ibid., 1:46, 195.
117. Ibid., 1:175. Niebuhr is working off the German translation of the second volume of *Either/Or*. At times he shows some familiarity with the English translations of David F. Swenson and Walter Lowrie, indeed reviewing portions of both men's work.

himself does not draw that contrast, perhaps sensing the potential in Kierkegaard for addressing social issues, a potential emphasized by such later receivers of Kierkegaard as Merold Westphal and Mark Dooley. In any case, as to social concerns, what is seen first is Kierkegaard's critique of culture. Thus Reinhold Niebuhr's younger brother, H. Richard, in 1951 identifies Kierkegaard as an example of Christ against culture in his highly influential *Christ and Culture*.[119]

The positive appropriation of Kierkegaard is most explicit in Reinhold Niebuhr's extensive analysis of the coming-about, character, and consequences of human sin. Recalling Tillich for a moment, we find Reinhold Niebuhr in 1952 criticizing Tillich for blurring the distinction between creation and fall by identifying estrangement and existence. He writes:

> Whatever difficulty those of us have who use the symbols of innocency and perfection in history, they seem to me no greater than the difficulty in this [Tillich's] symbolism which presupposes a state which is neither potential being nor actualized being in time.[120]

Reinhold Niebuhr draws explicitly on Haufniensis to recognize the anxiety that accompanies human existence but is not itself sin.[121] Yet, remembering perhaps his first pastorate in Detroit during the Great Depression, he feels compelled to write that sin is "inevitable but not necessary." The story of human sin is a tale of human freedom gone terribly wrong, but it does not derive from created human goodness.[122]

---

118. See, for example, Langdon Gilkey, *On Niebuhr* (Chicago: University of Chicago Press, 2001).
119. H. Richard Niebuhr, *Christ and Culture* (London: Faber & Faber, 1951). He discusses Kierkegaard in the "Christ and Culture in Paradox" chapter, but writes that "so far as he deals with the Christ and culture problem, it is much more in the spirit of exclusive Christianity than as a synthesist or dualist" (182–83).
120. Reinhold Niebuhr, "Biblical Thought and Ontological Speculation in Tillich's Theology," in Kegley and Bretall, *Theology of Paul Tillich*, 216–45 (223). The chapter famously closes with Niebuhr's description of the difficult task of "walking the tightrope" on the boundary between metaphysics and theology: "If Barth refuses to approach the vicinity of the fence because he doesn't trust his balance, Tillich performs upon it with the greatest virtuosity, but not without an occasional fall. The fall may be noticed by some humble pedestrians who lack every gift to perform the task themselves" (226–27).
121. R. Niebuhr, *Nature and Destiny*, 1:195.
122. Reinhold Niebuhr's Kierkegaardian struggle here recognizes that "[s]in is to be regarded as neither a necessity of man's nature nor yet as a pure caprice of his will. It proceeds rather from a defect of the will, for which reason it is not completely deliberate; but since it is the will in which

This much-commented-on distinction is supported by explicit reference to *The Concept of Anxiety,* though we have seen that he could as easily have cited Anti-Climacus's *The Sickness unto Death* where despair is recognized not as "something that lies in human nature as such."[123]

Perhaps SUD is most efficacious in the presupposition for Niebuhr's reflections on human sin, that is, in his understanding of the transcendence of the human spirit. If his Union Seminary colleague makes expansive use of the components of the human synthesis, Reinhold Niebuhr is effectively developing the significance of Anti-Climacus's emphasis on the relation as a "positive third."[124] He cites SUD's emphasis on consciousness as the decisive factor in the intensification of the self, involving the relation moving away from itself and coming back to itself.[125] This transcendent self has choices to make. They go badly and Reinhold Niebuhr devotes two chapters to his influential discussion of the sin of pride and sin as sensuality. The emphasis in the appropriation of Reinhold Niebuhr has certainly been on his thorough indictment of the pride of power, knowledge, and virtue. He sees "that pride is more basic than sensuality and that the latter is, in some way, derived from the former."[126] At this point, Reinhold Niebuhr has earned a pointed criticism brought forward especially by feminist interpreters of Kierkegaard. Wanda Warren Berry argues that Niebuhr lost sight of the human sin that occurs in the refusal to will to be oneself, the sin that Anti-Climacus associates with "the feminine."[127] She writes that a fuller appropriation of Anti-Climacus's complexity "might liberate each soul to the extent that it is oppressed, and humble it to the extent that it is oppressor."[128] While such criticism does make a good point, it does seem probable that *The*

---

the defect is found, and the will presupposes freedom, the defect cannot be attributed to a taint in man's nature" (ibid., 1:257).
123. SUD, 16.
124. SUD, 13.
125. SUD, 30. See R. Niebuhr, *Nature and Destiny*, 1:182–83.
126. R. Niebuhr, *Nature and Destiny*, 1:198.
127. SUD, 49–50.
128. Wanda Warren Berry as cited by Kyle A. Roberts, "The Logic of Paradox for a Theology of Human Nature," in KRSRR, Stewart, *Anglophone and Scandinavian Protestant Theology*, 143–55 (151).

THE THEOLOGICAL RECEPTION OF KIERKEGAARD

Nature and Destiny of Man sent many persons of faith to their libraries and bookstores in search of Kierkegaard.

Barth published the second edition of his commentary on Romans in 1922. Bultmann was the last of these "Neo-Orthodox" figures to die, in 1976. In those fifty-five years we see what arguably can be called the "high-water mark" in the theological reception of Kierkegaard in the Protestant world. Barth, Brunner, Bultmann, Tillich, the Niebuhrs—these voices dominated the theological scene in Protestantism. Were we to open the theological curtains farther, we would need to consider Catholic voices such as Erich Przywara (1889–1972), Eugen Biser (1918–2014), or even Thomas Merton (1915–1968). In the Jewish community surely Abraham Heschel (1907–1972) and Martin Buber (1878–1965) come to mind.[129] But these voices did not carry Kierkegaard into twentieth-century theological conversation with the same force as the half dozen we have discussed.

In any case, in the mid-twentieth century Kierkegaard was becoming available to the English-speaking public increasingly and effectively. David F. Swenson, Walter Lowrie, and Lee M. Capel were producing translations that served until Howard and Edna Hong launched their painstaking twenty-six-volume venture of translating *Kierkegaard's Writings*.[130] Accordingly, a body of Kierkegaard research was emerging. The Lutheran liberal arts colleges deserve some mention here. I am thinking of Reidar Thomte at Concordia College (MN), the Arbaughs at Augustana College (IL) and at Pacific Lutheran University (WA), Stanley Olsen at Augustana College (SD), and, *primus inter pares*, the Hongs at St. Olaf College (MN). To refer to a scholar who was not a Lutheran, but often sounded like one: Paul Holmer's work at the University of Minnesota and particularly at Yale University produced a whole generation of Kierkegaard researchers.[131]

---

129. See Jon Stewart, ed., *Catholic and Jewish Theology*, tome 3 of *Kierkegaard's Influence on Theology*, vol. 10 of KRSRR (Aldershot, UK: Ashgate, 2012).
130. Very worth noting as well is the Hongs' seven-volume translation of *Kierkegaard's Journals and Papers* for which they won the National Book Award in 1968.
131. Lee C. Barrett, a Holmer student himself and one of the most published Kierkegaard scholars coming out of Yale, provides a representative list: Bradley Dewey, Andrew J. Burgess, Robert C. Roberts, Timothy Polk, David J. Gouwens, and Lee C. Barrett. "Kierkegaard as Theologian: A

Substantive secondary scholarship was also appearing, such as James Collins's *The Mind of Kierkegaard* (1953), Martin Heinecken's *The Moment before God* (1956), Louis Dupré's *Kierkegaard as Theologian* (1963), and Paul Sponheim's *Kierkegaard on Christ and Christian Coherence* (1968). Back across the waters, one surely could well devote pages to the Swedish debate between Torsten Bohlin (1889-1950) and Valter Lindström (1907-1991)[132] as well as to Lutheran Bishop Per Lønning's (1928-2016) pondering of the "Moment" in Norway.[133] Most important for Kierkegaard research in the twentieth century was the establishment of the Howard and Edna Hong Kierkegaard Library at St. Olaf College in 1976, and the 1984 launching by Robert L. Perkins of the twenty-four-volume *International Kierkegaard Commentary*.

The Priority of the Future: Wolfhart Pannenberg and Jürgen Moltmann

To return to the reception of Kierkegaard in the constructive work of twentieth-century theology, the so-called "theologians of hope," Lutheran Wolfhart Pannenberg (1928-2014) and Reformed Jürgen Moltmann (b. 1926), were arguably the dominant Protestant theological voices heard in the last four decades of the twentieth century and their influence stretched well into the twenty-first. While Kierkegaard did not play as major a role in their writings as he did with the Neo-Orthodox, they do provide an interesting combination of appreciation and criticism. Pannenberg takes as his focus an emphasis familiar to us in the story of Kierkegaard's theological reception, finding in *The Concept of Anxiety* and *The Sickness unto Death* the "most penetrating development" of the "modern" view that seeks to understand sin in terms of the human being's relationship to himself.[134] Pannenberg's expression of that view reflects his underlying

---

History of Countervailing Interpretations," in Lippitt and Pattison, *Oxford Handbook of Kierkegaard*, 528-49 (542).

132. See Henriksen, *Methods and Results*, 141-52, for a useful summary.
133. Per Lønning, "*Samtidighedens Situation*": *en studie i Søren Kierkegaards kristendomsforståelse* (Oslo: Forlaget Land og Kirke, 1954).
134. Wolfhart Pannenberg, *Anthropology in Theological Perspective*, trans. Matthew J. O'Connell (Philadelphia: Westminster, 1985), 96.

conception of the nature of time and particularly the priority of the future therein. Moltmann is working on that large canvas as well and appropriates particularly the Kierkegaardian notion of the "Moment" when time and eternity intersect in "the passion of possibility."[135]

In Pannenberg's case, his concern to offer a genuinely public theology brings him to abandon the traditional creation/fall/redemption framework for theological anthropology. Thus, "[T]he aim is to lay theological claim to the human phenomena described in the anthropological disciplines."[136] The secular description may only provide a "provisional version . . . that needs to be expanded and deepened," but that process is only completed when the ultimate future yields its fruit. In the meantime, he writes:

> As a historical claim about the beginnings of human history, the idea that there was an original union of humankind with God which was lost through a fall into sin is incompatible with our currently available scientific knowledge about the historical beginnings of the race.[137]

While "there can be no loss of something that never existed," a point of departure that can be claimed is "the experience of humanness as entailing an obligation."[138] At that point, Pannenberg does claim Kierkegaard's word of the individual facing a task, for "the species itself is still in becoming through the course of human history."[139] He finds *The Sickness unto Death* to make an advance beyond *The Concept of Anxiety* in the notion of the "positive third" and will locate his own anthropology in that third's relation to itself.[140] The way this plays out is to ponder that dizzy self experiencing openness to the world as it seeks to center itself. He praises Kierkegaard's distinction between dread (anxiety) and fear, but rejects the distinction between anxiety

---

135. Curtis L. Thompson ("Jürgen Moltmann: Taking a Moment for Trinitarian Eschatology," in KRSRR, Stewart, *German Protestant Theology*, 185–221 [197]) points out that in that particular phrase, Moltmann is quoting Kierkegaard by way of Ernst Bloch, who "mistakenly attributes it to Kierkegaard's *The Moment*," while the phrasing actually is from *Either/Or*, 1:41.
136. Pannenberg, *Anthropology in Theological Perspective*, 19.
137. Ibid., 58.
138. Ibid., 57.
139. Ibid.
140. See Curtis Thompson, "Kierkegaaard's Anthropology Tantalizing Public Theology's Reasoning Hope," 241–74 in Stewart, KRSRR, Vol. 10, tome 2, 261–63.

and sin. After all, "does not dread for the self, that feeling of dizziness when freedom is left to its own resources, presuppose sin, which consists in human beings making themselves the center and standard of their own lives?"[141] But Pannenberg's work is, precisely in the end, a theology of hope, for in the eucharistic community there is an "anticipatory participation in the final destiny of human beings through a sharing in the spirit."[142]

In the case of Moltmann, his theology of hope is rooted in the cross. His groundbreaking 1972 book, *The Crucified God*, uses the subtitle to speak of "*The Cross of Christ as the Foundation and Criticism of Christian Theology*."[143] He writes of martyrdom as a public testimony to this link between "Golgotha and the eschatological end of the world."[144] He explicitly cites Kierkegaard's "attack on Christianity" as making the point that with the abandonment of martyrdom in an enculturated Christendom, "the gospel of the cross had lost its meaning and ultimately that established Christianity was bound to lose its eschatological hope."[145] It's not obvious how Golgotha is the basis of ultimate hope, but Moltmann is working with a concept of God's power that is not vanquished by oppressive powers. Over a quarter of a century later, Moltmann actually cites the famous journal reference that states, "Only omnipotence can take itself back while it gives away, and this relation is indeed precisely the independence of the recipient."[146]

So Kierkegaard had the categories right: the eternal and the temporal come together in "the passion of the possible" the Moment bequeaths. But Moltmann lumps Kierkegaard with Barth and Bultmann as losing the eschatological fulfillment in the kairotic moment.[147] Early in his career he was troubled by this side of what he saw in Kierkegaard, citing in 1959 Martin Buber's detection of a hidden

---

141. Pannenberg, *Anthropology in Theological Perspective*, 100.
142. Ibid., 532.
143. Jürgen Moltmann, *The Crucified God*, trans. R. A. Wilson and John Bowden (New York: Harper & Row, 1974).
144. Ibid., 58.
145. Ibid.
146. JP, 2:1251.
147. See Thompson, "Jürgen Moltmann," 196–97.

Marcionism in Kierkegaard and worrying in 1961 about Climacus's word of subjectivity as the truth.[148] In the book that gave its name to a movement, *The Theology of Hope* (1965), he wrote of Kierkegaard radicalizing Immanuel Kant's dualism and contributing to the death of God in Western culture.[149]

In the final third of the twentieth century, secondary literature grew exponentially, offering a dizzying range of avenues into the Kierkegaard corpus.[150] Paul Holmer's students from Yale have been among the most active, notably David Gouwens and Lee Barrett. There have been some voices that stand out for their distinctive commitment in the dissonance, such as the evangelical cadences of Stephen Evans, first curator of the Hong library, working to counter readings of the works of Johannes Climacus as elevating contradiction, and the sobering imperatives of Christian pacifist Vernard Eller, who named his twin sons Enten (Either) and Eller (Or). The number of women in the interpretive conversation has greatly increased. Julia Watkin, Sylvia Walsh, and Wanda Warren Berry may have led the way, but many follow in their wake and make clear that women do not speak with a single voice.

The Feminist Interpretation of Kierkegaard

That plurality continues and bridges the turn of the century. For example, on such a major volume as *Works of Love*, one can consult Amy Laura Hall's *Kierkegaard and the Treachery of Love* (2002) to get the full force of Kierkegaard's critique of preferential love. Or one can ponder M. Jamie Ferreira's *Love's Grateful Striving* (2001) to find a place for self in love's complexity.[151] Back in the last decade of the twentieth century, Sylvia Walsh and Céline Léon edited an incredibly

---

148. Ibid., 195–97.
149. Jürgen Moltmann, *The Theology of Hope*, trans. James W. Leitch (New York: Harper & Row, 1967), 169–70.
150. Barrett, "Kierkegaard as Theologian," 528–49, has an excellent summary of the "countervailing interpretations."
151. Ferreira is particularly known for her path-breaking *Transforming Vision*, where she discusses Kierkegaardian decision as a reorienting shift in perspective, an imaginative revisioning, not a sheer act of arbitrary will.

diverse gathering of voices in the book *Feminist Interpretations of Søren Kierkegaard*.[152] In their introduction, the editors state the interpretive challenge of this man whose attitude toward women "is at best ambiguous":

> On the one hand, he insists on an ultimate and fundamental equality of the sexes before God—even, in some instances, the greater perfection of woman—and singles out the feminine as the paradigm of religious existence. On the other hand . . . his entire production is bestrewn with stereotyped, degrading, and patriarchal remarks about women.[153]

Are those troubling remarks simply a reflection of the empirical condition of women in nineteenth-century Denmark and thus in Søren Kierkegaard's brain? Or does he hold "essentialist" views dismissive of women? What is the role of the author's use of irony and the complex pseudonymity of his writing?

The Sickness unto Death receives explicit attention in a number of the fourteen essays. Birgit Bertung stretches strenuously to see Kierkegaard ironically addressing the actual discriminatory behavior of human beings in his time period while also reflecting that attitude. She argues that, at best, Kierkegaard is saying that a "woman can exist" and "whether she does so is her own responsibility."[154] Céline Léon, on the other hand, goes to the second volume of *Either/Or* and writes critically of Kierkegaard's most explicit praise of women and marriage, finding "the delineation of the 'other sex' as relational, dependent, and oriented toward finitude and immediacy."[155] She remembers that Judge William opposes the emancipation of women (as did Kierkegaard), but knows as well of how some readers have found saving resource in SUD's recognition of the genders' religious equality. Recall Anti-Climacus's claim that "in the relationship to God . . . 'the distinction of man-woman vanishes' . . . for [in that relationship] . . . it holds

---

152. Sylvia Walsh and Céline Léon, eds., *Feminist Interpretations of Søren Kierkegaard* (University Park: Pennsylvania State University Press, 1997).
153. Ibid., 1.
154. Birgit Bertung, "Yes, a Woman *Can* Exist," in Walsh and Léon, *Feminist Interpretations*, 51–68 (65).
155. Céline Léon, "(A) Woman's Place Within the Ethical," in Walsh and Léon, *Feminist Interpretations*, 103–30.

for men as well as for women that devotion is the self and that in the giving of oneself the self is gained."[156] She ends up illustrating the editors' "at best ambiguous" claim. Perhaps there is hope in reaching beyond the ethical, but "conversely, it could be that professing belief in the virtual/abstract equality of both sexes will only place women at a vertiginous distance from the acquisition of rights without which their actual lives will never be enhanced."[157] Léon's coeditor, Sylvia Walsh, is not blind to the dangers in Anti-Climacus's description of what seem to be created differences between men and women. But, drawing on the writings of Carol Gilligan, Walsh finds that SUD, "pointing in the direction of androgyny within a common structure of selfhood for the sexes provides a conceptual basis for a fuller development of individuality and relatedness in both sexes."[158] The final essay in *Feminist Interpretation of Kierkegaard* is by Tamsin Lorraine, who, like Walsh, goes to Anti-Climacus to find a route to "a form of subjectivity of primary importance for the development of all human beings."[159]

Taking Another Look: Emmanuel Levinas and Jacques Derrida

Jürgen Moltmann writes of hope as a "passion for the *impossible,*" the not yet possible.[160] In doing that, he anticipates the postmodernist writings of a John D. Caputo or a Mark Dooley. We'll hold our discussion of postmodern reception to this chapter's final section, with its attention on the twenty-first century. But first we must give at least some attention to two twentieth-century figures who were major influences on that later development: Emmanuel Levinas (1906–1995) and Jacques Derrida (1930–2004). In both cases, the number of explicit references to Kierkegaard is not great, but the response is emphatic. The critical note is sounded more strongly by Levinas. Merold

---

156. SUD, 50.
157. Léon, "(A) Woman's Place," 127.
158. Sylvia Walsh, "On 'Feminine' and 'Masculine' Forms of Despair," in Walsh and Léon, *Feminist Interpretations,* 203–16 (212).
159. Tamsin Lorraine, "Amatory Cures for Material Dis-ease: A Kristevian Reading of *The Sickness unto Death,*" in Walsh and Léon, *Feminist Interpretations,* 307–34 (320), citing the editors' summary. Unlike Walsh, Lorraine does not envision an androgynous goal.
160. See Thompson, "Jürgen Moltmann," 201, citing Jürgen Moltmann, *Hope and Planning,* trans. Margaret Clarkson (New York: Harper & Row, 1971), 184.

Westphal (of whom more in a moment) has remarked on how the Frenchman and the Dane "together formed a radical challenge to main strands of the western philosophical tradition."[161] Certainly Levinas praises Kierkegaard "as a thinker who was suspicious of the tyranny of speculative reason and resistant to the totality of the system." He resonated with Kierkegaard's theory of a "persecuted truth" as opposed to "truth triumphant."[162] But he worried about an emphasis on subjectivity yielding an egoism, and a potentially violent one at that. Given Levinas's claim for the priority of the "face" of "the other," he could not stomach talk of the teleological suspension of the ethical. Westphal puts his finger on the crucial disagreement: "Levinas insists that the neighbor is always the middle term between me and God, while Kierkegaard insists that it is God who is always the middle term between me and my neighbor."[163]

Derrida defends Kierkegaard against Levinas's criticism. He reads Kierkegaard not to be speaking of himself as an ego, but of the subjectivity of any human existence; indeed, of something like what Levinas intends by *"the other."* Derrida specifically defends talk of "subjective existence in general" as "a noncontradictory expression."[164] Derrida's most extensive discussion of Kierkegaard is his 1992 work, *The Gift of Death*, where he ponders deeply Johannes de Silentio's evocation of Abraham's ascent to Mount Moriah in fear and trembling. That the pseudonymous author is "the silent one" who "cannot understand Abraham" speaks of how a text cannot be controlled by the author. Indeed, Abraham himself in saying "God himself will provide the lamb for the holocaust, my son" "responds without responding."[165] There is indeed a teleological suspension of the ethical for "absolute duty towards God and in the singularity of

---

161. Merold Westphal, *Levinas and Kierkegaard in Dialogue* (Bloomington: Indiana University Press, 2008), 1.
162. Ibid., 174.
163. Ibid., 5. He adds that this, perhaps, in the final analysis, is their only fundamental disagreement.
164. Marius Timmann Mjaaland, "Jacques Derrida: Faithful Heretics," in Stewart, *Kierkegaard's Influence on Philosophy*, Volume 11 Tome 2, *Francophone Philosophy* (Aldershot, UK: Ashgate, 2012), 112, citing Jacques Derrida, *Writing and Difference*, trans. Alan Bass (London: Routledge, 1978), 111–38 (110).
165. Jacques Derrida, *The Gift of Death*, trans. David Wills (Chicago: University of Chicago Press, 1995), 74.

faith implies a sort of gift or sacrifice that functions beyond both debt and duty"—"the gift of death."[166] Derrida is bearing witness to Kierkegaard's "open rupture" of the Hegelian system in that an "infinite otherness" breaks up the system from within.[167] This is truly deconstruction, suspicious of reforming tendencies that would amount only to changing the language of metaphysics. Thus Derrida writes:

> Hence, I never associated the theme of deconstruction with the themes that were constantly coming up during the discussion, themes of "diagnosis," of "after," or "post," of death (death of philosophy, death of metaphysics, and so on), of "completing" or of "surpassing" . . . of the "end." One will find no trace of such vocabulary in any of my texts.[168]

We'll see in the next section that the postmodernists will readily claim that their writing is not simply deconstruction.[169] Before coming to that, we need to note how in both Levinas and Derrida, the theme of responsibility assumes great importance. It's perhaps not a coincidence that in these same final decades of the twentieth century the role of the social-political dimension of the ethical received increasing attention in the secondary Kierkegaard scholarship. Merold Westphal, a preeminent Levinas scholar, has led the way in that development and has particularly emphasized the theology of what he calls "Religiousness C" in that regard. As opposed to a Barthian reading stressing the disjunction of the distinctively Christian Religiousness B over against the immanent Religiousness A, Westphal has argued for a continuity carried by the stages on life's way. He has noted a key shift in authorship moving beyond Johannes Climacus's emphasis on the inwardness of religious suffering. Later writings such as *Practice in Christianity*, *For Self-Examination*, and *Judge for Yourself*, all written after Kierkegaard's Easter week experience of forgiveness in 1847, identify Christ not merely as the Paradox but also as the Paradigm or Pattern.

---

166. Ibid., 63.
167. Mjaaland, "Jacques Derrida," 13.
168. Ibid., 124n52, citing Jacques Derrida, *Rogues: Two Essays on Reason*, trans. Pascale-Anne Brault and Michael Naas (Stanford: Stanford University Press, 2005).
169. See in anticipation Steven Shakespeare, "Kierkegaard and Postmodernism," in Lippitt and Pattison, *Oxford Handbook of Kierkegaard*, 469–83 (469–70).

In this Religiousness C we finally reach the teleological suspension of the ethical understood as our comfortable modes of behavior sustained by the social order. Thus Westphal remarks that "there is nothing about the gods of Religiousness A and B to keep them from being the echo of our social mores, the legitimizing servant of the Established Order, while the God of Religiousness C is essentially a danger to every Established Order."[170] What Christian faith must face is this: "Christ's life on earth was a continuous and ultimately fatal confrontation with the established order" and "Christians are called to just such a dangerous practice, dangerous to the established order and therefore dangerous to them."[171]

We ended our discussion of Kierkegaard's nineteenth-century reception with a lamenting question, "Where are the theologians?" That lament cannot credibly be made about the twentieth century. Indeed, the past century may have been the "high-water mark" in the theological reception. Let's see what is stirring in the twenty-first century.

The Twenty-First Century: Plural Postmodern Perspectives

Mark Dooley and John Caputo

As we consider a mere sixth of a century, succinctness will be sought. Kierkegaard continues to be a force being reckoned with, again in strikingly diverse ways and at times through surprising initiatives. Attracted by the allure of alliteration, we will speak of a plurality of perspectives as postmodern. Perhaps we may speak of the postmodern as a cultural configuration that gives shape to the late twentieth century's assaults on the optimism of doing theology on a firm foundation, as in the relative confidence characterizing even Neo-Orthodoxy's recognition of the fault line of divine difference and, later,

---

170. Merold Westphal, "Kierkegaard's Teleological Suspension of Religiousness B," in *Foundations of Kierkegaard's Vision of Community: Religion, Ethics, and Politics in Kierkegaard*, ed. George B. Connell and C. Stephen Evans (London: Humanities Press, 1992), 114. Westphal finds the shift dramatically illustrated by Kierkegaard's changing interpretations of the flogging of the disciples in Acts 5.
171. Merold Westphal, *Becoming a Self* (West Lafayette, IN: Purdue University Press, 1996), 198–99.

Pannenberg and Moltmann's appeal to a sure future. Or perhaps we will see twenty-first-century theologians dealing with a destabilizing discontent that may be seen as the flowering of seeds planted much earlier by such architects of suspicion as Marx, Nietzsche, and Freud, and, indeed, Søren Kierkegaard.

In any case, explicit talk of the postmodern has been a steady stream in the century's currents to this point. Once again Kierkegaard is present in or somehow behind the texts.[172] The wide swath of authors claiming the term postmodern may not permit us to speak of a unitary position, but surely one finds in many forms here a "posture" or "mood" recalling the reception's occasional emphasis on the "how" of Kierkegaard rather than the "what." A minimal amount of "what" survives in Kierkegaard's reception in deconstruction.[173] That relative imbalance perhaps represents the long reach of Jacques Derrida. In the previous section, we heard Derrida insisting that deconstruction attend to Kierkegaard's "open rupture" with Hegel's system and its likes. Suspicious of reforming initiatives that might reflect an unreformed return of the metaphysical, he emphasized in 2003 that themes of "post" were not to be found in his vocabulary.[174] But how clean is the cut between the deconstruction and postmodernism movements? Steven Shakespeare comments that critics of postmodernism often feature a "tendency to conflate postmodernism with deconstruction, identifying both with a nihilistic 'anything goes' approach to truth and interpretation."[175] That dismissive attitude is challenged by influential postmodern authors who argue that a fruitful way back into Kierkegaard runs through Derrida and the often-missed ethical import of his thought.

Thus at the century's turning (2001), Mark Dooley published *The Politics of Exodus: Kierkegaard's Ethics of Responsibility*, a sustained

---

172. Already in 1995, Martin J. Matuštík and Merold Westphal gathered fifteen authors, including such prominent figures as Jürgen Habermas, in *Kierkegaard in Post/Modernity* (Bloomington: Indiana University Press, 1995).
173. See Elsebet Jegstrup's collection of authors in *The New Kierkegaard* (Bloomington: Indiana University Press, 2004).
174. Mjaaland, op. cit., see above note 164 and 168.
175. Steven Shakespeare, "Kierkegaard and Postmodernism," in *The Oxford Handbook of Kierkegaard*, ed. John Lippitt and George Pattison, 469-70.

Derridean reading of Kierkegaard. He candidly declares in his introduction that he intends to "press the case for Kierkegaard as a 'proto-deconstructionist'" by elucidating the relationship between Derrida and Kierkegaard. Crucial here is Dooley's emphasis on the ethical-political implications of Derrida's writing. Here he takes issue with Mark C. Taylor, who appealed to Derrida in celebrating in *Erring* (1984) the death of God, self, history, and book, but in doing so missed the Frenchman's ethical call. Thus Dooley charges that Taylor "plays into the hands of those detractors . . . who claim that deconstruction is not only philosophically ineffective but also ethically and politically dangerous."[176] As one such detractor, he identifies no less a Kierkegaard interpreter than Sylvia Walsh. Dooley contends that "[Walsh's] apparent failure to take more than a cursory glance at the Kierkegaardian strategies appropriated by Derrida severely curtails and delimits her capacity to set forth guidelines as to how it might be possible to live poetically with others in the present age."[177] In *Living Poetically* (1994), Walsh plays off an ethical understanding of the self's development against a Romantic sense of self-creation surfacing again in deconstruction. One can imagine Dooley's critical reaction upon reading *Living Christianly* (2005) where Walsh emphasizes that Kierkegaard's "deeply reflected and original" description of Christian existence "has an objective foundation in both scripture and Christian tradition."[178]

So what does Dooley propose positively? He follows Taylor's lifting up of the Derridean emphasis on the live becoming of writing and deftly draws in Kierkegaard's pseudonym Hilarius Bookbinder (*Stages on Life's Way*) in his abandonment of the closure of the book. What we write goes out into the stream of life to be received by the reader

---

176. Mark Dooley, *The Politics of Exodus: Søren Kierkegaard's Ethics of Responsibility* (New York: Fordham University Press, 2001), 148. Early in his career, Taylor had contributed importantly to Kierkegaard research in *Kierkegaard's Pseudonymous Authorship: A Study of Time and the Self* (1975) and *Journeys to Selfhood: Hegel and Kierkegaard* (1980). Curtis L. Thompson, citing *The Moment of Complexity* (2001) and *After God* (2007), has pointed out to me that Taylor quite definitely moved beyond the stark reductions of *Erring*.
177. Dooley, *Politics of Exodus*, 152. He is responding to Walsh's 1994 work, *Living Poetically*.
178. Sylvia Walsh, *Living Christianly: Kierkegaard's Dialectic of Christian Existence* (University Park: Pennsylvania State University Press, 2005), 15.

in an inventive "repetition." Thus, space is made available for that reader, "the other," and who knows what will come of that? Indeed, Dooley finds an imperative in that interrogative, calling us to expect the impossible as Johannes de Silentio found happening in Abraham's ascent to Mount Moriah.[179] He's not done, for Dooley finds Derrida's treatment of Kierkegaard in *The Gift of Death* to suggest that the death of the self in self-denial entails "acts of excessive generosity" in which "we open up to the other by keeping a relation of foreignness to the [Hegelian] circle."[180] Living in such a faith, one breaks out of the economy of reciprocity in a genuine teleological suspension of the ethical. Dooley's book closes with an appropriation of *Works of Love* and what John Caputo has called "a mad economy or an economy of forgiving" in a love that *"does not seek its own, for there are no mine and yours in love."*[181]

John Caputo—there Dooley names the figure who is perhaps the most creative and influential appropriator of Kierkegaard in the postmodern stream.[182] Before giving Caputo at least a couple of paragraphs, we pause to note that this stream is broad and one might say virulent. Over by the left bank, we find Whiteheadian David Ray Griffin establishing already in 1983 a Center for a Postmodern World. Concerned with showing that nihilistically tending deconstruction does not own postmodernism, Griffin appealed to such "hard-core ideas" or "commonsense universals" as causality, freedom, genuine evil, and the existence of an actual world.[183] There's no appeal to Kierkegaard in this argument, though one remembers William James entertaining Harald Høffding at Harvard in 1904 and his enchantment with Kierkegaard's "understanding backwards, but living forwards."[184]

---

179. See Dooley, *Politics of Exodus*, 179; Dooley explicitly links this with Anti-Climacus and SUD where we see that "the self one wills to be, of course, is one that challenges the established order by emphasizing the primacy of existence and becoming."
180. Ibid., 200.
181. Ibid., 243.
182. That both Dooley and Caputo have chapters in Jegstrup's collection of "exclusively in the deconstructionist mode" receptions (*The New Kierkegaard*, ix) suggests again the complex mapping of postmodern thought.
183. See Gary J. Dorrien, *The Making of American Liberal Theology: Crisis, Irony and Postmodernity, 1950–2005* (Louisville: Westminster John Knox, 2006), 231–55.
184. Dorrien notes that such major figures in process thought as Bernard Meland and David Tracy do

Over on the right bank of this postmodern current, one can find Bethel Seminary in St. Paul where Kyle A. Roberts links the emergent (emerging) church with postmodernism since this "turn creates some intellectual (epistemological, hermeneutical) breathing room, and a cultural pause, for a conscious attempt at deepening the authenticity of Christian faith and reconsidering the meaning of 'church.'"[185] Beyond the right bank, one finds John Milbank and his "radical orthodoxy" seeking "to overcome the pathos of modern theology, and to restore in postmodern terms, the possibility of theology as a metadiscourse."[186] Seeking the safety of higher ground, he claims Kierkegaard shows that humankind is "open to transcendence" and Kierkegaard's emphasis on God's incarnation in a single individual "invents" "the logic of universality; it [Christianity] constituted this logic as an event."[187]

There's some rough going on this postmodern voyage, but John Caputo steers his craft not along the banks with their quiet eddies but boldly in the stream's middle, celebrating the excitement and surprise of the journey. He's very much on board with the call to justice voiced by Dooley. A perceptive commentator on Caputo, James H. Olthuis, stitches together Caputo fragments that claim in Derrida "the voice of prophetic Judaism": deconstruction is a "radical call to justice," the "undeconstructible."[188] He also joins Dooley in appreciative criticism of Mark C. Taylor. He acknowledges that "[w]e all work in the wake of Mark Taylor's *Erring* and we are in his debt." But he voices a strong dissent to Taylor's "a/theology," in which Taylor finds deconstruction to be "the final nail in the coffin of the old God, bringing the death of God movement to its most radical conclusion."[189] He agrees that "Kierkegaard took his stand with the 'singular individual,'" but he

---

cite Kierkegaard favorably. See also Paul R. Sponheim, *Love's Availing Power: Imaging God, Imagining the World* (Minneapolis: Fortress Press, 2011), for an effort to bring Whitehead and Kierkegaard into conversation.

185. Kyle A. Roberts, *Emerging Prophet: Kierkegaard and the Postmodern People of God* (Eugene, OR: Cascade, 2013), 151.
186. John Milbank, *Theology and Social Theory: Beyond Secular Reason* (Oxford: Blackwell, 1990), 1.
187. John Milbank, "Materialism and Transcendence," in *Theology and the Political: The New Debate*, ed. Creston Davis, John Milbank, and Slavoj Žižek (Durham, NC: Duke University Press, 2005), 401.
188. John D. Caputo, *Religion with/out Religion: The Prayers and Tears of John D. Caputo*, ed. James H. Olthuis (London: Routledge, 2002), 6.
189. Ibid., 158.

believes that "the God of the Scriptures has numbered every hair on our head and counted every tear."[190]

Caputo invites the reader to his dialogue with premodern thinkers, Augustine particularly, but as "a phenomenological, not a metaphysical or speculative enterprise."[191] In this venture, he identifies three "axioms of a religion without religion." The axioms seem stages on a postmodernist way, moving from "*I do not know who I am or whether I believe in God*" through "*I do not know whether what I believe in is God or not*" to "*How do I love when I love my God?*"[192] He finds his answer in the book of Amos (and Matthew 25), for the love of God

> has to do with the transformability of our lives, with the possibility of a transforming future, and with serving the poorest and most defenseless people in our society, with welcoming the strangers who make their way across our well-defended borders, the homeless and the abandoned, the ill and the aging.[193]

One can imagine what John Caputo would say, and do, in the refugee crisis of this century.

The Prophetic and the Pastoral

Certainly postmodern authors like Dooley and Caputo could be considered prophetic voices. In using that term, one could gather diverse figures who come together in receiving Kierkegaard as a writer whose ethical thinking holds great importance for contemporary justice concerns. Caputo and the like certainly qualify for that designation, as they read de Silentio's teleological suspension of the ethical to be calling the reader to a seemingly impossible justice way beyond and often against the cultural norms celebrated in the modernity enshrined in "the system." Many other very different authors join them in probing the ethical to serve justice. There can be dissent in that probing. Thus in 2005 we find the fresh publication

---

190. John D. Caputo, *On Religion* (London: Routledge, 2001), 51. Caputo dedicates his book "To Jacques Derrida, who loosened my tongue."
191. Ibid., 57.
192. Ibid., 132–34.
193. Ibid., 136.

of Michael Theunissen's *Kierkegaard's Concept of Despair*, originally published in German in 1993. Theunissen takes Anti-Climacus to task, arguing that he "thwarts his own intention to emphasize freedom" by "hypostazing" the "self" and "despair," thereby compromising the "real subject," "the concrete person."[194] But Merold Westphal speaks for a wide consensus of commentators in arguing that "the concept of 'task' is utterly fundamental to Kierkegaard's writings," citing explicitly *The Sickness unto Death*.[195] One could mention here several volumes in the continuing tide of Kierkegaard research. At the century's beginning, M. Jamie Ferreira published *Love's Grateful Striving*, her three-hundred-page commentary on *Works of Love*. She gives the reader the same scrupulous care with the texts and the creative imagination in interpretation one may remember from her much-discussed work of a decade earlier, *Transforming Vision*. In 2008 we find Edward Mooney gathering many established Kierkegaard scholars in *Ethics, Love, and Faith in Kierkegaard*. Then in 2014 there is John Lippitt pondering one of Kierkegaard's most contested themes in *Kierkegaard and the Problem of Self-Love*.

Our emphasis has been on attending to how Kierkegaard has been received in the constructive theological production of later authors.[196] For a twenty-first-century expression of that sort, we turn to two 2015 texts, Michael O'Neill Burns's *Kierkegaard and the Matter of Philosophy: A Fractured Dialectic* and Alison Assiter's *Kierkegaard, Eve and Metaphors of Birth*. O'Neill Burns might seem poorly suited for this volume since he proposes an explicitly "non-theological systematic account of the religious sphere of existence."[197] But theologians have plenty of reason to be interested in a reading of *The Sickness unto Death* that "allows us to

---

194. Michael Theunissen, *Kierkegaard's Concept of Despair*, trans. Barbara Harshav and Helmut Illbruck (Princeton: Princeton University Press, 2005), 118.
195. Merold Westphal, *Kierkegaard's Concept of Faith* (Grand Rapids: Eerdmans, 2014), 238. See also, ibid., 270, for his discussion of "the teleological suspension of Religiousness B" in "Religiousness C."
196. See again Heiko Schulz's useful sixfold typology in Stewart, KRSRR, "Germany and Austria," 307–10. Thus we have emphasized what Schulz terms "receptive production," though at times reception without production, "a reception that leaves no literary traces," has called for attention.
197. Michael O'Neill Burns, *Kierkegaard and the Matter of Philosophy: A Fractured Dialectic* (London: Rowman & Littlefield, 2014), xv.

consider the way in which the individual can exists [sic] religiously in a whole host of existential commitments."[198]

This "systematic account" is miles away from deconstruction's dedication to Kierkegaard's alleged dismantling of the Hegelian system. O'Neill Burns draws on a Marxist, materialist reclaiming of a Hegelian dialectic in which considering the religious "in wholly ontological terms" yields significant political consequences. He appeals particularly to Slavoj Žižek's reading of Kierkegaard in *The Parallax View*. Žižek, a Slovenian philosopher, sounds a familiar theme in speaking of Kierkegaard's effort to break the "closed circle" of Hegelianism. But with striking originality Žižek continues, writing of how "Kierkegaard's theology presents the extreme point of idealism: he admits the radical openness and contingency of the entire field of reality, which is why the closed Whole can appear only as a radical Beyond, in the guise of a totally transcendent God."[199] Žižek is pondering the "occurrence of an insurmountable *parallax gap*, the confrontation of two closely linked perspectives between which no neutral common ground is possible."[200] He will replace the colonizing notion of the polarity of opposites "with the concept of the inherent 'tension,' gap, noncoincidence, of the One itself."[201]

O'Neill Burns picks up on this to sketch "a dialectical system that makes fracture, rather than unity, the starting point of both thought and existence."[202] There's no minimalism in the sweep of O'Neill Burns's book. He takes the reader through *The Concept of Anxiety*'s critique of immediacy and *The Sickness unto Death*'s critique of reflection and arrives at *Works of Love*'s "higher immediacy" where we find "not faith in a necessarily transcendent God, but a faith in our ability to become ourselves in the midst of fracture and contradiction."[203] He emerges with a political ontology in which "individuals never simply collapse into political collectives but remain in a constant tension with

---

198. Ibid.
199. Slavoj Žižek, *The Parallax View* (Cambridge, MA: MIT Press, 2006), 79.
200. Ibid., 4.
201. Ibid., 7.
202. O'Neill Burns, *Kierkegaard*, xvi.
203. Ibid., 189.

themselves, other members of the collective and the ideas that orient their political activity."²⁰⁴ With a tone suggesting some bravado, O'Neill Burns closes his book by saying he has "no interest in keeping Kierkegaard chained to a conservative theological interpretation."²⁰⁵ One can readily grant that he has succeeded in severing any such chain. But is the theological substance of Kierkegaard so tidily dismissed? Alison Assiter, who also cites Žižek favorably, doesn't think so.

Assiter appreciates Žižek's reading of Kierkegaard, which "sees ultimate reality as comprising processes as opposed to things."²⁰⁶ For Žižek, this suggests a claim that reality is ultimately contingent. Assiter respectfully dissents for perhaps two reasons. One reason suggests the importance of conceiving reality in such a way that a prophetic word can be spoken to the troubles of the time. Kant's "practical reason" is hard to sustain if reality is ultimately chaotic. Such a view, she laments, "may lend itself to a nihilistic ethic that seems to me to be counterproductive in the contemporary world."²⁰⁷ A second reason seems to be that she has read Kierkegaard's *The Sickness unto Death*. She notes Anti-Climacus's witness that "for God . . . 'everything is possible.'" She astutely observes that "this notion of possibility need not entail that everything is simply wide open. . . . Rather, God is that which sets the process in motion."²⁰⁸

Assiter launches her highly original reception of Kierkegaard with a question rooted in Anti-Climacus's critique of his beloved Socrates. She asks, "How is it possible freely to do wrong?" Anti-Climacus, against the wise man of Athens, contended that sin is a matter of the will and thus it cannot be understood simply as ignorance. Assiter goes beyond or against Anti-Climacus in suggesting that somehow an ultimate grounding is to be found for such clear-eyed evil. At this point, she introduces a counterintuitive reading of Kierkegaard's remarks about women. Turning to Haufniensis's *The Concept of Anxiety*, she notes

---

204. Ibid., 190.
205. Ibid., 191.
206. Alison Assiter, *Kierkegaard, Eve and Metaphors of Birth* (London: Rowman & Littlefield, 2015), 4.
207. Ibid., 189.
208. Ibid., 128.

Christ being understood as withstanding temptation.[209] As fully human, this Christ finds his place in "a process system, beginning somewhere and continuing through generation and procreation."[210] For Haufniensis, then, there is an "evolution of freedom and the beginnings of the identification of sensuality with sin."[211] Back to the ground:

> God is that which sets the process in train and, in order to be capable of doing this, God must contain attributes that enable "him" to ground the rest of nature. This necessarily means that God is a capacity or power and that the rest of nature shares something of the same characteristics.[212]

At this point in Assiter's ambitious argument, a familiar figure appears, Friedrich Wilhelm Joseph Schelling. Haufniensis recognizes that "freedom involves the capacity to act in good or bad ways. . . . [Moreover] it is ultimately grounded in a Being that, like Schelling's Absolute—or his *ungrund*—contains the ground of both good and evil."[213] How shall this generating power be identified? Assiter claims the promise of her title and turns to the metaphor of birth. She offers a bold interpretation of Kierkegaard's writing on women. She turns the predominant feminist critique on its head, following instead the reading of Christine Battersby:

> Rather than denigrating "woman" for being relational, for being closer to nature than "man" and intertwined with others to a greater extent than the male, Kierkegaard, I believe, values these qualities to a greater extent than he does the "myth" of a perfectly autonomous, perfectly rational and whole "person."[214]

She hasn't forgotten the grounding power. Schelling, seeing "the natural world as inherently full of life and dynamism," deploys the

---

209. CA, 80.
210. Assiter, *Kierkegaard, Eve and Metaphors*, 129.
211. Ibid.
212. Ibid., 128.
213. Ibid., 91–92.
214. Ibid., 102. Cf. Christopher B. Barnett, *From Despair to Faith: The Spirituality of Søren Kierkegaard* (Minneapolis: Fortress Press, 2014), 183. Assiter's affirmation of Kierkegaard's writing on women is not unqualified. She dissents (*Kierkegaard, Eve and Metaphors*, 100) from his opposition to women's liberation in *Works of Love*.

metaphor "of the 'yearning' or the 'longing' of the 'one' to give birth to itself."[215] Developing the model involved, Assiter adds a prophetic word of an "ethic of care that incorporates care for the environment."[216]

Alison Assiter's dizzying daring reflects again the prophetic power of Kierkegaard to inspire new interpretations. Every reading is selective, and the omissions may arise in protest. Has Assiter forgotten about the "infinite qualitative difference" between the Creator and the creatures? But without doubt, she opens Kierkegaard's texts to challenging new readings. One wonders what might well be seen as a fitting descriptive telos for the reception of Kierkegaard in 2099? There will be more to say of this in the final section on "legacy," but for now it seems the story of the theological reception turns toward the pastoral.

In the pastoral, we do not leave the prophetic behind certainly, but in turning to the faith communities, we encounter a different register or a new key. This is perhaps the right note for us to strike in closing this sketch of the theological reception of Kierkegaard, for it is in the pastoral, after all, that the theological rubber most pointedly hits the road. Kierkegaard, we have been saying, wrote of the human venture before God. He wrote of the restless heart that finds peace, joy, and calling in the will and work of God known in a strange itinerant preacher named Jesus. In the first decade and a half of this troubled twenty-first century, people of faith continued to gather to hear the good news they claim(ed) in that story. Sometimes the voice of Kierkegaard shapes the telling of that story explicitly. Often it may not, but it is there sounding through the translations offered by a Barth or a Niebuhr, a Caputo or an Assiter.

It is striking that the pastoral telos is clearly in place in the Kierkegaard research of this first sixth of the twenty-first century. There's surely some rubber on the road as Christian theologians draw on Kierkegaard to give a reason for the hope that is in them (1 Peter 3:15). Scholars who have toiled for a half century with this Danish genius from a market town are still doing so, aiming to serve people

---

215. Assiter, *Kierkegaard, Eve and Metaphors*, 190.
216. Ibid., 191.

of faith. One thinks of Lee Barrett and his *Eros and Self-Emptying* (2013) in which he traces remarkable parallels and important divergences in Kierkegaard and Augustine as they write of the human desire for God and journey to God.[217] Or of Stephen Evans, who gathered many of his earlier writings in *Kierkegaard on Faith and the Self* (2006). Evans has voiced a sustained argument against reading Kierkegaard as an irrationalist reveling in self-contradiction. In 2013, Richard McCombs offered a strong second to Evans in *The Paradoxical Rationality of Søren Kierkegaard*, distinguishing Kierkegaard's understanding of the passionate human venture from Pascal's "mathematical cost-benefit analysis."[218]

These major research efforts are explicitly theological, and as such, they address the situation of practitioners in communities of worship.[219] Thus Jason Mahn, whom we cited in this book's first half, locates the Christian "as perched between confession and communion, between Friday and Easter."[220] Indeed, the church is not in an easy place, for there are new challenges intensifying the enduring pastoral imperative to afflict the comfortable and comfort the afflicted. How shall the church understand itself as it finds itself immersed in a religiously plural world? Does the church have a word to speak as climate change emerges as *the* issue of our time? The final chapter of this book will make a beginning in speaking of Kierkegaard in relation to these questions. But the account of the pastoral dimension of this century's theological reception should not close without mentioning a particular parish and its pastor, First Lutheran Church of West Seattle and Rev. Ronald F. Marshall. Marshall has published frequently in Kierkegaard circles and in 2013 gathered many of his essays and sermons in *Kierkegaard for the Church*. Marshall locates Kierkegaard solidly in the line of Martin Luther, sharing with the German reformer

---

217. On the Kierkegaard side of Barrett's profound study, one may consult as well Law's *Kierkegaard's Kenotic Christology*, which thoroughly relates Kierkegaard's use of the theme to diverse kenotic theologies of earlier and then-contemporary authors.
218. McCombs, *Paradoxical Rationality*, 211.
219. A comparable momentum may be seen in the increased attention to Kierkegaard's veronymous writings. Representative works would be George Pattison's *Kierkegaard's Upbuilding Discourses: Philosophy, Literature and Theology* (2002) and Christopher B. Barnett's *From Despair to Faith* (2014).
220. Mahn, *Fortunate Fallibility*, 203.

a deep attentiveness to the biblical writings.[221] The people of First Lutheran meet Kierkegaard through their pastor's sermons and articles in the church newsletter, but also otherwise. The year 2013 brought many conferences recognizing the bicentennial of Kierkegaard's birth. It also saw on November 17 a prominent Kierkegaard presence in the morning worship and adult education at First Lutheran, followed by the dedication of a Kierkegaard statue.[222] There he is, greeting each individual with the word from *Christian Discourses*: "I will seek my refuge with . . . the Crucified One . . . to save me from myself."

The depth and intensity of Kierkegaard's reception in West Seattle is no doubt exceptional, but it is highly likely that he is to be found frequenting many other places of worship in this twenty-first century. It's a long way from Spring Prairie, Wisconsin, and the 1840s to West Seattle and 2013. But at the continent's edge, there's the shadow of Linka Keyser Preus reading Kierkegaard in a Midwestern pioneer parsonage.[223] The pastoral telos of this enigmatic Danish religious author is there to be found across the miles and the centuries. We'll ask next what he brings us and where that might take us.[224]

---

221. Marshall, *Kierkegaard for the Church* (Eugene, OR: Wipf & Stock, 2013). For my appreciation and questions, see *Word and World* 34, no. 2 (Spring 2014): 216–20.
222. For this occasion, a poem was also commissioned and printed as a limited-edition broadside. The bicentennial booklet contained the service folder featuring Kierkegaard quotations, words, and music for his "favorite hymn" (JP 6:6673), "Commit Thy Way, Confiding," and a Kierkegaardian Fugue, as well as the program for the dedication and articles on the bicentennial from the *New York Times* and the *New Yorker*.
223. See above, pp. 79n7 and 90.
224. I borrow the "taking" language from Evans's chapter 19 title in *Kierkegaard on Faith and the Self*.

4

The Theological Legacy of Kierkegaard for Our Time

Kierkegaard's legacy is a gift to many fields, to aesthetics, for example.[1] We will focus here on his explicitly theological legacy. Legacy writing is a Janus-like task, for to speak of legacy is to speak of that which is transmitted and of that which is received. In between lies an ambiguous middle. We are asking what theological gifts Kierkegaard has for our time. In earlier chapters, our task has been more descriptive, though I have not claimed to offer "a view from nowhere." To attempt to write of legacy seems to invite a more constructive mood. I will write as a Christian theologian seeking to receive accurately and pertinently the offerings of Kierkegaard as an earlier laborer in the theological task. It is fitting to do so, I believe. Already in the biographical sketch, the point was made that our orienting text was written by Anti-Climacus, the pseudonym Kierkegaard says "regards himself to be a Christian on an extraordinarily high level."[2] That may

---

1. See Peder Jothen, *Kierkegaard, Aesthetics, and Selfhood: The Art of Subjectivity* (Aldershot, UK: Ashgate, 2014).
2. JP, 6:6433.

seem more than sufficient warrant for reading *The Sickness unto Death* in straightforwardly theological terms. Yet, ever a dialectical thinker, in that journal entry, Kierkegaard softly places some kind of metaphorical question mark alongside the exclamation point by the introductory word that "one seems to be able to detect" this self-estimation in Anti-Climacus. All the same, there's more than enough invitation in that striking journal entry, and more importantly in Anti-Climacus's book itself, to lure us into this constructive task. So, to sum up, we ask: what legacy do we seem able to detect in the Kierkegaard represented centrally by SUD?

Getting the Direction Right: Confessing Faith ... Sin

To make a first point in getting from there to here we'll reclaim our title, "Existing before God: Søren Kierkegaard and the Human Venture." I'm arguing in this book that those nine words carry much of the theological energy in *The Sickness unto Death*. To get the direction right for this movement of appropriation is crucial. Thus the gift and task of the creature's relationship to God will structure our statement of legacy. Perhaps we do well to begin "from below," where we belong, with the creatures. Human existence, Anti-Climacus (and arguably Kierkegaard) is telling us, is a venture. The self is not simply given but comes to be ("becomes") as the given relation "relates itself to itself." This is a passionate affair, one that profoundly involves the human act of choosing. The existentialists got something right about that matter of passionate choosing, a matter that echoes Anti-Climacus perhaps particularly on the place of possibility in the components of the human relationship to oneself. One may well feel with Martin Heidegger that one is "thrown" into life and that circumstance is indeed anxiety-producing, as the German learned from the Danish pseudonym Vigilius Haufniensis. Moreover, our choosing is fraught with ambiguity—indeed, is "unjustifiable," as Sartre saw. The Frenchman came to conclude that "man is a useless passion."[3]

---

3. See our discussion above in chapter 3 and notes 91 and 92 there.

But what the existentialists did not see is that this human venture in dialectical passion is always already in relationship to a creator God. Every human being exists "before God," whether or not she knows or acknowledges that. In speaking of God, we do not leave our viewing point "from below," for it turns out that in Anti-Climacus's reading of things, this humble location is precisely where God is. As Anti-Climacus puts it, every human being has God as a criterion, a "measuring stick." That's saying something, because between every human being and God there is "an infinite qualitative difference." Karl Barth got something right about that.[4] Barth was insistent that, as he put it, God is in heaven and we are on earth. But one struggles with Barth to find much place for the creaturely role in what takes place on earth. Anti-Climacus develops more fully the actual relationship between God and the creature. The distinction between Creator and creature is not about distance, but about difference. Recall the emphasis on intimacy in Anti-Climacus's phrasing: "Christianity teaches that … this individual human being exists *before God* . . . may speak with God any time he wants to, assured of being heard by him—in short, this person is invited to live on the most intimate terms with God!"[5]

There's a calling in this intimate relationship. The self is called so to relate to itself as to create a dynamic equilibrium, and that can only happen in and for the self "by relating itself to that which has established the entire relation."[6] In that relating, the self "rests transparently in the power that established it," and that, Anti-Climacus reiterates in his final sentence, "is the definition of faith."[7] The emphasis on transparency provides a powerful contrast to the "shut-in-ness" (*Indesluttethed*), which Haufniensis links with demonic anxiety. So, to refer again to the poles of Kierkegaard's twentieth-century reception, in his formulation of the self before God, Anti-Climacus is at work somewhat against the grain in the passionate venturing of the existentialists and in Barth's battle cry of the infinite

---

4. Above, chapter 3, and note 57.
5. SUD, 85.
6. SUD, 14.
7. SUD, 131.

qualitative difference. But he holds the connecting points together in dialectical tension and in doing so qualifies and modifies both partial appropriations profoundly. Thus Merold Westphal recognizes already in *Fear and Trembling* (1843) that "God is given [to Abraham, to us] as a subject by whom I am addressed; nor am I an object but rather a decentered subject. . . . We have a subject-subject relation, not a subject-object relation."[8] In the complexity of Kierkegaard's writing of the empowered creature interrupted by the Creator, there's a call to the counselor and the pastor to talk with each other as they together seek equilibrium for the self. One may hope Kierkegaard's voice would reach countless practitioners dedicated to the maturation and healing of the human spirit.

It's clear healing is needed. We see that now in the explosion of violence and equally in matters of omission, where care for the other simply seems to go missing. The self turned in upon itself (Luther) or shut in within itself in weakness or in strength (Kierkegaard) seems to dominate the narrative of our time too. How is one to understand this and what's to be done about it? Anti-Climacus has a stark correction for the hopeful communicative strategy of anyone following the tutelage of Kierkegaard's beloved Socrates. We'll need here again to be able to speak dialectically. On the one hand, Anti-Climacus offers a strong second to Haufniensis's emphasis on individual responsibility in the messy stretches of life. He calls us to recognize that the messiness is not merely a matter of making a mistake here or there, the sort of problem that could well be corrected by better education. The problem is different and deeper, as Anti-Climacus reads the Christian faith. He speaks of sin being "rooted in willing."[9] To talk of the difference between the Creator and the creature is a good start on getting the direction right, but Anti-Climacus calls us to see that "[s]in is the one

---

8. Merold Westphal, "Divine Givenness and Self-Givenness," in *Kierkegaard as Phenomenologist: An Experiment*, ed. Jeffrey Hanson (Evanston, IL: Northwestern University Press, 2010), 39–56 (40).
9. SUD, 93; including in culpable ignorance, see SUD, 92. Anti-Climacus is insistent in his critique. See the series of references in "The Socratic Definition of Sin" in SUD, 87–96. Yet a few pages later he can reclaim Socratic ignorance, pleading that we should not forget "that as far as it was possible for a pagan he was on guard duty as a *judge* on the frontier between God and man, keeping watch so that the deep gulf of qualitative difference between them was maintained" (99).

and only predication about a human being that in no way, either *via negationis* [by denial] or *via eminentiae* [by idealization], can be stated of God."[10] The deepest difference facing the self is not between the eternal and the temporal, but between faith and sin. The individual's call to faith runs through repentance. And we are not done yet, for that faith goes on to "fasten the end," that volitional end, by adding "the doctrine of hereditary sin."[11] Perhaps our troubles are grim enough and our despair deep enough in this early twenty-first century to bring us to hear Kierkegaard on the promise of the human calling, the perilous character of the human predicament, and his witness to God's response to that predicament. Given that sense of our location, what are the chances that Kierkegaard could help us in our time?

Meeting the World: Faith Facing the Other

As Kierkegaard is received more fully into this twenty-first century, there may likely be many surprising turns. In some ways, life in this high-tech, information-driven world seems so different from the Denmark of the mid-nineteenth century. Emmanuel Levinas wrote of how "the Stranger . . . disturbs the being at home with oneself."[12] Space limitations permit us only to sample the surprises. While Levinas is making his point about the face of the other much more broadly, his vivid phrasing catches something of the interruption we sense in our experience of religious diversity. Questions press upon us in this experience. To mention only three: (1) Why do religious claims so often seem to yield violence toward others holding different claims or professing no faith? (2) Can the vast plurality of claims only be reconciled by recognizing them all as false? (Indeed, the suggestion arises that perhaps these claims do not actually refer to any reality existing objectively beyond the claiming.) (3) Getting to the point for Christians, how can a loving Creator so arrange things that there is "no other name" (Acts 4:12) by which salvation is to be had but the name of

---

10. SUD, 122.
11. SUD, 93.
12. Emmanuel Levinas, *Totality and Infinity: An Essay on Exteriority*, trans. Alphonso Lingis (Pittsburgh: Duquesne University Press, 1969), 251.

an itinerant first-century figure of whom much of humanity has never heard through no fault of their own?

Kierkegaard scholars are having a go at these questions. From India, we have Varughese John's pondering of Kierkegaard in relationship to Hinduism and concluding that "there cannot be a proper understanding of subjectivity outside Christ and His revelation."[13] "Evidential apologetics" "could provide an occasion for a divine encounter," but would be more valuable "for someone whose spiritual eyes are already open."[14] An opposing tack is taken by David R. Law in backing away from the theme of Christian faith possessing a sort of revelational bank account of propositions. He argues that Kierkegaard may well be read as a "negative theologian." Indeed, he writes that Kierkegaard "seems to be more apophatic than the negative theologians . . . by severing the bond that exists . . . between God and the human being" and giving faith precedence over knowledge.[15] Thus "Kierkegaard does not make the transition to the *via mystica* but stops at the *via negativa*."[16] The reading I have offered of *The Sickness unto Death* leaves me restless with Law's conclusion, for we have looked at Anti-Climacus as witnessing emphatically to a creational connection spanning the abyss of the infinite qualitative difference. As creator, God is categorically different from *and* intimately related to the creatures. This divine transcendence does create something real in the creature, whether that be the spirit's disequilibrium until it rests in God or the creature facing a God who is not locked in impotent perfection but in omnipotent love becomes a servant, a becoming that Climacus finds to be "precisely the teaching."[17]

Perhaps the most sustained foray into this field is Aaron Fehir's *Kierkegaardian Reflections on the Problem of Pluralism*. Fehir recognizes that on the face of things in Kierkegaard's writings, one cannot claim him as a religious pluralist. Indeed, he quotes Climacus in CUP on

---

13. Varughese John, *Truth and Subjectivity, Faith and History: Kierkegaard's Insights for Christian Faith* (Eugene, OR: Pickwick, 2012), xviii.
14. Ibid., 144.
15. David R. Law, *Kierkegaard as Negative Theologian* (Oxford: Clarendon, 1993), 214–15.
16. Ibid., 217.
17. PF, 55.

what has been identified here as the third problem regarding those "who are excluded through no fault of their own, but by the accidental circumstance that Christianity has not yet been proclaimed to them."[18] Yet Fehir spends most of his pages persistently showing that one can claim Kierkegaard in 2015 as a colleague in even-handed interreligious dialogue.[19] Part of his strategy is to provide a series of parallels where Kierkegaardian Christian emphases meet companion notions in pure land Buddhism, Judaism, and Taoism (in its polemical stance toward Confucianism; Fehir resists being read as a pure relativist). Somehow these parallels fail to close the deal; one is left wanting more.

There is more, the move to the "how" as distinguished from the "what." The argument takes off from Climacus's (in)famous "parable of the penitent pagan" praying to an idol but "with all the passion of infinity."[20] Fehir summarizes: "If essential truth is subjectivity, then the primary thing is not the *what* of religious doctrine, but the *how* of religious faith." He has in mind CUP's italicized statement that *"[i]f only the how of this relation is in truth, the individual is in truth, even if he in this way were to relate himself to untruth."*[21] This emphasis on the "how" is familiar to us by now, appearing not only in atheistic existentialism but also in emphatically Christian writers such as Paul Holmer. The emphasis underlies Fehir's presentation of the parallels he finds in the Buddhist notion of "skillful means" and the Taoist view of *tz'u* or love. James Giles offers a similar two-pronged approach, offering Buddhist parallels to Anti-Climacus's emphasis on the universality of despair (all life is suffering) and its healing (faith in Amida Buddha as your deepest self) and then an ingenious reduction of SUD's theme that "with God everything is possible."[22] Giles writes: "Kierkegaard's philosophical point is not that such a lifting out of despair depends on the actual existence of a god for whom all things are possible. It

---

18. CUP, 1:582–83.
19. Aaron Fehir, *Kierkegaardian Reflections on the Problem of Pluralism* (Lanham, MD: Lexington, 2015), chapters 4–6.
20. CUP, 1:201. Fehir, *Kierkegaardian Reflections*, xv, credits the phrase to Erik Hanson in a paper, "Was Kierkegaard a Christian Inclusivist?" delivered to the Society of Christian Philosophers.
21. CUP, 1:199.
22. SUD, 38.

is rather that the way out of despair depends on the *belief* that there exists such a God."[23] Thus the way is open to a nontheistic but religious understanding of reality.

This emphasis on the Christian "how," on subjectivity as the truth, is in my view a necessary but insufficient resource for a Christian commitment to open interreligious conversation. Giles's facile emphasis on belief resembles what in the twentieth century was paraded as "the power of positive thinking." As for Climacus, Fehir's favorite, chapter 2 in this book has presented CUP's insistence that the dialectical paradox of Religiousness B and the "pathetic" subjectivity of Religiousness A need to be held together.[24] Moreover, Anti-Climacus clearly presents an understanding of Christianity that stresses decisively such elements of the "what" as sin and the atonement. Something more is needed if one is to support a Christian dialogical openness to persons of other faiths. In *Kierkegaard and the Paradox of Religious Diversity*, George B. Connell draws the particularism highlighted by Varughese John and the universalism suggested by Aaron Fehir together in an "unresolved tension."[25] But he is not paralyzed by this paradox. Rather he is driven to ask two very promising questions:

> But what if religious faith contains within itself key resources for encouraging respectful, cooperative engagement with others? What if religious faith offers unique disincentives to disrespectful, coercive, damaging interactions?[26]

Positively, he appeals to the call in *Works of Love* to love the Other, every other. Negatively, he draws on Kierkegaard's use of pseudonymity and indirect communication to undermine any coercive manipulation of the individual's relationship with God. In like fashion, in my final subsection I'll reflect on Anti-Climacus's claims for the "what" of

---

23. James Giles, ed., *Kierkegaard and Japanese Thought* (London: Palgrave Macmillan, 2008), 9.
24. See above, p. 59n121, and Climacus's reference, CUP, 1:568, to using the understanding to believe against the understanding.
25. George B. Connell, *Kierkegaard and the Paradox of Religious Diversity* (Grand Rapids: Eerdmans, 2016), 24.
26. Ibid., 181.

Christian faith in relation to a question arising from within that faith itself. In the radicality of his response, the author of *The Sickness unto Death* may open a way to a fruitful practice of the faith in our religiously diverse time.

Living in Hope, Honestly before God

It is exciting to contemplate living before God as Anti-Climacus describes it. We sense the rising intensification of the self that takes place as Anti-Climacus defines "before God" in terms of the persons of the Trinity. There is gratitude and joy in knowing a God who not only speaks the creature into life by saying "Become!" but also adds "Become something even in relation to me!"[27] Yes there's excitement here, but also fear and trembling, for with the gift comes the task of a calling. Moreover, if the opposite of sin is not virtue but faith,[28] then the calling seems most basically a call to faith. A question arises with its challenge. What if Anti-Climacus is spot on in his metaphor for the human condition when he describes the guilty person fleeing the scene of his crime on an express train, where the telegraph wires under the coach carry his description and the order for his arrest? Do we not indeed "personally bring our denunciation with us" in this venture of life? If our counselor reminds us that all that is asked is faith, we cry out "Who, then, can be saved?" (Matt 19:25 RSV). Echoing in that asking is the original thrust of the Greek *sozomai*, "Who can be healed, made well?" This is not, first of all, a question about who outside Christianity can be saved, but the question of who inside Christendom can be.

Kierkegaard wrote that in Denmark, where everyone was of course a Christian, he found his task to be to make things more difficult. Well, he succeeded. Take the Christ chapter in SUD. Anti-Climacus writes of how "[a] self directly before Christ is a self . . . intensified by the inordinate accent that falls upon it because God allowed himself to be born, become man, suffer, and die also for the sake of this self."[29] Surely

---

27. CD, 127.
28. SUD, 82, 124.
29. SUD, 113.

these are the good tidings of the gospel. But who can believe it? Who does believe it? Anti-Climacus voices the call to faith persistently, but never without the warning mention of the "possibility of offense." In that same Christ chapter, he writes of how Christianity makes every person a single individual "and here everything that heaven and earth can muster regarding the possibility of offense . . . is concentrated."[30] How sobering it is to be told that "you can do what you want to, but judgment is at hand."[31] Jason Mahn finds a parallel between the spiritless Christendom that Kierkegaard attacked and today's pervasive secularism with its buffered selves, "invulnerable, immune from failure."[32] Well, perhaps we will allow some speaking of failure, but that can be set religiously within an evolutionary schema of creation, fall, and redemption. Kierkegaard makes such protective covering difficult, for he drives us to recognize "clear-eyed evil," where the language of mistake can no longer gloss over the human predicament.[33] A few may perhaps juggle their way through this narrow pass, saying "I believe; help my unbelief!" (Mark 9:24). More likely our word is "Who, then, can be saved?"

We've spoken of venturing in dialectical passion before God. Is there another side here, something bearing on the self, called but convicted, buffered but facing judgment? There is. Recall Anti-Climacus's summary statement:

> First of all, Christianity proceeds to establish sin so firmly as a position that the human understanding can never comprehend it; and then it is this same Christian teaching that again undertakes to eliminate this position in such a way that the human understanding can never comprehend it.[34]

---

30. SUD, 122.
31. Ibid.
32. Jason A. Mahn, "Becoming a Christian in Christendom," in *Why Kierkegaard Matters: A Festschrift in Honor of Robert L. Perkins*, ed. Marc A. Jolley and Edmon L. Rowell Jr. (Macon, GA: Mercer University Press, 2010), 166–78 (173). He is drawing on Charles Taylor's analysis of a secularism that does not so much displace religion as "replace" it within itself.
33. See above, p. 71n175, in chapter 2, where I take issue with my esteemed colleague Arnold B. Come in his language of the self's "failure" and "recovery" in *Kierkegaard as Theologian*. Come's response to me is in the postlude, 368–74. See also above, pp. 129–30, in chapter 3, where Alison Assiter goes to the other extreme in suggesting an ultimate ground for our acts of freely choosing evil. I take it that Haufniensis would say simply that "sin presupposes itself."
34. SUD, 100.

What's going on with Anti-Climacus as he goes on to say that "sin is to be completely forgotten," eliminated "as completely as if it were drowned in the sea"?[35] Perhaps he's remembering that which lies behind the book's title and explicitly pervades the chapters that follow: the infinite qualitative difference between God and the creatures. In our calling and in our sinning, we live before a God who is infinitely and qualitatively different from us. Perhaps Kierkegaard was thinking of that difference when he wrote in his journal of how "it is incomprehensible that omnipotence is not only able to create the most impressive of all things—the whole visible world—but is able to create the most fragile of all things—a being independent of that very omnipotence."[36] Anti-Climacus writes of the faith that there is such a God for whom everything is possible. Such a person of faith, we are told, "does not collapse. He leaves it entirely to God how he is to be helped, but he believes that for God everything is possible."[37]

Does that mean that God forgives even the one who takes offense at the gospel? The one who declares Christianity a falsehood, the one who decides to have no opinion about this message? But is not the sin against the Holy Spirit, Anti-Climacus's final topic, understood to be the unforgivable sin? We do know that a little later in his journal Kierkegaard wrote that "what the atonement expresses is . . . that God has remained unchanged while men changed, or it *proclaims* to men altered-in-sin that God has remained unchanged."[38] With Anti-Climacus, we have the ringing assertion that "God is separated from man by the same chasmal qualitative abyss when he forgives sins."[39] Yet in that final section, Anti-Climacus writes again that even "[God] cannot remove the possibility of offense."[40] One gets dizzy trying to follow the twists and turns here. Is there a way beyond this vertiginous impasse? Perhaps. We closed our analysis of and commentary on SUD in chapter 2 by taking note of the footnote that occurs two pages

35. Ibid.
36. JP, 2:1251.
37. SUD, 39.
38. JP, 2:1348.
39. SUD, 122.
40. SUD, 126.

before SUD closes. There, Anti-Climacus thanks God "for requiring only faith."[41] We'd still have our question, as did Anti-Climacus, for the note closes with a question: "But I wonder whether faith is to be found on earth!" That's been our question in these closing pages, "Who, then, can be saved?" But the footnote's prayer closes with a complexifying plea concerning the required faith: "And I pray that you will continue to increase it."

Perhaps Anti-Climacus was looking ahead a year to his next book, *Practice in Christianity*. This work also states the requirement for being a Christian in strong terms. But here in the thrice-repeated preface Anti-Climacus says that he states the requirement so strictly "so that I might learn not only to resort to *grace* but to resort to it in relation to the use of *grace*."[42] What might it mean in our use of grace to resort to grace as we ask the question, "Who, then, can be saved?" To return to the previous section, how might we resort to grace in using grace in matters of interreligious dialogue? Could we carry that preface into the other questions we anxiously ask? Climate change, for example: what can be saved, made whole, regarding this planet? Perhaps Alison Assiter is not off on a wild goose chase in finding Kierkegaard's employment of the metaphor of birth lending itself "to an ethic . . . an ethic of care that incorporates care for the environment."[43]

Putting a footnote and a preface together, we find some shifting of the ground regarding agency with respect to the question of who and what can be saved. God becomes the subject of active verbs. Is there nothing for us to do? The *Festschrift* for Robert L. Perkins includes a remarkable article by Andrew J. Burgess on "Kierkegaard's Call for Honesty." Burgess notes PC's moral, but focuses especially on what Kierkegaard says about honesty in his last writings. The *Kirkekamp* was a vehement critique of Christendom's lack of honesty. Kierkegaard calls for honesty toward the other creatures, but particularly toward the Creator.[44] But in closing, Burgess returns to PC's final paragraph of

---

41. SUD, 129.
42. PC, 7, 73, 149.
43. Assiter, *Kierkegaard, Eve and Metaphors*, 191.
44. Andrew J. Burgess, "Kierkegaard's Call for Honesty," in ed. Jolley and Rowell (Macon, GA: Macon

part 1, where the subject is the individual who receives the invitation: "Come here to me, all you who labor and are burdened, and I will give you rest" (Matt 11:28). What will such an invited one, poised over the possibility of offense, do? Anti-Climacus continues:

> Whether one will succeed in becoming essentially Christian, no one can tell him. But anxiety and fear and despair are no help either. Honesty [*Oprigtighed*] before God is the first and the last, honestly to confess to oneself where one is, in honesty before God continually keeping the task in sight.[45]

In such honesty, one gives up trying to hide from God. One could say that the self of such a person "rests transparently in the power that established it." Anti-Climacus uses the last words of *The Sickness unto Death* to remind us that "this formula . . . is the definition of faith."[46] Kierkegaard calls us into the human venture still and does so dialectically. So his readers will find their passion engaged fully, living in hope. It is a fitting legacy for this theological poet of the paradox.

University Press, 2010), *Why Kierkegaard Matters*, 38–49, makes helpful distinctions between the different Danish terms translated as "honest."
45. PC, 66.
46. SUD, 131.

Bibliography

Adams, Noel S. "Kierkegaard's Conception of Indirect Communication in 'The Dialectic of Ethical and Ethical Religious Communication' of 1847." *Søren Kierkegaard Newsletter* (August 2006): 10–15.

Assiter, Alison. *Kierkegaard, Eve and Metaphors of Birth*. London: Rowman & Littlefield, 2015.

Barbour, Ian G. *Religion in an Age of Science*. San Francisco: HarperCollins, 1990.

Barnett, Christopher B. *From Despair to Faith: The Spirituality of Søren Kierkegaard*. Minneapolis: Fortress Press, 2014.

Barrett, Lee. *Eros and Self-Emptying: The Intersections of Kierkegaard and Augustine*. Grand Rapids: Eerdmans, 2013.

———. "Karl Barth: The Dialectic of Attraction and Repulsion." In *German Protestant Theology*. Tome 1 of *Kierkegaard's Influence on Theology*. Vol. 10 of KRSRR, edited by Jon Stewart, 1–42. Aldershot, UK: Ashgate, 2012.

———. "Kierkegaard as Theologian: A History of Countervailing Interpretations." In *The Oxford Handbook of Kierkegaard*, edited by John Lippitt and George Pattison, 528–49. Oxford: Oxford University Press, 2013.

———. "The Paradox of Faith in Kierkegaard's 'Philosophical Fragments': Gift or Task?" In *"Philosophical Fragments" and "Johannes Climacus."* Vol. 7 of IKC, edited by Robert L. Perkins, 261–84. Macon, GA: Mercer University Press, 1994.

———. "Paul Tillich: An Ambivalent Appropriation." In *German Protestant Theology*. Tome 1 of *Kierkegaard's Influence on Theology*. Vol. 10 of KRSRR, edited by Jon Stewart, 335–76. Aldershot, UK: Ashgate, 2012.

Barth, Karl. *The Epistle to the Romans*. Translated by Edwyn C. Hoskyns. 2nd ed. London: Oxford University Press, 1933.

———. *The Humanity of God*. Translated by Thomas Wieser and John Newton Thomas. Richmond, VA: John Knox, 1960.

———. "Mein Verhältnis zu Søren Kierkegaard." *Orbis Litterarum* (1963): 97–100.

Barth, Karl, and Emil Brunner, eds. *Natural Theology: Comparing "Nature and Grace" by Professor Dr. Emil Brunner and the Reply "No!" by Dr. Karl Barth*. Translated by Peter Fraenkel. London: Centenary Press, 1946.

Beauvoir, Simone de. *The Ethics of Ambiguity*. Translated by Bernard Frechtman. New York: Philosophical Library, 1948.

Bertung, Birgit. "Yes, a Woman *Can* Exist." In *Feminist Interpretations of Søren Kierkegaard*, edited by Sylvia Walsh and Céline Léon, 51–68. University Park: Pennsylvania State University Press, 1997.

Bringle, Mary Louise. *Despair: Sickness or Sin? Hopelessness and Healing in the Christian Life*. Nashville: Abingdon, 1990.

Brunner, Emil. "Søren Kierkegaard's Budskap." *Janus* (1939).

Bultmann, Rudolf. *Kerygma and Myth: A Theological Debate*. Edited by Hans Werner Bartsch. Translated by Reginald H. Fuller. New York: Harper & Row, 1961.

———. "The Primitive Christian Kerygma and the Historical Jesus." In *The Historical Jesus and the Kerygmatic Christ: Essays on the New Quest of the Historical Jesus*. Translated by Carl E. Braaten and Roy A. Harrisville, 15–42. New York: Abingdon, 1964.

Burgess, Andrew J. "Kierkegaard, Brorson, and Moravian Music." In *Practice in Christianity*. Vol. 20 of IKC, edited by Robert L. Perkins, 211–43. Macon, GA: Mercer University Press, 2004.

———. "Kierkegaard's Call for Honesty." In *Why Kierkegaard Matters: A Festschrift in Honor of Robert L. Perkins*, edited by Marc A. Jolley and Edmon L. Rowell Jr., 38–49. Macon, GA: Mercer University Press, 2010.

Camus, Albert. *Resistance, Rebellion and Death*. Translated by Justin O'Brien. New York: Knopf, 1961.

Caputo, John D. *On Religion*. London: Routledge, 2001.

———. *Religion with/out Religion: The Prayers and Tears of John D. Caputo*. Edited by James H. Olthuis. London: Routledge, 2002.

Christoffersen, Svein Aage. "Gisle Christian Johnson: The First Kierkegaardian in Theology?" In *Anglophone and Scandinavian Protestant Theology*. Tome 2 of *Kierkegaard's Influence on Theology*. Vol. 10 of KRSRR, edited by Jon Stewart, 191–202. Aldershot, UK: Ashgate, 2012.

Come, Arnold B. *Kierkegaard as Humanist: Discovering My Self*. Montreal: McGill-Queen's University Press, 1995.

———. *Kierkegaard as Theologian: Recovering My Self*. Montreal: McGill-Queen's University Press, 1997.

———. *Trendelenburg's Influence on Kierkegaard's Modal Categories*. Montreal: Inter Editions, 1991.

Connell, George B. *Kierkegaard and the Paradox of Religious Diversity*. Grand Rapids: Eerdmans, 2016.

———. *To Be One Thing: Personal Unity in Kierkegaard's Thought*. Macon, GA: Mercer University Press, 1985.

Cuff, Joyce M., and Curtis L. Thompson. *God and Nature: A Scientist and a Theologian Conversing on the Divine Promise of Possibility*. New York: Continuum, 2012.

Davenport, John J., and Anthony John Rudd, eds. *Kierkegaard after MacIntyre: Essays on Freedom, Narrative and Virtue*. Chicago: Open Court, 2001.

Derrida, Jacques. *The Gift of Death*. Translated by David Wills. Chicago: University of Chicago Press, 1995.

———. *Rogues: Two Essays on Reason*. Translated by Pascale-Anne Brault and Michael Naas. Stanford: Stanford University Press, 2005.

———. *Writing and Difference*. Translated by Alan Bass. London: Routledge, 1978.

Dooley, Mark. *The Politics of Exodus: Søren Kierkegaard's Ethics of Responsibility*. New York: Fordham University Press, 2001.

Dorrien, Gary J. *Kantian Reason and Hegelian Spirit: The Idealistic Logic of Modern Theology*. Chichester, UK: John Wiley & Sons, 2012.

———. *The Making of American Liberal Theology: Crisis, Irony, and Postmodernity, 1950–2005*. Louisville: Westminster John Knox, 2006.

Evangelical Lutheran Worship Minneapolis: Augsburg Fortress, 2006.

Fehir, Aaron. *Kierkegaardian Reflections on the Problem of Pluralism*. Lanham, MD: Lexington Books, 2015.

Ferreira, M. Jamie. *Love's Grateful Striving: A Commentary on Kierkegaard's Works of Love*. Oxford: Oxford University Press, 2001.

———. *Transforming Vision: Imagination and Will in Kierkegaardian Faith*. Oxford: Clarendon, 1991.

Garff, Joakim. *Søren Kierkegaard: A Biography*. Translated by Bruce H. Kirmmse. Princeton: Princeton University Press, 2005.

Giles, James, ed. *Kierkegaard and Japanese Thought*. London: Palgrave Macmillan, 2008.

———, ed. *Kierkegaard on Freedom*. New York: Palgrave, 2000.

Gilkey, Langdon. *On Niebuhr: A Theological Study*. Chicago: University of Chicago Press, 2001.

Glenn, John D. Jr. "The Definition of the Self and the Structure of Kierkegaard's Work." In *The Sickness unto Death*. Vol. 19 of IKC, edited by Robert L. Perkins, 5–21. Macon, GA: Mercer University Press, 1987.

Gouwens, David J. *Kierkegaard as Religious Thinker*. Cambridge: Cambridge University Press, 1966.

Grøn, Arne. "The Human Synthesis." In *Anthropology and Authority: Essays on Søren Kierkegaard*, edited by Poul Houe, Gordon D. Marino, and Sven Hakon Rossel, 27–32. Amsterdam: Rodopi, 2000.

Hall, Amy Laura. *Kierkegaard and the Treachery of Love*. Cambridge: Cambridge University Press, 2002.

Hannay, Alastair. *Kierkegaard: A Biography*. Cambridge: Cambridge University Press, 2001.

———. "Kierkegaard and the Variety of Despair." In *The Cambridge Companion to Kierkegaard*, edited by Alastair Hannay and Gordon D. Marino, 329–48. Cambridge: Cambridge University Press, 1998.

———. "Something on Hermeneutics and Communication in Kierkegaard After All." *Søren Kierkegaard Newsletter* (September 2001): 8–14.

Hartshorne, Charles, and William L. Reese, eds. *Philosophers Speak of God*. Chicago: University of Chicago Press, 1953.

Hegel, Georg Wilhelm Friedrich. *The Phenomenology of Mind*. Translated by J. B. Baillie. New York: Harper Torchbooks, 1967.

———. *The Phenomenology of Spirit*. Translated by J. B. Baillie. New York: Harper, 1967.

BIBLIOGRAPHY

———. *The Philosophy of Right*. Translated by T. M. Knox. Chicago: Encyclopedia Britannica, 1951.

———. "The Spirit of Christianity and Its Fate." In *Early Theological Writings*, translated by T. M. Knox and Richard Kroner, 182–301. Chicago: University of Chicago Press, 1948.

Heidegger, Martin. *Being and Time*. Translated by John Macquarrie and Edward Robinson. Oxford: Basil Blackwell, 1967.

Henriksen, Aage. *Methods and Results of Kierkegaard Studies in Scandinavia: A Historical and Critical Survey*. Copenhagen: Ejnar Munksgaard, 1951.

Hirsch, Emanuel. *Kierkegaard-studien*. Gütersloh: C. Bertelsmann, 1933.

Holmer, Paul L. "On Understanding Kierkegaard." In *A Kierkegaard Critique: An International Selection of Essays Interpreting Kierkegaard*, edited by Howard A. Johnson and Niels Thulstrup, 40–53. New York: Harper, 1962.

Hong, Howard V., and Edna H. Hong, eds. *The Essential Kierkegaard*. Princeton: Princeton University Press, 2000.

Ibsen, Henrik. *Letters of Henrik Ibsen*. Translated by J. Nilsen Laurvik and Mary Morison. New York: Duffield, 1908.

Jansen, F. J. Billeskov. "Brandes." In *The Legacy and Interpretation of Kierkegaard*. Vol. 8 of *Bibliotheca Kierkegaardiana*, edited by Niels Thulstrup and Marie Mikulová Thulstrup, 204–8. Copenhagen: Reitzel, 1981.

Jegstrup, Elsebet, ed. *The New Kierkegaard*. Bloomington: Indiana University Press, 2004.

John, Varughese. *Truth and Subjectivity, Faith and History: Kierkegaard's Insights for Christian Faith*. Eugene, OR: Pickwick, 2012.

Jothen, Peder. *Kierkegaard, Aesthetics, and Selfhood: The Art of Subjectivity*. Aldershot, UK: Ashgate, 2014.

Kauffman, Stuart. *At Home in the Universe: The Search for Laws of Self-Organization and Complexity*. New York: Oxford University Press, 1995.

Kegley, Charles W., and Robert W. Bretall, eds. *The Theology of Paul Tillich*. New York: Macmillan, 1952.

Kierkegaard, Søren. *The Book on Adler*. Edited and translated by Howard V. Hong and Edna H. Hong. Princeton: Princeton University Press, 1995.

———. *Christian Discourses / The Crisis and a Crisis in the Life of an Actress*. Edited and translated by Howard V. Hong and Edna H. Hong. Princeton: Princeton University Press, 1997.

———. [Vigilius Haufniensis, pseud.] *The Concept of Anxiety*. Edited and translated by Reidar Thomte. Princeton: Princeton University Press, 1980.

———. *The Concept of Irony, with Continual Reference to Socrates / Notes on Schelling's Berlin Lectures*. Edited and translated by Howard V. Hong and Edna H. Hong. Princeton: Princeton University Press, 1989.

———. [Johannes Climacus, pseud.] *Concluding Unscientific Postscript to "Philosophical Fragments."* Edited and translated by Howard V. Hong and Edna H. Hong. 2 vols. Princeton: Princeton University Press, 1992.

———. [Victor Eremita, pseud., ed.] *Either/Or*. Edited and translated by Howard V. Hong and Edna H. Hong. 2 vols. Princeton: Princeton University Press, 1992.

———. *Eighteen Upbuilding Discourses*. Edited and translated by Howard V. Hong and Edna H. Hong. Princeton: Princeton University Press, 1990.

———. [Johannes de Silentio, pseud.] *Fear and Trembling* / [Constantin Constantius, pseud.] *Repetition*. Edited and translated by Howard V. Hong and Edna H. Hong. Princeton: Princeton University Press, 1983.

———. *For Self-Examination / Judge for Yourself!* Edited and translated by Howard V. Hong and Edna H. Hong. Princeton: Princeton University Press, 1990.

———. *"The Moment" and Late Writings*. Edited and translated by Howard V. Hong and Edna H. Hong. Princeton: Princeton University Press, 1998.

———. [Johannes Climacus, pseud.] *Philosophical Fragments / Johannes Climacus*. Edited and translated by Howard V. Hong and Edna H. Hong. Princeton: Princeton University Press, 1985.

———. *The Point of View*. Edited and translated by Howard V. Hong and Edna H. Hong. Princeton: Princeton University Press, 1998.

———. [Anti-Climacus, pseud.] *Practice in Christianity*. Edited and translated by Howard V. Hong and Edna H. Hong. Princeton: Princeton University Press, 1991.

———. [Anti-Climacus, pseud.] *The Sickness unto Death*. Translated by Alastair Hannay. London: Penguin, 1989.

———. [Anti-Climacus, pseud.] *The Sickness unto Death: A Christian Psychological*

Exposition for Upbuilding and Awakening. Edited and translated by Howard V. Hong and Edna H. Hong. Princeton: Princeton University Press, 1980.

———. *Søren Kierkegaard's Journals and Papers*. Edited and translated by Howard V. Hong and Edna H. Hong, assisted by Gregor Malantschuk. 7 vols. Bloomington: Indiana University Press, 1967-78.

———. [Hilarius Bookbinder, pseud., ed.] *Stages on Life's Way*. Edited and translated by Howard V. Hong and Edna H. Hong: Princeton: Princeton University Press, 1988.

———. *Upbuilding Discourses in Various Spirits*. Edited and translated by Howard V. Hong and Edna H. Hong. Princeton: Princeton University Press, 1993.

———. *Without Authority*. Edited and translated by Howard V. Hong and Edna H. Hong. Princeton: Princeton University Press, 1997.

———. *Works of Love*. Edited and translated by Howard V. Hong and Edna H. Hong. Princeton: Princeton University Press, 1995.

Kirmmse, Bruce H. "'I Am Not a Christian'—A 'Sublime Lie'? Or 'Without Authority,' Playing Desdemona to Christendom's Othello." In *Anthropology and Authority: Essays on Søren Kierkegaard*, edited by Poul Houe, Gordon D. Marino, and Sven Hakon Rossel, 129-36. Amsterdam: Rodopi, 2000.

———. "Kierkegaard and the End of the Danish Golden Age." In *The Oxford Handbook of Kierkegaard*, edited by John Lippitt and George Pattison, 28-43. Oxford: Oxford University Press, 2013.

———. *Kierkegaard in Golden Age Denmark*. Bloomington: Indiana University Press, 1990.

Law, David R. "A Cacophony of Voices: The Multiple Authors and Readers of Kierkegaard's *The Point of View for My Work as an Author*." In *The Point of View*. Vol. 22 of IKC, edited by Robert L. Perkins, 12-47. Macon, GA: Mercer University Press, 2010.

———. *Kierkegaard as Negative Theologian*. Oxford: Clarendon, 1993.

———. *Kierkegaard's Kenotic Christology*. Oxford: Oxford University Press, 2013.

———. "The Point of View for My Work as an Author." In *The Point of View*. Vol. 22 of IKC, edited by Robert L. Perkins, 12-47. Macon, GA: Mercer University Press, 2010.

Lawson, Lewis. "Small Talk on the 'Melancholy Dane.'" In *The Legacy and Interpretation of Kierkegaard*. Vol. 8 of *Bibliotheca Kierkegaardiana*, edited by

Niels Thulstrup and Marie Mikulová Thulstrup, 178–97. Copenhagen: Reitzel, 1981.

Léon, Céline. "(A) Woman's Place Within the Ethical." In *Feminist Interpretations of Søren Kierkegaard*, edited by Sylvia Walsh and Céline Léon, 103–30. University Park: Pennsylvania State University Press, 1997.

Levinas, Emmanuel. *Totality and Infinity: An Essay on Exteriority*. Translated by Alphonso Lingis. Pittsburgh: Duquesne University Press, 1969.

Lippitt, John, and George Pattison, eds. *The Oxford Handbook of Kierkegaard*. Oxford: Oxford University Press, 2013.

Lønning, Per. *"Samtidighedens Situation": en studie i Søren Kierkegaards kristendomsforståelse*. Oslo: Forlaget Land og Kirke, 1954.

Lorraine, Tamsin. "Amatory Cures for Material Dis-ease: A Kristevian Reading of *The Sickness unto Death*." In *Feminist Interpretations of Søren Kierkegaard*, edited by Claudia Walsh and Céline Léon, 307–34. University Park: Pennsylvania State University Press, 1997.

Loungina, Darya. "Russia: Kierkegaard's Reception through Tsarism, Communism and Liberation." In *Southern, Central and Eastern Europe*. Tome 2 of *Kierkegaard's International Reception*. Vol. 8 of KRSRR, edited by Jon Stewart, 247–83. Aldershot, UK: Ashgate, 2009.

Luther, Martin. *Martin Luther's Basic Theological Writings*. Edited by Timothy F. Lull. Minneapolis: Fortress Press, 1989.

———. *Table Talk*. Edited and translated by Theodore G. Tappert. Vol. 54 of *Luther's Works*. Philadelphia: Fortress Press, 1967.

Mahn, Jason A. "Becoming a Christian in Christendom." In *Why Kierkegaard Matters: A Festschrift in Honor of Robert L. Perkins*, edited by Marc A. Jolley and Edmon L. Rowell Jr., 166–78. Macon, GA: Mercer University Press, 2010.

———. *Fortunate Fallibility: Kierkegaard and the Power of Sin*. New York: Oxford University Press, 2011.

Malik, Habib C. *Receiving Søren Kierkegaard: The Early Impact and Transmission of His Thought*. Washington, DC: Catholic University of America Press, 1997.

Marino, Gordon D. "The Place of Reason in Kierkegaard's Ethics." In *Kierkegaard after MacIntyre: Essays on Freedom, Narrative, and Virtue*, edited by John J. Davenport and Anthony John Rudd, 113–28. Chicago: Open Court, 2001.

Marshall, Ronald F. *Kierkegaard for the Church: Essays and Sermons.* Eugene, OR: Wipf & Stock, 2013.

Martensen, Hans L. *Between Hegel and Kierkegaard: Hans L. Martensen's Philosophy of Religion.* Translated by Curtis L. Thompson and David Kangas. Oxford: Oxford University Press, 1997.

Matuštík, Martin J., and Merold Westphal, eds. *Kierkegaard in Post/Modernity.* Bloomington: Indiana University Press, 1995.

McCarthy, Vincent. "Martin Heidegger: Kierkegaard's Influence Hidden and in Full View." In *KRSRR*, Vol. 9, *Kierkegaard and Existentialism*, edited by Jon Stewart, 95–125. Aldershot, UK: Ashgate, 2011.

McCombs, Richard. *The Paradoxical Rationality of Søren Kierkegaard.* Bloomington: Indiana University Press, 2013

McKim, Mark G. *Emil Brunner: A Bibliography.* Lanham, MD: Scarecrow, 1996.

Melanchthon, Philip. *The Loci Communes of Philip Melanchthon.* Translated by Charles L. Hill. Boston: Meador, 1944.

Milbank, John. "Materialism and Transcendence." In *Theology and the Political: The New Debate*, edited by Creston Davis, John Milbank, and Slavoj Žižek, 393–426. Durham, NC: Duke University Press, 2005.

_____. *Theology and Social Theory: Beyond Secular Reason.* Oxford: Blackwell, 1990.

Miles, Thomas. "Ludwig Wittgenstein: Kierkegaard's Influence on the Origin of Analytic Philosophy." In *German and Scandinavian Philosophy.* Tome 1 of *Kierkegaard's Influence on Philosophy.* Vol. 11 of KRSRR, edited by Jon Stewart, 209–41. Aldershot, UK: Ashgate, 2012.

Mjaaland, Marius Timmann. "Jacques Derrida: Faithful Heretics," in *Kierkegaard's Influence on Philosophy.* Vol. 11 of KRSRR, Tome 2, *Francophone Philosophy*, edited by Jon Stewart, 111–38. Aldershot, UK: Ashgate, 2012.

Moltmann, Jürgen. *The Crucified God: The Cross of Christ as the Foundation and Criticism of Christian Theology.* Translated by R. A. Wilson and John Bowden. New York: Harper & Row, 1974.

_____. *Hope and Planning.* Translated by Margaret Clarkson. New York: Harper & Row, 1971.

_____. *The Theology of Hope: On the Ground and the Implications of a Christian Eschatology.* Translated by James W. Leitch. New York: Harper & Row, 1967.

Nakazato, Satoshi. "Japan: Varied Images through Western Waves." In *The Near*

East, Asia, Australia and the Americas. Tome 3 of *Kierkegaard's International Reception*. Vol. 8 of KRSRR, edited by Jon Stewart, 149–74. Aldershot, UK: Ashgate, 2009.

Niebuhr, H. Richard. *Christ and Culture*. London: Faber & Faber, 1951.

Niebuhr, Reinhold. "Biblical Thought and Ontological Speculation in Tillich's Theology." In *The Theology of Paul Tillich*, edited by Charles W. Kegley and Robert W. Bretall, 216–45. New York: Macmillan, 1952.

———. *The Nature and Destiny of Man: A Christian Interpretation*. 2 vols. New York: Charles Scribner's Sons, 1941–43.

O'Neill Burns, Michael. *Kierkegaard and the Matter of Philosophy: A Fractured Dialectic*. London: Rowman & Littlefield, 2014.

Pannenberg, Wolfhart. *Anthropology in Theological Perspective*. Translated by Matthew J. O'Connell. Philadelphia: Westminster, 1985.

Pascal, Blaise. *Pensées*. Translated by W. F. Trotter. New York: E. P. Dutton, 1958.

Pattison, George. *Kierkegaard's Upbuilding Discourses: Philosophy, Literature and Theology*. London: Routledge, 2002.

———. "Lev Shestov: Kierkegaard in the Ox of Phalaris." In *Kierkegaard and Existentialism*. Vol. 9 of KRSRR, edited by Jon Stewart, 355–73. Aldershot, UK: Ashgate, 2011.

———. "Philosophy and Dogma: The Testimony of an Upbuilding Discourse." In *Ethics, Love, and Faith in Kierkegaard: Philosophical Engagements*, edited by Edward F. Mooney, 156–62. Bloomington: Indiana University Press, 2008.

Pelikan, Jaroslav. *From Luther to Kierkegaard*. St. Louis: Concordia, 1950.

Perkins, Robert L., ed. *International Kierkegaard Commentary*. 24 vols. Macon, GA: Mercer University Press, 1984–2001.

Podmore, Simon D. *Kierkegaard and the Self Before God: Anatomy of the Abyss*. Bloomington: Indiana University Press, 2011.

Polk, Timothy. *The Biblical Kierkegaard: Reading by the Rule of Faith*. Macon, GA: Mercer University Press, 1997.

Poole, Roger. *Kierkegaard: The Indirect Communication*. Charlottesville: University Press of Virginia, 1993.

Prenter, Regin. "Luther and Lutheranism." In *Kierkegaard and the Great Traditions*. Vol. 6 of *Bibliotheca Kierkegaardiana*, edited by Niels Thulstrup and Marie Mikulová Thulstrup, 121–73. Copenhagen: Reitzel, 1981.

Roberts, Kyle A. *Emerging Prophet: Kierkegaard and the Postmodern People of God.* Eugene, OR: Cascade, 2013.

———. "The Logic of Paradox for a Theology of Human Nature." In *Anglophone and Scandinavian Protestant Theology.* Tome 2 of *Kierkegaard's Influence on Theology.* Vol. 10 of KRSRR, edited by Jon Stewart, 143–55. Aldershot, UK: Ashgate, 2012.

Rose, Tim. *Kierkegaard's Christocentric Theology.* Aldershot, UK: Ashgate, 2001.

Rudd, Anthony John. "On Straight and Crooked Readings: Why the *Postscript* Does Not Self-Destruct." In *Anthropology and Authority: Essays on Søren Kierkegaard,* edited by Poul Houe, Gordon D. Marino, and Sven Hakon Rossel, 119–27. Amsterdam: Rodopi, 2000.

Sartre, Jean-Paul. *Being and Nothingness: An Essay on Phenomenological Ontology.* Translated by Hazel E. Barnes. New York: Philosophical Library, 1956.

———. "Existentialism Is a Humanism." In *Existentialism from Dostoevsky to Sartre,* edited by Walter Kaufman, 287–311. New York: Meridian, 1989.

Schröer, Henning. *Die Denkform der Paradoxalität als Theologisches Problem.* Göttingen: Vandenhoeck & Ruprecht, 1960.

Schulz, Heiko. "Germany and Austria: A Modest Head Start: The German Reception of Kierkegaard." In *Northern and Western Europe.* Tome 1 of *Kierkegaard's International Reception.* Vol. 8 of KRSRR, edited by Jon Stewart, 307–419. Aldershot, UK: Ashgate, 2009.

———. "A Phenomenological Proof? The Challenge of Arguing for God in Kierkegaard's Pseudonymous Authorship." In *Kierkegaard as Phenomenologist: An Experiment,* edited by Jeffrey Hanson, 101–27. Evanston, IL: Northwestern University Press, 2010.

———. "Rudolf Bultmann: Faith, Love and Self-Understanding." In *German Protestant Theology.* Tome 1 of *Kierkegaard's Influence on Theology.* Vol. 10 of KRSRR, edited by Jon Stewart, 105–44. Aldershot, UK: Ashgate, 2012.

Shakespeare, Steven. "Kierkegaard and Postmodernism." In *The Oxford Handbook of Kierkegaard,* edited by John Lippitt and George Pattison, 464–83. Oxford: Oxford University Press, 2013.

Shaw, George Bernard. *Major Barbara.* New York: Brentano's, 1907.

Søltoft, Pia. "Anthropology and Ethics: The Connection between Subjectivity and Intersubjectivity as the Basis of a Kierkegaardian Anthropology." In

Anthropology and Authority: Essays on Søren Kierkegaard, edited by Poul Houe, Gordon D. Marino, and Sven Hakon Rossel, 41–48. Amsterdam: Rodopi, 2000.

Sorainen, Kalle. "Brøchner." In *The Legacy and Interpretation of Kierkegaard*. Vol. 8 of *Bibliotheca Kierkegaardiana*, edited by Niels Thulstrup and Marie Mikulová Thulstrup, 198–203. Copenhagen: Reitzel, 1981.

———. "Høffding." In *The Legacy and Interpretation of Kierkegaard*. Vol. 8 of *Bibliotheca Kierkegaardiana*, edited by Niels Thulstrup and Marie Mikulová Thulstrup, 209–14. Copenhagen: Reitzel, 1981.

Sponheim, Paul R. "America." In *Kierkegaard Research*. Vol. 15 of *Bibliotheca Kierkegaardiana*, edited by Niels Thulstrup and Marie Mikulová Thulstrup, 9–36. Copenhagen: Reitzel, 1987.

———. "God's Changelessness: The Triumph of Grace in Law and Gospel as 'Archimedean Point.'" In *"The Moment" and Late Writings*. Vol. 23 of IKC, edited by Robert L. Perkins, 101–28. Macon, GA: Mercer University Press, 2009.

———. *Kierkegaard on Christ and Christian Coherence*. New York: Harper, 1968.

———. *Love's Availing Power: Imaging God, Imagining the World*. Minneapolis: Fortress Press, 2011.

———. "Relational Transcendence in Divine Agency." In *Practice in Christianity*. Vol. 20 of IKC, edited by Robert L. Perkins, 47–68. Macon, GA: Mercer University Press, 2004.

Stewart, Jon. "France: Kierkegaard as a Forerunner of Existentialism and Poststructuralism." In *Northern and Western Europe*. Tome 1 of *Kierkegaard's International Reception*. Vol. 8 of KRSRR, edited by Jon Stewart, 442–74. Aldershot, UK: Ashgate, 2009.

———, ed. *Kierkegaard Research: Sources, Reception and Resources*. 18 vols. Aldershot, UK: Ashgate, 2007–16.

———. *Kierkegaard's Relations to Hegel Reconsidered*. Cambridge: Cambridge University Press, 2003.

Svendsen, Paulus. "Norwegian Literature." In *The Legacy and Interpretation of Kierkegaard*. Vol. 8 of *Bibliotheca Kierkegaardiana*, edited by Niels Thulstrup and Marie Mikulová Thulstrup, 9–39. Copenhagen: Reitzel, 1981.

Theunissen, Michael. *Kierkegaard's Concept of Despair*. Translated by Barbara Harshav and Helmut Illbruck. Princeton: Princeton University Press, 2005.

Thompson, Curtis L. "Emil Brunner: Polemically Promoting Kierkegaard's Christian Philosophy of Existence." In *German Protestant Theology*. Tome 1 of *Kierkegaard's Influence on Theology*. Vol. 10 of KRSRR, edited by Jon Stewart, 65–103. Aldershot, UK: Ashgate, 2012.

———. *Following the Cultured Public's Chosen One: Why Martensen Mattered to Kierkegaard.* Copenhagen: Museum Tusculanum Press, 2008.

———. "Jürgen Moltmann: Taking a Moment for Trinitarian Eschatology." In *German Protestant Theology*. Tome 1 of *Kierkegaard's Influence on Theology*. Vol. 10 of KRSRR, edited by Jon Stewart, 185–222. Aldershot, UK: Ashgate, 2012.

———. "Wolfhart Pannenberg: Kierkegaard'ss Anthropology Tantalizing Pullbic Theology's Reasoning Hope." In *German Protestant Theology*. Tome 1 of *Kierkegaard's Influence on Theology*. Vol. 10 of KRSRR, edited by Jon Stewart, 241–74. Aldershot, UK: Ashgate, 2012

Thulstrup, Niels. *Kierkegaard's Relation to Hegel*. Translated by George L. Stengren. Princeton: Princeton University Press, 1980.

Tillich, Paul. *Love, Power and Justice: Ontological Analyses and Ethical Applications.* New York: Oxford University Press, 1960.

———. *On the Boundary: An Autobiographical Sketch*. New York: Charles Scribner's Sons, 1966.

———. *Systematic Theology*. 3 vols. Chicago: University of Chicago Press, 1951–63.

Töpfer-Stoyanova, Desislava. "Bulgaria: The Long Way from Indirect Acquaintance to Original Translation." In *Southern, Central and Eastern Europe*. Tome 2 of *Kierkegaard's International Reception*. Vol. 8 of KSRSS, edited by Jon Stewart, 285–99. Aldershot, UK: Ashgate, 2009.

Updike, John. "Incommensurability: A New Biography of Kierkegaard." *The New Yorker*, March 28, 2005, 71–76.

Vidal, Dolors Perarnau, and Óscar Parcero Oubiña. "Spain: The Old and New Kierkegaard Reception in Spain." In *Southern, Central and Eastern Europe*. Tome 2 of *Kierkegaard's International Reception*. Vol. 8 of KRSRR, edited by Jon Stewart, 18–29. Aldershot, UK: Ashgate, 2009.

Walsh, Sylvia. *Discourses at the Communion on Fridays*. Bloomington: Indiana University Press, 2011.

———. "Kierkegaard's Theology." In *The Oxford Handbook of Kierkegaard*, edited by John Lippitt and George Pattison, 292–308. Oxford: Oxford University Press, 2013.

———. *Living Christianly: Kierkegaard's Dialectic of Christian Existence*. University Park: Pennsylvania State University Press, 2005.

———. "On 'Feminine' and 'Masculine' Forms of Despair." In *The Sickness unto Death*. Vol. 19 of IKC, edited by Robert L. Perkins, 129–34. Macon, GA: Mercer University Press, 1987.

———. "Reading Kierkegaard with Kierkegaard against Garff," *Søren Kierkegaard Newsletter* 38 (July 1999): 4–8.

Walsh, Sylvia, and Céline Léon, eds. *Feminist Interpretations of Søren Kierkegaard*. University Park: Pennsylvania State University Press, 1997.

Watkin, Julia. *Historical Dictionary of Kierkegaard's Philosophy*. Lanham, MD: Scarecrow, 2001.

Welz, Claudia. "J. P. Sartre: Kierkegaard's Influence on His Theory of Nothingness." In *Kierkegaard and Existentialism*. Vol. 9 of KRSRR, edited by Jon Stewart, 323–46. Aldershot, UK: Ashgate, 2011.

Westphal, Merold. *Becoming a Self: A Reading of Kierkegaard's "Concluding Unscientific Postscript."* West Lafayette, IN: Purdue University Press, 1996.

———. "Divine Givenness and Self-Givenness in Kierkegaard." In *Kierkegaard as Phenomenologist: An Experiment*, edited by Jeffrey Hanson, 39–56. Evanston, IL: Northwestern University Press, 2010.

———. "Jon Stewart, Kierkegaard's Relations to Hegel Reconsidered." *Søren Kierkegaard Newsletter* 48 (September 2004): 10–15.

———. "Kenosis and Offense: A Kierkegaardian Look at Divine Transcendence." In *Practice in Christianity*. Vol. 20 of IKC, edited by Robert L. Perkins, 19–46. Macon, GA: Mercer University Press, 2004.

———. *Kierkegaard's Concept of Faith*. Grand Rapids: Eerdmans, 2014.

———. "Kierkegaard's Teleological Suspension of Religiousness B." In *Foundations of Kierkegaard's Vision of Community: Religion, Ethics, and Politics in Kierkegaard*, edited by George B. Connell and C. Stephen Evans, 110–29. London: Humanities Press, 1992.

———. *Levinas and Kierkegaard in Dialogue*. Bloomington: Indiana University Press, 2008.

Wingren, Gustaf. *Creation and Law.* Translated by Ross Mackenzie. Philadelphia: Muhlenberg, 1961.

Wolf, Herbert C. *Kierkegaard and Bultmann: The Quest of the Historical Jesus.* Minneapolis: Augsburg, 1965.

Žižek, Slavoj. *The Parallax View.* Cambridge, MA: MIT Press, 2006.

Index of Names

Abraham, xxiii, 49, 72n186, 82, 111, 118–19, 123, 136
Adams, Noel S., xxvii, xxviii
Assiter, Alison, 126–30, 144
Augustine, 91, 99, 125

Barnett, Christopher B., 60n135, 131n219
Barrett, Lee C., 8n78, 62n136, 67n159, 93, 96–98, 103, 104n103, 110, 112n131, 115, 131
Barth, Karl, xi–xii, 78, 93–97, 111, 115, 117, 135
Beauvoir, Simone de, 101, 103
Berry, Wanda Warren, 110, 115
Bloch, Ernst, 113n134
Bohr, Niels, 89n41
Bohlin, Torsten, 112
Brandes, Georg, 79, 84–88, 90–93
Bringle, Mary Louise, 16n8
Brøchner, Hans, 85–86
Brunner, Emil, 93, 95, 98–101, 105, 110
Buber, Martin, 93, 110, 115

Bultmann, Rudolf, 93, 95, 98–101, 105, 110, 115
Burgess, Andrew J., 48n59, 55n96, 110, 144–45n44

Camus, Albert, 101–2, 104
Caputo, John D., 117–18, 120–25, 130
Christoffersen, Svein Aage, 80n9
Clausen, H. N.. xvii, xix
Coles, Robert, 105
Come, Arnold B., 14n2, 15, 37n14, 40n23, 59n123, 60n127, 71n175, 142n33
Connell, George B., 8, 140

Darwin, Charles, 85
Derrida, Jacques, 117–19, 121–23
Descartes, Rene, 15
Dilthey, Wilhelm, 92
Dooley, Mark, 109, 117, 120, 122–25
Dorrien, Gary J., 93, 95, 106, 124n184
Dostoevsky, F., 99

Evans, Stephen, 115, 132n224

Fehir, Aaron, 138–40
Ferreira, M. Jaimie, 59, 116, 126
Feuerbach, Ludwig, 85
Freud, Sigmund, 121

Garff, Joakim, xxn16, xxiin22, xxiv, xxvin37
Giles, James, 139–40
Gottsched, Hermann, 91
Gouwens, David J., 40n25, 52n82, 68n159, 110, 115
Griffin, David Ray, 123
Grundtvig, N. F. S., xvii, xix, 22, 85

Habermas, Jürgen, 121n172
Haecker, Theodor, 93
Hall, Amy Laura, 58n117, 115
Hannay, Alastair, xxiin18, xxviin41, xxixn51, 6n8, 14n2, 30, 81n13
Hartshorne, Charles, 37, 107n109
Hauge, H. N., 80
Hegel, Georg Wilhelm Friedrich, xvi–xvii, 9n20, 10, 26, 28, 37n14, 44, 56, 84, 94, 117, 121, 127
Heiberg, Johan Ludvig, xvi–xviii
Heidegger, Martin, 93, 101–5, 134
Henriksen, Aage, 87
Heschel, Abraham, 110
Hirsch, Emanuel, xvi, 96, 105
Høffding, Harald, 47, 79, 84, 86–89, 94, 124

Holmer, Paul L., xiii, 24, 63n142, 88n37, 112, 115, 139
Hong, Edna H., xiii, xxvn33, xxxn54, 5n68, 7n12, 47n53, 50, 84n23, 112
Hong, Howard V., xiii, xxvn33, xxxn54, 5n68, 7n12, 47n53, 50, 84n23, 88, 112
Howitt, Mary, 89
Husserl, Edmund, 93

Ibsen, Henrik, xvi, 79–83, 90

James, William, 88, 124
Jaspers, Karl, 93
John, Varughese, 138, 140
Johnson, Gisle Christian, 80–81

Kafka, Franz, 92
Kangas, David, xixn12
Kant, Immanuel, xvi, 36n12, 115, 128
Kauffman, Stuart, 58n111
Kierkegaard, Michael Pedersen, xx–xxin12
Kierkegaard, Søren: The Book on Adler, xxi–xxii, xxviii, 46; Christian Discourses, xxv, xxix, 38, 40, 103–4; The Concept of Anxiety, xxiv, 5, 28, 37, 44, 90–91, 93, 98–99, 105, 110, 113, 129; The Concept of Irony with Continual Reference to Socrates, xxiii, 37, 91–92;

INDEX OF NAMES

Concluding Unscientific Postscript to Philosophical Fragments, xix, xxiii–xxvii, 6, 8, 38, 42, 48, 52, 59, 91, 99, 138–40, 144; The Crisis and a Crisis in the Life of an Actress, xxviii; Discourses at the Communion on Fridays, xxxn53, 7n11; Eighteen Upbuilding Discourses, xxv, 9, 36n12, 40n25, 102; Either/Or, xxiii, xxv, 11, 23, 83, 86, 105, 109n117, 113n134, 116; Fear and Trembling, xxiii, 49, 86, 99, 136; For Self-Examination, xxix, 58, 120; Søren Kierkegaard's Journals and Papers, 30, 68, 73; Judge For Yourself, 61, 120; The Moment, xxix, 53n96, 61, 80–81, 86–87, 91–94, 113n134; Philosophical Fragments, xix, xxiii, xxv, xxx, 5, 37, 42, 48, 52, 59–60, 67, 90–92, 99–100; Point of View for My Work as an Author, xii, xxiin26, xxvii, 86; Practice in Christianity, xxv–xxviii, xxxn54, 36, 41, 52–53, 58, 62, 67, 73, 87, 94, 99, 104, 120, 144; Repetition, xxiii; The Sickness unto Death, *passim*; Stages on Life's Way, xxiv–xxv, 49, 123; The Unchangeableness of God, xxx; Upbuilding Discourses in Various Spirits, xxv; Works of Love, xxv, xxix, 52, 54, 78, 94, 99, 115, 121, 129n214–15, 138

Kirmmse, Bruce H., xv, xvii–xix, xxin17, xxvin35, 69n162, 82

Lammers, Gustav Adolph, 80–82
Law, David R., 67n159, 131n217, 138
Lehmann, Orla, xvii, xix
Léon, Céline, 116–17
Levinas, Emmanuel, 117–18, 137
Lindstrom, Valter, 112
Lippitt, John, 126
Lønning, Per, 112
Loungina, Darya, 77n5
Lowrie, Walter, 82, 105, 109n117, 110
Lukács, Georg, 83
Lund, Ane Sørensdatter, xx
Luther, Martin, 8n78, 35, 39, 41n29, 48n59, 51–54, 59–62, 64, 71, 92, 100, 108, 132, 136

Mahn, Jason A., 9, 19n18, 31–32, 35n9, 55n98, 131, 142
Malik, Habib C., 78n1, 81n12, 84n26, 88, 89n41,
Marino, Gordon D., xiii, 57n122
Marshall, Ronald F., xiii, 59n129–62n135, 131
Martensen, Hans Lassen, xvii–xx, 10n26, 44n41, 47n53, 84–85, 89, 99
Marx, Karl, 106, 121, 235
May, Rollo, 105

McCombs, Richard, 55n98, 131
Melanchthon, Philip, 66
Meland, Bernard, 101n85, 124n184
Merton, Thomas, 110
Moltmann, Jürgen, 112–15, 117, 121
Mynster, J. P., xvii–xix, xxi, xxix, 10n26, 83

Niebuhr, H. Richard, 99, 109–10
Niebuhr, Reinhold, xii, 99, 104–5, 108–10, 130
Nielsen, Rasmus, 83–84, 88
Nietzsche, Friedrich, 87, 90–93, 121

O'Connor, Flannery, xxiin21
Olsen, Regine, xxi–xxiii, 87, 92
O'Neill Burns, Michael, 126–28

Pannenberg, Wolfhart, 112–14, 121
Pascal, Blaise, 47, 66, 93, 129
Pattison, George, 17n10, 36n12, 55n95, 73, 131n219
Pelikan, Jaroslav, xiii, 59n129
Percy, Walker, xxiin21, 77, 105n100
Perkins, Robert L., xxiiin28, xxxn54, 3, 23, 112, 142
Plato, 16, 37n14
Podmore, Simon D., 35n9, 65
Polk, Timothy, 71n174, 110
Poole, Roger, xxv
Prenter, Regin, 61n129
Preus, Linka Keyser, 79, 90, 132

Rilke, Rainer Maria, 92

Rose, Tim, 68n159
Rudd, Anthony John, 57n122, 63

Sartre, Jean-Paul, xii, 101–3, 134
Schelling, Friedrich Wilhelm Joseph, 106, 109, 129
Schleiermacher, Friedrich, xvi, xix, 85, 94
Schrempf, Christoph, 91–92, 102
Schulz, Heiko, 78, 90, 99–100, 126n196
Shakespeare, Steven, 121
Shaw, George Bernard, 64
Shestov, Lev, 73n185–86
Socrates, 2, 16, 32, 35n14, 41–43, 45, 54–55, 128, 136
Søltoft, Pia, 23n24
Sponheim, Paul R., xix, xxiin56, 10n26, 44n41, 61n129, 68n159, 105n100, 112, 124n184
Stewart, Jon, 77
Strauss, David Friedrich, 85
Svendsen, Paulus, 80n10–82n16
Swenson, David F., 90, 105, 109n117, 110

Taylor, Charles, 142n32
Taylor, Mark C., 122–25
Theunissen, Michael, 126
Thompson, Curtis L., xiii, xixn12, 9n20, 24, 98–99, 113n135, 122n176
Thomte, Reidar, xiii, 110
Thulstrup, Niels, xiii, xviin7

INDEX OF NAMES

Tillich, Paul, xiii, 101, 104–8, 110
Tolstoy, Leo, 79
Trendelenburg, Friedrich Adolf, 10n26
Töpfer-Stoyanova, Desislava, 78n3

Uchimura, Kanzo, 90
Unamuno, Miguel de, 79, 83
Updike, John, xxiin21, xxiv, 77

Vidal, Dolors Perarnau, 77n6

Walsh, Sylvia, xxin16, xxvin35, xxx, 7n11, 9–10n23, 28n67, 43n38, 115–17, 122
Watkin, Julia, xviiin11, xxii, xxiv, xxvii, 9n20, 43n38, 115
Westphal, Merold, xviin7, 59n129, 95, 109, 118–20, 126, 136
Whitehead, A. N., 88, 122n184
Wingren, Gustaf, 17n10
Wittgenstein, Ludwig, 63

Zinzendorf, Count N. L., xxi
Žižek, Slavoj, 127–28

www.ingramcontent.com/pod-product-compliance
Lightning Source LLC
Chambersburg PA
CBHW071201070526
44584CB00019B/2873